The String Play

To my friend and colleague

Thérèse Mc Kinney

with happy memories of
our Bolzano workshop.

All good wishes.

Phyllis Young

Dec 1986

(This is a Christmas gift
from Janet Ferguson.)

University of Texas Press, Austin

The String Play

The Drama of Playing and Teaching Strings

PHYLLIS YOUNG • Illustrations by Sally Blakemore

First Edition, 1986

Requests for permission to reproduce material from
this work should be sent to Permissions, University of
Texas Press, Box 7819, Austin, Texas 78713.

Library of Congress Cataloging-in-Publication Data

Young, Phyllis, date.
  The string play.

  Includes index.
  1. Stringed instruments, Bowed—Instruction and
study.   I. Blakemore, Sally.   II. Title.
MT259.Y695   1986   787′.01′07   85-22481
ISBN 0-292-77606-3
ISBN 0-292-77607-1 (pbk.)

To my husband, Jimmie—
the principal character of my life
and the star of my supporting cast.

Contents

Credits

Through the years I have learned from and been helped by many people. Although there is no way every person could be cited here, I wish to express my special gratitude to:

My husband, Jimmie, whose love and loyal support in all my activities since we were university students has been matchless.

My parents, who were a continual source of loving encouragement.

My cello teachers, in the order of their appearance—Jeanette Barbour, Yvonne Tait, Homer Ulrich, Horace Britt (with whom I studied the longest), and André Navarra. Each played an important role. I especially sense Mr. Britt's positive approach to life and music making illuminating many pages of this book, most specifically in Scene 56. Scene 129 is based on information he gave me.

George Neikrug for his pedagogical influences. I marvel not only at his uncanny teaching ability but also at his generosity in sharing his knowledge and perceptions with me since our association began some years ago as colleagues on the music faculty at the University of Texas at Austin. It is my impression that from him I have learned some of the concepts included in Scenes 1, 4, 5, 7, 19, 30, 35, 41, 42, 43, 55, 58, 59, 60, 64, 67, 68, 71, 86, 89, 105, 108, 109, 118, 126, and 169, although he may not identify with them. I view his suggestions after reading the manuscript as priceless.

Albert Gillis, the first director of the University of Texas String Project, and Dr. E. William Doty, former dean of the UT-Austin College of Fine Arts, for showing faith in my potential during my early teaching years. I especially note Albert's influence in Scene 106.

Stephen Clapp for the many hours he has spent combing every page of the manuscript and for his invaluable suggestions. I grew to admire Stephen, his talent, his productivity, and his caring attitude when he, too, was on our distinguished UT-Austin music faculty.

Dr. Anne Witt, former assistant director of the UT String Project, for her thought-filled suggestions after reading the manuscript.

Dr. Anne Mischakoff for her detailed review of the manuscript in its final stages, her encouraging feedback, and her valued advice.

Dr. Gerald Fischbach, who, with his visionary leadership as director of the International Workshops, has brought me in close contact with hundreds of progressive string teachers throughout the world. Although he may not recognize it, I feel his direct influence in Scene 63.

Dr. Samuel Applebaum, the late Paul Rolland, Dr. Robert Klotman, and Margaret Rowell for the tremendous support they have given me since they first observed my work with the University of Texas String Project in the early 1960s. To have the friendship and confidence of such distinguished string educators, whose own individual contributions are enormous, has meant a great deal to me. Naturally I feel their pedagogical influences. I have freely adopted the terms *balanced action* and *sequential action*, which I learned from Paul. I also wish to thank Sam for his enthusiastic reading of the manuscript of *The String Play*.

The authors of the following books, which I consulted often when writing about the various styles of bowing: *Principles of Violin Playing & Teaching* by Ivan Galamian, published by Prentice-Hall; *The Teaching of Action in String*

Playing by Paul Rolland and Marla Mutschler, published by Illinois String Research Associates; *Dictionary of Bowing Terms for Stringed Instruments* by Barbara Garvey Seagrave and Joel Berman, published by the American String Teachers Association; *Orchestral Bowing Etudes* by Samuel Applebaum, published by Belwin-Mills; *The Art of Cello Playing*, Second Edition, by Louis Potter, Jr., published by Summy-Birchard Music; and *The Modern Conductor*, Third Edition, by Elizabeth A. H. Green, published by Prentice-Hall.

Dr. Shinichi Suzuki, whose innovative and enlightened teaching method has made an enormous impact on my teaching as well as my expectations of students' levels of performance. He has shown us what can be done. The wonder child is no longer a phenomenon.

People from whom I learned, either directly or indirectly, little pieces of information which I have woven into at least a portion of a scene: Evangeline Benedetti, Scene 15; Jeanne Moore, Scene 35; Christopher Bunting, Scene 37; Gabor Rejto, Scene 38; Robert Culver, Scene 64; William Pordon, Scene 72; Mary Lindsay, Scene 88; Nannie Jamieson and Max Rostal, Scene 89; Dr. George Robinson, Scene 93; Dr. Marla Mutschler, Scene 98; Amanda Vick Lethco, Scenes 96 and 185; Richard Gill, Scene 102; Dr. Donald L. Hamann, Scene 105; Dr. Marvin Rabin, Scene 108; David Wiebe, Scene 113; William Primrose, Scene 116; Leonard Rose, Scene 117; Dr. Charles Ervin, Scene 133; Gene Pledge, Scene 152; and Dorothy Delay, Scene 167. It is possible these people will have no identity with the scene following their names.

The many string teachers of the public schools, private studios, Suzuki schools, and universities for their enthusiastic welcome of *Playing the String Game* and their requests for a follow-up book. Their feedback regarding my Texas-born ideas, which I have introduced in workshops in many different geographical locations, has been irreplaceable.

The American String Teachers Association, which has taken the lead in making it possible for string teachers to share ideas and to learn from each other through its conventions, workshops, and its beautiful journal, *American String Teacher*. With its permission I have used in Chapter 2 some sentences from my President's Message in the Summer 1979 issue.

The University Research Institute of the University of Texas at Austin for a grant to help with the final manuscript preparation.

Catherine Aal, with her upbeat enthusiasm as she spent hours typing and retyping the manuscript. Also, Marilyn Ross, who typed an earlier version.

Sally Blakemore for her terrific drawings.

Those super professionals at the University of Texas Press. What a Supporting Cast!

And that constant stream of wonderful young people who have passed through my studio and classroom doors over a period of many years. They have provided the inspiration, the motivation, and the challenges to keep my teaching of music a fresh and exciting adventure. Without the students, *The String Play* would have no reason or justification for existence.

Opening Notes

The purpose of this book is to share ideas with a special breed of people. It was written for any person who has been drawn to the fascinating challenge of getting four strings stretched over a hollow box to vibrate so they express his or her innermost feelings. Let's face it: We are not the run-of-the-mill! Surrounded by our personal computers, our microwaves, our cordless telephones, and our cable television, we know that our most treasured possession is of a simple, basic design—one that was perfected by the end of the seventeenth century. And we don't push a button to activate it; nor do we move a cursor. We use our own bodies, minds, and souls.

The ideas in *The String Play* were sprouted, weeded, and cultivated in my studio and classroom at the University of Texas at Austin. They usually came in response to a desperate need: I loved a student so much that I simply couldn't let him down. I had to find a solution to the problem which prevented the full realization of his dream of playing the cello beautifully.

It is my sincere hope that the 185 Scenes will help string students and players of various ages and levels of advancement, except the very young and the beginners. Most are applicable to any bowed instrument—a violin, viola, cello, or double bass. Each is rooted in at least one basic principle which underlies the technique and musicianship of the most advanced player. The same silk thread which runs through the intricate, complex tapestry of the artist can be woven into the apprentice's sampler. The person who instinctively approaches the instrument in such a manner that these principles are at work is quickly labeled "talented." Experience tells us that the number of people accredited with this positive attribute can be multiplied many times if these basic principles are set into motion.

To my colleagues who are teachers and to university or conservatory students preparing to become teachers: I would be thrilled if this book, along with presenting some new information and a new way of looking at the old, should help trigger your own creative ideas. Of all the comments I have received about *Playing the String Game*, this is the one that has been the most gratifying to me. String teaching is a fascinating profession when each sunrise brings a fresh day of discovery of new ways to help people learn to express their inner beauty through music. With each new student we are born again. I continually marvel at the giving spirit of the string teacher and the orchestra director. To us, it is not the dollars we make; it is the difference we make.

The 185 Scenes of *The String Play* can be incorporated into the study of any music or method. They are not intended to replace any existing method. I encourage that they be freely altered to complement the personality and style of the teacher, his instrumental technique, and the age and personality of the student. Except perhaps in Chapter 6, "The Children's Theater," which is intended to be read aloud, I would expect no one to use my exact words.

Some of the ideas and insights found throughout the book first revealed themselves in strange places at surprising times—in the car, at the grocery store, in the post office, at the breakfast bar. It often appeared that their scheduled departure time was the same as the moment of arrival. Thus, with each new idea, speed was necessary to capture the kernel, later to be examined, reviewed, and tested as to its full meaning and usefulness.

Often it turned out to be something as simple and supposedly obvious as the jar of mayonnaise sitting in the front of the refrigerator shelf at eye level, just waiting to be found! Yet, when the idea was brought into the studio, my students' advancement leaped forward.

A word to the kids who are studying a stringed instrument: My compliments to you! You are developing a skill that will enrich your entire lives. Some fads come and go but you are investing your time, talent, and energy in something of lasting value. I have never heard an adult say that he or she regretted studying music in youth but I have heard the opposite at least 2,059 times!

My hat is off to the parents of string students! Your priorities are in line! What a unique position you are in to help and to encourage your youngster's music making. If you have studied the instrument, the worth of your assistance is obvious. If you have not, you may at times be in a better position to see the jar of mayonnaise than others, who see all the complexities. I trust *The String Play* will help and interest you and will at times bring a smile to your lips.

The book was not designed to be read from beginning to end like a novel or textbook. Instead, I picture the string student, the parent, or the teacher picking it up at a casual moment and reading one or possibly two episodes at a time, skipping around at will, much like we enjoy the short anecdotes and articles in the *Reader's Digest*. Each Scene is self-contained; if references to other Scenes are recommended, they are listed in its Inner Drama. When there is a specific need, the "Cue Sheets" at the end of the book stand ready to help.

Most of the book was written from the viewpoint of a string teacher or player but Chapter 6, "The Children's Theater," brings a different outlook. Aren't we always astonished at what we can learn when we perceive a subject through another set of eyes? Perhaps I have said enough.

On to the drama of playing and teaching strings . . .

The String Play

1 The Play

Cast of Characters

- Student(s)
- Teacher
- Supporting Cast of parents, family, other students, and friends

Setting

The action takes place every day in many places throughout the world. Time: Present.

About the Characters

The characters in this play are real people and traditionally are not played by actors or actresses. They have had no professional theatrical training and may be of any age, race, or sex. However, in most productions the person who plays the role of Teacher arrived on planet Earth some years before the person(s) who portrays the Student(s). He also has had significantly greater training and experience in making music.

As the play progresses, the part of Student melds into the part of Teacher; thus, one person moves into a dual role. He becomes his own Teacher, yet remains the Student through the final act. He learns from everyone and everything.

Unlike other plays the parts are not filled by a casting director. Each of the principal characters—the Student(s) and the Teacher—has chosen to play in this real life drama. He has also selected the instrument to serve as his stage voice, though not without influence from the Supporting Cast.

Production Crew

The musician who plays the role of Teacher also serves as director, producer, technical advisor, script writer, program coordinator, publicity agent, stage manager, audio engineer, and lighting designer. He manages to focus the spotlight on the Student(s) throughout every scene. The script and the entire production are designed for the benefit of the Student(s) and for the people whose lives will be touched by the music.

Props

- A violin, viola, cello, or double bass
- A bow for each instrument
- Rosin
- Music
- A music stand
- Records or cassettes
- Additional props that may be required for some scenes

About the Play

Though it may appear commonplace and involves people in everyday life, this play is a dramatic production. It is the story of miracles.

- The miracle that human beings can reach beyond their physical realm and express their inner beauty through music.

- The miracle that sound waves travel and that living creatures have ears to receive them and minds to interpret them.

- The miracle that, with a hank of hair attached tightly to the ends of a stick and drawn across a string, one can evoke from a hollow box some of the most glorious sounds known.

- The miracle that these sounds can be far more than just pleasing tones, that they can take on personality, character, and a spiritual beauty.

- The miracle that some people have felt called upon to design and make instruments to serve as tools and that others have been driven to compose music and write it on paper as a heritage for generations to come.

- The miracle that people have been given a body with the ability to move and to develop meticulous skills, a mind able to direct and to remember, and a soul to guide the operation so a meaningful combination of sounds can be brought forth from an instrument.

- The miracle that people have the gift of imagination within their power, the ability to feel emotions, and the motivation to express them.

- The miracle of the human hand, its uniqueness in adaptability, and its ability to respond and perform on command.

- The miracle of being able to learn, to give, and to share.

- The miracle of love.

This is a drama of people and music.

2 The Nature of the Production

Plays are looked on by most people as an entertainment form that is produced on a stage before an audience who expects to be amused, captivated, amazed, or moved. The String Play is an exception. It is the total experience of learning to play and perform on a stringed instrument. For some, this involves many years in which the play is interwoven into the professional and personal life of the player. For others, it is primarily a home and school activity to be enjoyed with friends and family. In either case the teacher-producer-director has the major responsibility for the script and production design during the first decade or more.

Various Kinds of Productions

A wide variety of methods of production have been used to help music students learn to play instruments. Most methods have evolved from the work and style of one generation building on the previous one, plus ideas and insight that come when the need arises. Some methods stress one aspect more than others. Except for those which have a specified sequence of music to be learned, most methods remain nameless or are broadly labeled the _____ school.

From time to time one method or influence will stand out. Like a comet in the sky, it appears to come out of nowhere and makes a great impact on many people. In these methods and in other schools which have staged productions with positive results, certain characteristics prevail.

- The consideration of the total design from the moment the curtain rises.

- The focus on using a model to help the mind's ear and eye "hear" and "see" the final production.

- The isolation of each gesture and technique.

- A well-designed step-by-step plot.

- The mutual respect of the participants in the play.

- An awareness of the influence of the supporting cast.

- The time-honored belief in the necessity of careful home practice.

- The presence of the human qualities called patience, faith, courage, discipline, humor, and love.

The Script

The music teacher has a unique position as a script writer. Though she studies and plans a logical sequence of music, activities, and approaches for the lesson or class, she must be an adept quick-change artist. From moment to moment her actions and words must bounce off unexpected conditions and the moods and reactions of the students. Armed with multiple pedagogical tools that seem to expand with each new experience, the teacher also becomes a master of improvisation. She meets the magic of the moment.

As she designs and modifies her script, the music teacher totally respects the uniqueness of each human being. Indeed, this very uniqueness of each individual student is what keeps the work of the string teacher so fascinating. Why else would it be possible for a veteran teacher to exude genuine enthusiasm as she guides yet another student in a technique, such as vibrato? After thirty or forty years of watching hundreds of students pass across her stage, this could seem deadly repetitious. Even for the most imaginative teacher who is able to capture the spirit of reliving each new experience with every student, the freshness would almost inevitably grow stale if people were all alike. Surely a more challenging field would be sought after the third or fourth year.

The script is written and rewritten as new experiences pop up every day in the life of a string teacher. The possibilities are endless because she deals with so many aspects of the student as a human being. Unlike the history professor, she concerns herself with a variety of shapes and sizes of hands, arms, and bodies and the way they move. Unlike the math teacher, she deals with the expression of heartfelt emotions prompted by countless personal experiences. And what art teacher spends time thinking of ways to help the student's mind learn to move with the lightning speed demanded of the orchestral musician? Not to mention the many facets of the personality with which she must work in order to build the confidence needed for a public performance. Thus, with each student she learns, and miraculously her attitude is forever young. Her script never turns yellow with age.

Production Techniques

Three primary techniques are used by the modern music teacher: imitation, dialogue, and mime. Imitation is by far the most effective and prevalent method for the very young child. Dialogue and mime are necessities in the teaching of less young students.

Because no tone is emitted from a stringed instrument without a physical action on the part of the player, the study of movement is a focal point and frequently the most baffling part of string teaching. To express in words how to move the human body in order to achieve certain results can be the most challenging part of the string teacher's job. Certainly such sentences as "Hold this note a little longer," "Make a crescendo here," and "Play this phrase with more feeling" are child's play in comparison.

On the other hand, the study of muscles and tendons in the physical anatomy might conceivably equip the teacher with necessary ammunition to eradicate every problem and to explain every technique. The secret appears not to lie here, however. What student, for example, could possibly learn to pick a flower from the ground by a detailed technical description of the complex workings of the muscular system and of the kinesthetic senses involved? The obvious initial solution is to demonstrate the action or to provide a flower too beautiful to resist. The answer on a continuing basis lies with the mental image.

The Mental Image

For the young actor cast in the role of an old man, undoubtedly his first intuitive mental process is the visualization of an elderly person. The same is true with the picking of a flower. Though no one may be on hand to give a demonstration for imitation purposes, the actor has stored in his mental photo library an action shot he can instantly see with his mind's eye. It tells him instinctively what to do.

When isolated from all others, almost every physical action required in string playing has been experienced by the student somewhere or sometime in everyday life. With the exception of very young children, most students have a rich background of experiences either firsthand or vicariously through movies or television. When a student walks through the door of a studio or classroom, he appears to be carrying only his instrument and music. But with him he brings an immense library of practical material applicable to string pedagogy. He has been filming and cataloging for years.

If the teacher's words can trigger the flash of an instant picture or feeling from the enormous storehouse in the brain, the student has had a notable head start. Though some people have intuitively used this technique through the ages, only in recent years have the effects of mental imagery on the brain waves and the chemicals of the body been proven in scientific laboratories. No longer can an intelligent, informed person label such activity a child's game. Somehow the miracle of creation has provided man and woman with the capability to achieve certain goals within limits if the image of the desired goal is tattooed on the brain.

Tapping Creativity

The use of mental imagery and fantasy in teaching appears to help tap the inborn creativity of the student's mind. Unlike some other subjects in which instruction focuses on the presentation of facts and the encouragement of logical thinking, music teaching lends itself to the freeing and developing of the imaginative potential, which some researchers believe to be centered in the very special right side of the brain.

The music found on the printed page or in recordings had its beginning in the creative mind.

So, why should the music student or the teacher, as they work together toward developing the skills to transform it to their own self-created sound waves, be afraid to use the imagination? Without this precious human quality, no music would exist.

Scene by Scene

Just as life itself is made up of a series of moments, the String Play is composed of momentary episodes interspersed between performances of music. For convenience sake these may be called Scenes. Deep in the core of each Scene is a concept or principle. The approach of learning an isolated technique or principle by relating it to an everyday, vicarious, or fictional experience may at times appear indirect but in truth it cuts straight through to the core. The results are direct.

The Scene Design

The 185 Scenes on the following pages are designed for students of violin, viola, cello, or double bass unless otherwise indicated. Except for the episodes in the chapter entitled "The Children's Theater," each Scene is composed of at least three parts: the suggested words and actions for the teacher to use, the Cue to Use, and the Inner Drama, which explains the technical or pedagogical purposes behind the Scene. In some Scenes an additional section entitled Props or Musical Setting has been included.

The titles are used in the book for identification purposes only. Rarely will they be used in the studio or classroom. Instead, the script will flow out of the teacher's other instructions. Some teachers, however, may use the titles as a two- or three-word reminder to the student of something already learned.

The reader is advised to freely alter the script to adapt to her personality and to the age, experience, and personality of the student(s). In fact, it is believed that many students and parents will find most of them helpful, even without a teacher's interpretation. Though a few may require more than one student, the great majority of the Scenes are designed for either an individual or a class teaching situation. Some Scenes overlap in purpose since the need for disguised repetition is a well-known principle in teaching. Students soon learn to ignore a repeated admonition or to label it as nagging.

The following Scenes are grouped according to categories, not in the order they should appear in lessons. It is intended that the teacher will determine the appropriate order of presentation of the Scenes for each class or student. Or, at the appropriate moment of need, she will call forth one. The six "Cue Sheets" at the end of the book provide a quick reference. *Naturally the music itself should always remain the dominant feature of every music lesson.*

Before the introduction of the Scenes it is assumed that the student will have already had some training on a stringed instrument. He will have learned to hold the instrument and bow and to play some music. The stage is set.

THE CURTAIN RISES

3 The Drama of the Bow

The unique BOW & RIGHT ARM DANCING DUO enters stage right. From their graceful, sweeping motions to their leaps through the air, they move as a perfectly synchronized team. At times they shoot across the string like an arrow, only to come to a halt in mid-flight. What a performance they give with their bouncing steps in a countless combination of rhythms and angles! Their clever and well-timed choreography wins the admiration of all!

But what makes this dynamic pair so unique in a world filled with dancers? Why is it an out-of-the-ordinary treat? Rather than dancing *to* music, it dances *to make* music.

The forty-seven Scenes in this chapter are designed to help build better bow technique. They may be used in any order and are intended to be interspersed with the music. It is assumed that the double bass students are using French bows although most of the principles remain the same for the German bow. Additional Scenes related to bowing can be found in later chapters. *As always, the music itself must play the dominant role throughout every lesson.* For quick references to subject matter and specific needs, the reader is advised to refer to the "Cue Sheets" following Chapter 8.

SCENES FOR BETTER BOWING

Coconut Cream Pie
SCENE I

Musical Setting: A lyric phrase requiring great sensitivity

Teacher: "I brought you some imaginary homemade pie today! In fact, we have two kinds— apple pie with two crisp crusts and some coconut cream pie topped with whipped cream. Please help yourself to an invisible fork.

"If you will close your eyes, I will serve each of you a generous piece. . . . Now with your eyes still closed, take a bite."

Before the forks reach the mouths, the teacher calls out, "Freeze!

"Open your eyes. If this had been real pie, would you have known before you tasted it whether I had served you coconut cream pie or apple pie? You could? How?"

The students will explain that they would have felt the texture of the pie when they cut into it.

"But how? None of you ate with your fingers!"

Together it is evolved that one can feel through the fork.

"The same is true with our bows. When we hold the bow sensitively and focus our attention on the place where the hair meets the string, the hand will feel almost as though it is touching the string. Even with our eyes closed, we know if we are bowing near or far from the bridge or on a thick or thin string. Let's feel through our bows as we play this phrase again. It will make the music sensitive and alive!"

Cue to Use

Anytime the teacher wishes to improve the expressiveness of a student's playing and the sensitivity of her bow hand. It probably should be held on reserve for a day when the lesson or class needs an added spark.

Inner Drama

In this scene the teacher highlights the phenomenon of being able to feel something through an inanimate object, which in itself has no sensory perception. This magic occurs in many situations. The dental hygienist, for example, depends on feeling through a steel instrument to detect a tiny rough bump on a tooth under the gums. This signals to her that there is a deposit on the enamel to be scraped clean. The miracle lies in the human hand—not in the object being held.

The teacher enjoys thinking of a possible dinner scene in the youngster's home that evening. Should a parent ask, "Judy, what did you do in your music lesson today?" surely "the same old thing" would be an unlikely answer. Anything out of the ordinary is more apt to be remembered. The teacher's goal is to make an indelible impression on the youngster's mind.

Weather Report
SCENE 2

Without instruments the teacher and students stand holding their bows.

"Check your bow hold. Is your thumb nicely curved and opposite the second finger? Monkey see, monkey do!"

With no words of explanation, the teacher turns his back to the students and begins speaking rapidly and enthusiastically in the style of an old-time TV weather reporter. As he talks, he points to an invisible map of the United States and outlines the temperature figures with the tip of the bow.

"We had balmy weather on the East Coast to-

day. Boston 68. New York 72. The hot spot in the nation was down in Greenville, South Carolina—94! A few snow flurries in Nebraska! Lincoln 28. Eight inches of snow in Greeley, Colorado—a brisk 18 degrees! San Francisco, a pleasant 65. Sunshine in Austin, Texas 73.

"Now let's take a look at Australia! Cloudy skies in Melbourne today—22. Cooler but clear on the West Coast—Perth 15. Sydney was rainy and 24. Sunshine in Brisbane—28. Stay tuned to KTBC-TV. In a moment we will have the local forecast for tomorrow."

Cue to Use

Anytime the teacher wishes to emphasize control of the bow tip and senses that a change of pace is in order.

Inner Drama

The teacher has witnessed wonderful improvement in bow technique of his students after such scenes as this TV weather report. His primary goal is for each student to learn to manage her bow with the utmost skill and accuracy. He knows that, with each activity removed from the responsibility of producing sounds with the instrument, the bow will be viewed as an increasingly friendly object.

The teacher's secondary goal is to have a quick change of pace during the lesson or class. Most certainly after they have learned the weather in both the United States and Australia and have switched their thinking from Fahrenheit to Celsius, the students will feel refreshed on return to music making.

An added bonus is that the students will tend to look on their teacher with more interest after he has demonstrated a flair as a weather reporter!

Scrubbies
SCENE 3

Musical Setting: A passage requiring fast separate bow strokes

The teacher tosses a "scrubbie" to each student.
"Let's get this place cleaned up!"

Everyone shakes the scouring pads as though they are scrubbing an imaginary kitchen. While they work, the teacher talks.

"Great! Look how your upper arm also shakes! The under part of it quivers like jelly! Watch it!"

Together it is discovered that the inside of the

passive upper arm shakes a different direction than the hand.

"This is nature's way of balancing the arm! Because of it we can work a long time without getting tired. Now scrub in the direction of short down- and up-bows. Note how the jelly shakes best. . . . Good!"

The teacher and students return to their instruments and play some fast détaché strokes in various parts of the bow with the same balanced action. If necessary, the location of the elbow will be changed.

"Let your elbow float and the underside of your arm jiggle like jelly."

Cue to Use

1. Anytime for the improvement of fast détaché bowing and for the understanding of balanced action.
2. Whenever the right elbow and upper arm appear stiff or move in the same direction as the hand in fast détaché, tremolo, or sautillé bowing.

Props

Brightly colored "scrubbies" sold in grocery stores. They are shaped like balls about three inches in diameter and made of plastic mesh. Their traditional function is to aid in the scouring of pots and pans.

Inner Drama

The action described in this scene is only one of many daily activities which require balanced ac-

tion. As a variation on this scene the teacher may wish to have the student raise his elbow either too high or too low to show how the action is blocked. Finding exactly the right position of the elbow and the feeling that it floats is half the trick. The word *relax* is not the solution if the position is wrong.

A Pattern
SCENE 4

Teacher: "I'll show you the pattern for bowing this passage. Free your hand and oil your joints. My hand will be the motor."

Without using bows the teacher's right hand holds the student's right hand, moving it in the bowing pattern he wishes to establish. The shape, speed, size, and character of the motions will be the same as his own when performing the musical passage. After a number of repetitions while both teacher and student chant or sing, the teacher says:

"Now you have the feel of it! Let's hear you play this music using the same pattern."

Cue to Use

Anytime that the bowing motion is not effective, but most especially when the student's arm appears to be moving in an unnatural manner.

Inner Drama

This scene describes a standard method employed by physical therapists with their patients to re-establish neurological pathways that for one reason or another have been obliterated. By repeating an action many times new pathways are established. Instead of working from the usual brain-hand direction, this method begins with the hand and moves back to the brain.

Although used for a different reason, the hand-brain route can also be very effective with string students when something looks wrong. If all joints—including the shoulder, elbow, and wrist—are oiled, the motion in the hand seems to tell the arm just how far and in what manner to move. It ensures that the impulses start in the right place—the hand. Should the pattern fade with time, the student's own left hand can serve as the patterning motor in home practice.

This scene is easily adaptable to left hand techniques, especially in the study of vibrato.

A Swim in Molasses

SCENE 5

*Musical Setting: A melodic phrase requiring a
full, singing tone*

Teacher: "Let's fill up the room with some rich
thick molasses! Don't worry, no one will drown!
It only comes up to our shoulders. Now let's take
a swim!"

The teacher pantomimes the breast stroke and
the students imitate.

"Look how our hands and arms are pulling the
molasses aside! I feel the pull coming right from
my back out to my fingertips. . . .

"Presto! The molasses has vanished! We are
swimming through air. This feels quite different,
doesn't it? My arms feel loose and flimsy!

"Now let's try water. That's better. . . . Now
the room is filled with molasses again. Our hands
and arms feel different yet! I wonder why?"

With the teacher's guidance the students will
point out that the molasses offers much resistance, the air none, and the water some.

"Yes, *resistance* is the key word! When we pull
anything, we must feel that we are pulling against
something.

"But where did the molasses and water come
from? I don't see any. . . .

"Right! They originated in our minds. This is
called imagination!"

The teacher and students return to their
instruments.

"Let's pull some beautiful bow strokes. Sink
the bow hair deep into the string. The contact
itself creates some resistance but, as the bow
moves, our imaginations can help us! With imagination we can pull up-bows as well as down-bows!
Feel the resistance!"

Cue to Use

Anytime the teacher wishes to help the student improve the sustaining quality of her tone
through the pulling action.

Inner Drama

The teacher believes that one of the most powerful keys to a beautiful, sustained tone is the pulling action. He wishes to relate this sensation to
a nonmusical activity which has been enjoyed
by the student. The teacher also knows that
anything as preposterous as swimming through
molasses can awaken the fantasy in the young
person's mind and be highly motivating.

In the act of pulling, two sets of opposing
muscles are at work. The resulting tone quality is
distinctively different than that produced by other
actions.

Kangaroos and Roadrunners
SCENE 6

While holding her instrument in playing position, the teacher says:

"Australia has a very special animal—the kangaroo! Kangaroos come in several sizes. Some are red, others are gray, but they all jump to go places."

The teacher places her bow on a string at the frog. Without sound, it suddenly springs up and lands on the same string at the tip. After a moment it springs back to the frog. She does this in an unhurried manner although the initial thrust of each spring is vigorous. When she calls, "Join me!" the students move their bows like jumping kangaroos.

"After your bow lands, check the distance between its hair and the bridge. Try to make it land on the exact same spot of the string each time and stay there a moment before springing back. Let's practice this until it is perfect. . . .

"America does not have kangaroos but its southwestern states have something Australia does not have. Roadrunners!"

The teacher and the students zip their bows quickly and almost silently from the frog to the tip very close to the string; then, after a moment of rest, they return speedily to the frog.

"Again, check the distance between your bow hair and the bridge. If it is not the same at both ends of the trip, try again. Think of the top of the bridge near the string you are playing on as the curb of the road. Keep the roadrunner's feet at the same distance from the curb! He, too, has his own style of going places.

"Good! Now that you have done that several times, let's hear some slow whole bows with a beautiful deep tone. Allow the weight to sink into the string."

Cue to Use

1. Anytime the sounding point, the spot on the string where the bow crosses, changes its distance from the bridge for no musical reason.
2. Whenever the bow hand does not look properly aligned with the arm.
3. Anytime the bowing action appears sluggish.

Inner Drama

Who possibly could resist a kangaroo or a roadrunner? The teacher knows that this double feature will greatly improve the student's ability to keep the sounding point consistently the same

distance from the bridge when using a whole bow. Though the spring of the kangaroo is energetic, there is still plenty of time for feedback before the landing. Thus, the muscles can make any necessary corrections en route. As an added benefit, the act of springing the bow from one end to the other usually throws the hand and the arm into perfect alignment. It also tends to liven up the bow action. The roadrunner motion, on the other hand, is ballistic and allows no time for feedback.

Spreading Mayonnaise
SCENE 7

Musical Setting: A melodic phrase requiring long, sensitive bow strokes

Without instruments the teacher and students hold their bows horizontally with their left hands at the tip.

"With our right hands let's spread some invisible mayonnaise across the top of the bow stick! Spread it from one end to the other and back. . . .

Note how flexible your fingers are. Now play some music keeping the same touch."

Cue to Use

1. Anytime to increase sensitivity and flexibility in the bow hand.
2. Whenever the student appears to be clutching her bow.
3. Anytime to make the bow changes smoother.

Inner Drama

The teacher believes that the touch is the final determiner of the degree of sensitivity in playing a stringed instrument. In perhaps no other instrument does the player have such personal contact with the medium through which music is produced.

All string students have what seems like dozens of things to think about at the same time. In the process of learning to play it can be easy to overlook one of the most important elements of all—the link between the human body and the tools for making music.

Spotlight on Bowing
SCENE 8
(Especially designed for groups but can be adapted to the private lesson)

The teacher distributes four flashlights to the students and keeps one for himself. They all face a blank wall as the lights are dimmed.

"The lights of each of your flashlights will be the string notches of the bridges. David, your light will be the A, Teresa's will be D, Ann's G, and Tinka's the other string. Let's get the notches lined up the same distance apart in a nice curve, just like the top of your bridge. Hold your lights still. Now with the spotlight from my flashlight I will trace the route of the bow."

The teacher selects any kind of bowing he wishes to demonstrate. With the moving ball of light he can show the shape of the stroke, the speed of the motion, the distribution of the bow, and the rhythmic pattern. In addition, he can dramatize string crossings or the unique characteristics of any bowing. For example, the teacher can show the swing of the spiccato stroke and how it hits the string at the bottom of each arc.

Many possibilities exist for dramatizations requiring only two flashlights as it often is not necessary to have all four strings represented. After his demonstration the teacher switches roles with a student.

"Now my spotlight will be the string. Your light will provide the action!"

Cue to Use

Anytime to demonstrate specific bowing techniques, the speed and contour of a bow stroke, and string crossings.

Props

Five or fewer flashlights and a room that can be dimmed.

Inner Drama

The teacher had discovered that such a flashlight drama can clearly depict the speed and contour of a bow stroke. Before trying the flashlights he had on occasion drawn diagrams during a lesson to serve as a visual aid. This had helped some students part of the time.

Naturally nothing substitutes for a visual aid and aural demonstration by the teacher with his instrument. However, the teacher has noticed that often the student's eyes do not focus on the action being emphasized. For example, her eyes may be captured by the vibrato motion while the teacher demonstrates a bow stroke. With the lights dimmed, the single moving light magnetizes all eyes and the lesson is tattooed on the brain. Besides, it is great fun for both the student and the teacher!

Tickle the Floating Hand
SCENE 9

The teacher places her right hand on top of the student's bow stick, directly above the sounding point, where the bow hair contacts the string. She leaves it suspended there while the student bows, gently adjusting the pressure so the tone quality is pleasing.

"The bow tickles my floating hand as it glides past! Listen to that lovely sound! Now, while you continue bowing, I will remove my hand. Try to get the same sound!"

Cue to Use

Anytime the teacher wishes to improve the student's tone. It is especially useful if the bow drifts on the string, the bow stick is not at the best angle, the supported weight is not focused toward the sounding point, or the bow hand lacks flexibility.

Inner Drama

By adding a little weight at the sounding point the teacher has helped to provide a model tone. No model is more effective for the building of a beautiful tone than one in which the student has had an active participation. When the floating hand is removed, most students will automatically adjust their hands and arms to produce the same sound. If not, the teacher will help change the angle of the bow and/or the arm so the energy flows to the sounding point. Energy directed to any other location, other than the left hand, is a waste. Parents can assist their children with this at home. However, it is easy for a cello student to tickle his own left hand while playing open strings.

If there is already too much pressure in proportion to the speed of the bow and/or the distance from the bridge, the teacher can ask the student to move the bow faster and to lighten it. Then the teacher will adjust her hand until a pleasing sound is found. This scene can also be used to encourage more flexibility of the right hand since the responsibility of providing pressure has been relegated to the floating hand.

Red Lights
SCENE 10

Teacher: "Put an imaginary red light bulb on the tip of the right elbow. Attach another one to the tip of the bow. . . . Imagine that the room is dark. Now practice some silent string crossings at a tempo not very fast.

"As one red light goes up, the other will go down! They work as a team!"

Cue to Use

When the bow and arm fail to work as a unit in string crossings, particularly with the larger instruments.

Inner Drama

The teacher considers that there is an optimum position of the bow and arm for each string. When the bow moves from one string to another, it is important for the hand, arm, and bow to keep the same relationship with each other. He believes that one of the easiest ways to check this rela-

tionship is to focus on the movement of the bow tip and the elbow.

This scene is not applicable to string crossings which alternate between two strings at a fast tempo because it would result in far too much motion in the elbow and upper arm.

Shooting Arrows
SCENE 11

Musical Setting: A phrase or passage which requires some martelé bow strokes

Teacher: "Help yourself to an imaginary bow and arrow."

The teacher and students practice shooting arrows.

"Let's note what happens when we shoot an arrow. Take a look at the timing. We use our energy to get the bow and arrow set in a perfect position so the arrow is ready to shoot forward. But the arrow will not budge an inch as long as we continue to apply the energy. It is only on the *release* of energy that the arrow will start on its trip! Shoot some more arrows and notice this very special timing. . . ."

The students and teacher return to their instruments.

"Now let's 'shoot' some martelé strokes. Place your bow on the string. Sink the hair in deep. Now abruptly let go of some of the pressure and the bow will shoot across the string! When the bow finishes its trip, whether it is long or short, the hair should remain on the string. Now again pinch the hair against the string, suddenly release some pressure, and let your bow shoot back to the starting point."

Cue to Use

Anytime to improve the student's martelé bowing and most especially the timing of the application of pressure.

Inner Drama

Through this scene the teacher has conveyed several important concepts regarding the martelé stroke: its ballistic characteristic, the necessary application of pressure before the motion begins, and the fact that the bow hair should remain on the string. It stresses that the motion of the bow is brought about by the release of some pressure—not by the initial application of pressure. This characteristic makes martelé uniquely different from most bow strokes.

If an up-bow of a martelé stroke ends near the frog, the bow may be lifted slightly and reset on the string in order to avoid a crunch.

The teacher may wish to point out that the bow and arrow comprise one of the earliest inventions and that they were used at least thirty thousand years ago, if not earlier. People depended on them for food and clothing. This definitely was before the day of the microwaves!

This scene may be followed immediately by Scene 21, *The Archer Takes Time.*

Five Dollars for the First Inch
SCENE 12

Teacher: "Let's say that you are being paid $6.00 for every good bow stroke! The purchaser will pay $5.00 for the first inch of the bow drawn and only $1.00 for the remainder of the stroke.

"Make sure that the first inch sounds beautiful!"

Cue to Use

1. Whenever one part of the student's bow strokes does not sound good and needs more attention.
2. Anytime the string fails to respond at the beginning of a bow stroke.

Inner Drama

Naturally the teacher will use this scene sparingly since it smacks of being commercial. However, she has learned from experience that it captures the imagination of most students and the immediate improvement of sound is usually quite dramatic! At least, a sleepy ear will wake up and listen to the beginning of the bow strokes. Even if the problem is in the left hand, it usually is quickly corrected.

Since prices rise and fall as the market fluctuates, on another day the going rate for a different portion of the bow stroke may be higher. This scene was particularly designed for successive bow strokes, not isolated ones.

Hammer and Nails
SCENE 13

The teacher distributes some imaginary hammers and nails to the students and sets them to work.

"I notice that all of you are focusing your attention on the nail heads! Why is that? Let's try it another way. Watch the hand that holds the hammer instead."

Most assuredly there soon will be lots of "ouches" and sore thumbs stuck into mouths.

"The purpose of the hammer is to drive the nail into the wood. The purpose of the bow is to get its rosined hair to catch the string and set it into motion. In both cases, if we concentrate on the goal itself, we get better results. Let's watch the string vibrate beautifully as we draw the bow across it."

Cue to Use

Anytime the student bows perfunctorily or focuses her attention on the bow hold, rather than on the sounding point.

Inner Drama

The teacher believes that having a clearly stated goal is of immense importance. While no one has any doubt about the reason for hammering a nail, often the string student is so preoccupied with the many facets of string playing that she appears to draw the bow across the string without a real purpose in mind. The immediate improvement of resonance is usually quite noticeable when her attention is attracted to the goal of getting the string to vibrate.

Salting a Sweet Potato
SCENE 14

Musical Setting: A phrase or passage which requires a big, full tone

Teacher: "Picture a giant, buttered sweet potato in front of each of us. Let's salt it from one end to the other. Use lots of energy."

After the students have salted the sweet potato while moving their right arms in the direction of down- and up-bow strokes the teacher says: "Notice how loose your elbow feels when you shake the salt with your hand. Does the underside of your upper arm jiggle like jelly? If this isn't happening, raise or lower your elbow until you find the position where the fat of your upper arm jiggles the best. The elbow height will be slightly different for each portion of the bow stroke."

After the sweet potato is successfully salted, the teacher continues: "Now let's do the same thing while holding the bow."

Gradually, the teacher will help the students transfer this action to the instrument. The goal is to draw the bow in the air a few inches above the

appropriate air route for each string, shaking the hand and bow frog in a bye-bye motion throughout the stroke.

"Watch the tip of the bow. Of course, it, too, will shake slightly but try to keep it on the path set by the hand and the frog. Now let's draw some beautiful tones. Have your hand and arm in a position which would allow you to raise your bow at any moment and salt the potato!"

Cue to Use

1. Anytime, except in the early training, for the improvement of the bow arm and tone production.
2. Whenever the teacher believes that the hand and arm are not aligned to the best advantage and the student is unable to play with equal volume in all parts of the bow.

Inner Drama

The teacher has discovered through experience that this unique exercise can have miraculous results with most students. Usually the tone is instantly improved. Since this salting action requires the support of the weight of the bow and could put a strain on the hand, it should not be done in the very early training. Also, practice of it should be limited to very short time durations.

The teacher is particularly aware that any form of knocking throws the hand and arm into the best possible relationship so that the power line

between the player's back and hand is immediately open. She believes that this knocking action, which is at a 90° angle to the bow stick, is a vital step toward an expressive technique.

Fabric Store
SCENE 15

Teacher: "A fabric store is fun to visit! Have you noticed how the customers walk around touching the fabric?"

The teacher produces some swatches of material for the students to feel.

"Look how we do this! . . . Each of us uses the same part of our fingers! If we could visit fabric stores any place in the world—in Australia, Italy, Alaska, or Texas—we would find that almost every person feels the fabric the same way we do. There appears to be a spot in our fingers especially designed for feeling. It is someplace near the fingerprint or first joint.

"Now let's feel our bow sticks with the same sensitive spots. It helps not to hold the bow too tightly. Draw some bow strokes and be aware of this sensitivity."

Cue to Use

Anytime the student holds her bow tightly or with a lack of sensitivity.

Props

Some samples of fabric if easily available. If not, the student can feel her clothing.

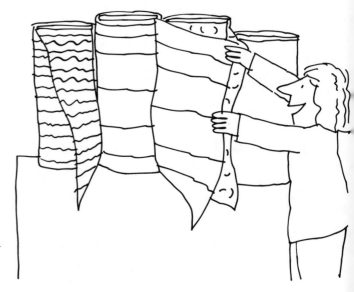

Inner Drama

The teacher's goal is to help the student be aware of another miracle of the human body and use it in string playing. While he has noted that some successful musicians appear to hold their bows with a part of the fingers that is relatively insensitive, the teacher has found that concentration on this precious quality of the human hand has helped many of his students.

If a student should try to relate this scene to her thumb, the teacher will explain that the mechanics of bowing require that the thumb be treated differently. The contact with the frog and the bow stick is traditionally on the inside corner of the thumb's tip.

Focus Here!
SCENE 16

Teacher: "Place the middle of your bow on the D string. Let's check that balance. X marks the spot! Focus here!"

With her index finger the teacher squashes the student's bow stick down to the hair directly above the spot it contacts the string. Probably the stick will change its angle somewhat when the weight is focused on the string by the teacher and the student will unconsciously make adjustments in the position of his bow hand.

Then the teacher removes her finger and suspends her own bow about twelve or fifteen inches above the student's bow. Her goal is to make it perfectly parallel to the student's bow.

"Lift your bow almost up to my bow. Good! Now lower it down to the string. Keep it at exactly the same angle. Use my bow as your guide.

"Do this several times so you can remember it. This is how your hand and arm should feel when *this* part of the bow is focused on *this* spot on *this* string.

"Let's hear you start a bow stroke from this spot. The tone will jump out at you!"

Cue to Use

1. Anytime to help the student discover and remember the appropriate angle of the bow and the kinesthetic feelings in the hand and arm.
2. Whenever the tone sounds weaker in certain parts of the bow.

Inner Drama

The teacher's goal is to help the student focus his attention on the sounding point and find the ap-

propriate angle of the bow and distribution of arm weight. *Focus Here!* can be repeated on any string using any part of the bow. Naturally it is not possible to squash the stick down to the hair at either extreme end of the bow.

Pea Soup
SCENE 17

Teacher: "Picture a little man sitting on top of your bow stick near the tip eating pea soup. Now practice changing from an up-bow to a down-bow near the frog. Watch the little man with your mind's eye. Be careful that he doesn't splash the green soup over his tan suit! Change directions so smoothly that his eating is never disturbed!"

Cue to Use

1. Anytime, not too early in the training, when the student's bow tip rolls or shows too much movement of any kind during a bow change at the frog.
2. Whenever the bow changes need to be smoother.

Inner Drama

The teacher realizes that some students become very tense if too much attention is called to their muscular actions. However, anything that affects one end of the bow also affects the other. For example, when the stick rolls at the tip, it also rolls concomitantly at the frog. If the change is abrupt at the frog, it will also be abrupt at the tip. By focusing the attention on the opposite end of the bow with a specific goal in mind, most students will automatically make the adjustments necessary to correct the problem.

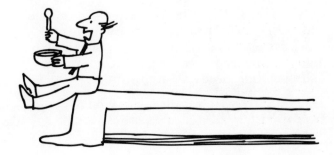

Boom-m-m
SCENE 18

Musical Setting: A passage or phrase requiring fast, articulated bow strokes on the string

Teacher: "Let's sing a scale at a moderate tempo with the word "BOOM" on each note. Keep the hum of the "m" going until you sing the next pitch. . . . Good!

"Now imitate this sound with your instrument. Begin each bow stroke with an accent by increasing both the pressure and the speed. Keep the bow moving in one direction or the other. It will be nonstop. . . .

"This kind of bowing is called accented détaché. Now play the scale faster! Your hand and forearm will move back and forth like you are erasing a pencil mark."

Cue to Use

1. Anytime, except in the very early training, to help the student learn or improve accented détaché bowing. It should be preceded by a study of martelé bowing and accents.
2. Whenever the student tries to use martelé bowing in a passage too fast for its effectiveness.

Inner Drama

The use of both consonant and vowel sounds is essential to fine string playing. The teacher's goal is to make instrumental music seem to have lyrics as does vocal music. The use of a word, such as "BOOM," can help the student immeasurably in home practice because her own voice can serve as a model.

One of the primary differences between accented détaché and martelé strokes is that the motion usually does not stop at the end of a détaché stroke unless a rest is notated. One stroke makes the next. Thus, a passage can be played much faster with accented détaché than with martelé. The reader may wish to refer to *The Ladybug Ride*, Scene 23, at this time.

A Good Bridge
SCENE 19

Teacher: "The wrist is like a good bridge! It gives but never collapses! Monkey see, monkey do!"

The teacher places the fingers of his right hand on top of his own left forearm in a position somewhat like a bow hold. As he talks, he very gently jiggles his right hand and wrist up and down. The fingers sink into the flesh, the thumb hangs loose, and the wrist is at the same level as the hand or slightly higher. The students imitate.

"Good! Your wrist is strong and flexible! It is the bridge between your arm and hand. When I tap on it, I can feel it give. Engineers also build their bridges to give a little. The ability to yield under pressures makes a bridge much stronger. In fact, it is necessary.

"Now let's try it in two undesirable ways. Make your wrist feel so hard and stiff that it remains rigid when I tap on it. . . . This would make the tone sound hard. We don't want that!

"Try it the opposite way. Let your wrist collapse. Feel the dead weight on your left forearm? That is what the bow would feel! The dead weight would crush the string's vibrations and the tone could not be beautiful.

"Find the good way again. Support your wrist but let it give a little as I tap on top of it. . . . Perfect! Now let's hear some beautiful tones!"

Cue to Use

1. Anytime the student's wrist looks rigid or collapsed.
2. Whenever the power flow from the student's back to the bow hand appears to be broken.
3. Anytime the weight on the bow seems to be dead rather than live and supported.

Inner Drama

The magic combination of strength and flexibility is stressed in this scene. It aids in finding the height of and feel in the wrist to open the power line from the player's back to the bow.

Through experience the teacher realizes the effectiveness of introducing a motion or kinesthetic feeling without the instrument or bow, then transferring it.

He also knows the way to ensure that the student experiences a particular internal sensation is to test it by doing the opposite. The surest way to find a relaxed state of a group of muscles, for example, is to consciously make them very tense, then relax them.

Glow in the Dark
SCENE 20

Teacher: "Paste an imaginary glow-in-the-dark tape reflector on the middle of your bow stick. Perhaps you would like to shape it as an eagle with outspread wings!

"Now turn off the lights in your mind's eye and play your piece. Watch the glowing eagle fly! . . . Does it make an interesting design? Does its speed vary?

"On a bowed instrument interesting movements make interesting music!"

Cue to Use

1. Whenever the bow motions are consistently one speed and the music lacks expression.
2. Anytime for bow distribution.

Inner Drama

The imaginary glow-in-the-dark tape helps the student to concentrate on one aspect of his music making. Sometimes almost everything a player does seems correct yet the music lacks zest. Varying the bow speeds and distributing the bow in different patterns can do much to liven a performance. Can anyone cite a famous creative dancer whose motions lack variety in speed and quality?

The Archer Takes Time
SCENE 21

Musical Setting: A passage or phrase which requires successive martelé strokes

Teacher: "The archer takes time to prepare her bow and arrow each time she shoots. The string player needs time to prepare her bow before 'shooting' a martelé stroke. She presses the bow hair into the string *before* the bow moves.

"With practice we can get faster but no composer would expect us to be superhuman. He realizes there is a limit to the number of martelé strokes we can play in a set period of time just as the archer also has a limit to the number of arrows she can shoot in one minute!"

Cue to Use

1. Whenever the student establishes a tempo too fast for martelé strokes. It should be preceded by *Shooting Arrows*, Scene 11.
2. Anytime the student tries to use martelé strokes in a fast passage and the teacher wishes to suggest that accented détaché be used instead.

Inner Drama

It is a fact of life that some bow strokes are better suited to a fast tempo than others and the wise composer keeps this thought in mind. When the

tempo is too fast for successive martelé strokes, the accented détaché stroke may be substituted. Well aware that trying to play a passage too fast with martelé bowing can cause tension in the arm, the teacher's goal is to prevent this from happening. The reader may wish to read *Boom-m-m*, Scene 18, at this time.

Colorful Skyways

SCENE 22
(Designed for a group)

Nine students are invited to participate. One will sit with her instrument. The teacher produces four strands of heavy yarn or ribbons in various bright colors.

"Jim and Meredith, I'd like for each of you to take one end of this red ribbon and stretch it across the D string like a bow. Let the middle of the ribbon touch the string. Center it between the two neighboring strings.

"Barbara and Sue, stretch this yellow ribbon across the A string."

Four more students will stretch ribbons across the other two strings, also at the sounding point.

"What a beautiful sight! It shows us the skyways in which we navigate our bows. Note the angle for each string and take a mental photo for your film library!

"Now let's return to our instruments and play on each of the strings while keeping this colorful picture in mind."

Cue to Use

Anytime the teacher would like to call attention to the bow route for each string.

Props

Heavy yarn or ribbons about forty-two inches long in four brilliant colors.

Inner Drama

The teacher's goal is to help the students form an unforgettable picture that makes them conscious of the various bow routes. Though he did not mention comparison of skyways, the distinct difference between each route is so obvious that it most certainly makes an indelible impression on each viewer.

The Ladybug Ride
SCENE 23

*Musical Setting: Fast passages requiring a
separate bow stroke for each note*

Teacher: "Imagine that you have a pet ladybug
who loves to ride on your bow arm! Her favorite
place to sit is on your upper arm above the elbow.

"But she has learned that the faster you play
separate bow strokes, the farther down the arm
she must travel to get a good ride. Sometimes she
sits on your forearm below the elbow. If you play
faster, she moves down to your wrist. When you
play really fast, she sits on top of your hand or
your fingers to get an exciting free ride!"

Cue to Use

Anytime the student uses too much upper arm in
playing fast passages with separate bows.

Inner Drama

The idea of focusing on one movable spot can
help students in bowing and in vibrato. The body
is designed so that the faster the action, the more
it moves to the outer extremities. Feet can move
faster than legs, and hands can move faster than
arms. Fingers can move faster than hands.

Fast alternating down- and up-bows require
smaller motions because there simply is not time
to cover a distance. Anyone writing a message
quickly does not use the big arm motions of the
sign painter.

Go Ahead—We'll Catch Up!
SCENE 24

*Musical Setting: A melody or passage to be
played legato*

Without a bow, the teacher pantomimes several
whole bow strokes using free paintbrush-type
motions.

"As I approach the end of a down-bow, I can
almost hear the arm say 'I think I'll start on back.'

"The fingers answer: 'That's OK. Go right
ahead. We want to go on just a little farther.
Don't worry. We'll take the bow with us but catch
up with you later!'

"The arm changes direction a moment or two
before the hand and fingers. Let's see you do
this. . . . Good! Now try it with your instrument
and bow."

Cue to Use

When the teacher wishes to introduce or review
smooth bow changes with the emphasis on hand
and finger flexibility. It is not suggested for the
very early training.

Inner Drama

The teacher is aware that the ability to make
smooth changes in bow direction at both ends of
the bow is essential for the singing quality associated with stringed instruments. The action described in this scene is called sequential. It has
been noted that in many actions in everyday life,
including walking and painting, the motion is
initiated by the large muscles and reaches the
smaller muscles of the outer extremities last.

The principle of sequential action or stroke
continuation also applies to the change from an
up-bow to a down-bow. It can occur in any portion of the bow. Since the bow hold while playing
at the frog looks and feels somewhat different
than when playing at the tip, the teacher has
called attention only to the change at the tip in
this scene. His goal is to isolate techniques as
much as possible in order to hasten learning.
Later, of course, he will spotlight the bow change
at the frog.

Pantomime is used first for two reasons: the
motion is easier to do when the fingers are freed
of the responsibility of holding the bow, and there
is no sound to distract the player's concentration.

Two for the Price of One!
SCENE 25

*Musical Setting: A dotted rhythmic figure of two
notes to be played energetically with separate
bows or with "hooked" bowing, e.g., a sixteenth note followed by a dotted eighth note,
or the reverse*

The teacher distributes a rubber band to each
student.

"Hold one end of the rubber band with your
left hand. Quickly stretch the other end with
your right hand in the direction of a down-bow
and immediately release it. Watch the rubber
band snap back! Good! Do this several times. . . .

"Now try this a different way. Let your right
hand ride back with the rubber band on its return
trip. . . . Good!

"Place your bow on the string about six or
eight inches from the tip. Play a short, fast down-

stroke and let the bow and hand snap back like the rubber band. . . . Good!"

After the students do this several times, the teacher guides them in reversing the bowing, starting the first of the two-note figure with an up-bow near the frog. Gradually, she leads them back to the music.

"You get two notes for the price of one! The price is one spurt of energy on the short note. Jab the short note!"

Cue to Use

Anytime a musical figure with dotted rhythm played with separate bows or with "hooked" bowing lacks vitality.

Props

A rubber band for each student.

Inner Drama

The teacher believes that the principle of two notes for the price of one described in this scene is vital to good music making. It adds rhythmic vitality to appropriate passages and keeps the bow action from sounding labored. An imaginary rubber band is readily available and can quickly be stretched as the musician plays the short note of a dotted rhythmic figure. The energy for the longer note is provided by the release of the rubber band and requires no added effort on the part of the player.

This principle of placing the impulse on only the shorter of the two notes applies whether it falls on or off the beat. The technique is also applicable to "hooked" bowing, in which the short note is played in the same direction as the preceding longer note. The spurt of energy is still directed to the short note and there is a stop on the dot of the longer note.

The bowing described in *Two for the Price of One!* is termed piqué by some musicians. Its literal translation is "pricked" and it can be played at a very fast tempo.

Mosquito Bites
SCENE 26

Teacher: "Look at those big imaginary mosquitoes landing on our left arms! Monkey see, monkey do."

The teacher slaps his arm as though he is killing a mosquito. As he repeats this two or three times, the students mimic.

"Fortunately, I brought along some imaginary salve for insect bites. Help yourself."

The teacher and students gently rub the soothing ointment on the bites.

"Good! Look how your hand applies the salve. . . . Now watch me again."

The teacher's right hand approaches his left arm vigorously as though he intends to slap it. About an inch from the arm his hand suddenly stops, then gently glides into a caressing motion. It moves slowly as though applying ointment.

"Something seems wrong! What could it be?"

The students will point out that the first part of the motion looked like a slap but the second part was a caress.

"Exactly! The first step in any motion is called the 'preparatory motion.' In both instances—the slapping of the mosquito and application of the ointment—the preparatory motion required that the action hand be moved to the injured site. It just happens that the hand required the same shape for both actions. It did this correctly! So, why were you surprised that I applied the salve instead of hitting a mosquito?"

With the teacher's guidance the students discover that the preparatory motion of a slap is strong, fast, and vigorous. However, from the moment the right hand collects some imaginary salve to rub on the bites, its motions would normally be slow and gentle.

"The preparatory motion of any action should have the same characteristics as the action itself. In fact, it should forecast what is going to happen!

"The same principle holds true in string playing. The preparatory motion of the bow arm should predict the mood of the musical passage to be played. Let's try this now with your music. First we will determine the mood of each passage. Then we will send out good forecast signals."

Cue to Use

1. Anytime the teacher wishes to highlight the preparatory motion.
2. Whenever the student's preparatory motions do not match the mood of the music.

Inner Drama

The teacher believes that the source of most technical problems lies in the preparatory motion, not in the motion itself. He welcomes any opportunity to highlight this important yet often neglected facet of string playing.

He also recognizes that much of the drama of string playing depends on the preparatory motion and that its emphasis can make the difference between a good performance and a distinguished one. The message of the music comes across more convincingly if the forecast signals are clear and accurate.

Pinocchio's Bow
SCENE 27

Musical Setting: A note of very long duration to be played with one bow stroke

Teacher: "How long can you hold a note on a down-bow?"

He takes out an imaginary pocket watch and starts counting seconds: "One, two, three . . ."

When the tip of the bow is reached, the teacher says: "Not bad! But you can do better! Let me show you some secrets.

"First, tilt the bow stick so most of the hairs touch the string. That will make your bow grow six inches longer! Second, move the bow closer to the bridge where the string is very taut. That will add another seven inches! Try drawing a long slow stroke again. Hug the string!"

As the teacher marks time, the student will draw another down-bow.

"Remember how Pinocchio's nose grew? Now you have a Pinocchio bow!"

Cue to Use

Whenever the time seems appropriate for the student to learn to draw long, slow bows. It should not be used too early in the training and definitely not during the early use of vibrato.

Inner Drama

The teacher is aware that no sensitive student chooses a sounding point very near the bridge unless encouraged. It is much easier to draw the bow near the fingerboard because the margin for error is far greater. When bowing near the bridge, the ratio of speed, pressure, and the distance of the contact point from the bridge becomes more crucial. If not perfect in all parts of the bow, a squeak or a scratch can result. Isolating a single technique and perfecting it is the surest route to mastery.

The Thud and the Bounce
SCENE 28

Musical Setting: A composition with a variety of bowing styles

Teacher: "Monkey see, monkey do! My hand is a rock. It is dropping into some mud with a thud!"

The teacher drops her hand on a desk or on the palm of her other hand. The students imitate.

"Now it is a rubber ball bouncing off a sidewalk!"

After several bounces the teacher calls attention to how the hand felt different before it moved.

"It also felt different while dropping. The hand had already taken on an identity!"

The teacher and students pick up a stapler, paper clip box, wallet, or any small object and move it like a stone or a ball, holding it throughout the action.

"Whatever personality we choose can be transferred to the object we hold in our hand while it moves. The same is true of the bow. When we hold the bow, it, too, can take on the identity of a stone, a rubber ball, or anything we choose. The trick is to decide on the identity before moving a muscle. Let's try this with our instruments. Give the bow strokes personality!"

Cue to Use

1. Anytime the student's bowing lacks personality.
2. Whenever it takes several notes for the student to get into a passage that requires a different style of bowing than used in the preceding passage.

Props

Any small object, such as a stapler, paper clip box, or wallet, already present in the studio or classroom.

Inner Drama

The teacher believes that the initial thrust of any motion is the most important and that usually the character of the complete motion is predetermined before any movement is made. Although she did not call attention to the power of mental imagery in this scene, she is confident that the student visualized a stone and a rubber ball. As a teacher, she is constantly impressed with the miraculous link between the imagination and the human hand.

The Race Horse
SCENE 29

Musical Setting: A phrase or passage which requires some martelé bow strokes

The teacher and students place their bows on the string ready to play a martelé stroke.

"As I pinch the stick, the hair pinches the string. The bow yells, 'Let me go!' Then I stop the pinching and the bow and arm speed on their way.

"The bow reminds me of a race horse held behind the starting gate! He, too, seems to yell, 'Let me go!' When the gate is flung open, he speeds on his way!"

Cue to Use

Anytime, except in the very early training, for the improvement and understanding of martelé bowing.

Inner Drama

The teacher dramatizes three features of martelé bowing in this scene: the application of pressure, the release of pressure at the appropriate moment, and the speed of the motion. He is well aware that most youngsters are fond of animals and will remember pedagogical devices that highlight them. The newspaper and television cartoonists capitalize on the young person's identification with animals and her acknowledgement that they, too, have feelings.

The teacher encourages the daily practice of martelé bowing because he believes that it serves as a good test for the bow hold and the balance of the bow on the string. If the beginning of a martelé stroke is not clear, it serves as a signal that something is wrong.

Naturally the teacher takes care that the sound is pleasing and that this stroke is surrounded by material requiring beautiful pulled tones with smooth bow changes. It is important that the student not get in the habit of stopping at the end of every bow stroke as is the case with martelé bowing.

A Hunk of Cheese
SCENE 30

Teacher: "Try using your bow as a knife. Think of the string as a hunk of cheese. Cut a groove in it!"

Cue to Use

Anytime the bow drifts around on the string.

Inner Drama

Slicing with a knife implies a very sharp focus. No one would think of allowing the blade to drift across the top of the cheese.

The teacher uses every opportunity to help the student realize that the bow is a tool that has been designed for a specific purpose. It, like a knife, must be controlled and guided by the person using it. Should the student hold the bow tightly like some people do a knife, the teacher explains that the cheese is of a soft variety. The truly convincing teacher seems to have an answer to almost everything!

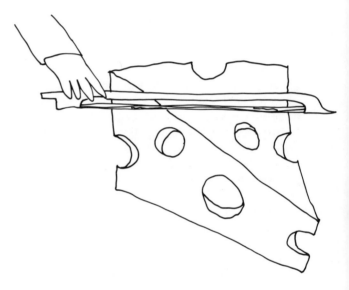

Mary Poppins Landings
SCENE 31

The teacher and students tie a cut rubber band around the wooden tip of each bow. The rubber band should run in the same direction as the hair and be tied tightly.

"Now we'll practice bringing the bow in from the sky like Mary Poppins!"

From a secret location the teacher produces some small colorful paper umbrellas. With his help an umbrella is installed at the tip of each bow. The toothpick handle is inserted between the rubber band and the bow stick.

"First, let's place the bow hair near the tip on the A string to check the angle of your bow and the position of your arm."

The teacher makes an attempt to pull a student's bow away from the string by very gently tugging up on the bow stick above the spot where the hair contacts the string.

"Glue the bow hair to the string! Don't let me pull it off!" Most students will automatically adjust the bow and arm to the optimum position and angle.

"Good! Now raise your bow about eight or twelve inches above the string. Move the bow and arm as one piece. . . . Practice landing on the string like Mary Poppins. Watch both the umbrella and the right hand. Move them exactly the same distance so the landing will be smooth without a jolt or a jiggle!"

After repeating this many times at the tip, the students will also practice landing in all parts of the bow and on the other strings.

"Now that you have seen an umbrella attached to your bow, I know you can always imagine one. Practice these Mary Poppins–type landings. They will do wonders for your bowing skills!"

Cue to Use

Anytime, both in early or later training, for the review of lifting and placing the bow and for the improvement of bow control. It should be preceded by *Focus Here!*, Scene 16.

Props

Small colorful paper umbrellas. These are inexpensive ornamental toothpicks about four inches long and are readily available at party shops and some variety stores. They are designed to embellish hors d'oeuvres, cocktails, and sandwiches.

Inner Drama

This scene helps the student find the optimum position of the bow and arm so the weight is focused on the spot the bow hair contacts the string. This place is frequently termed the sounding point. The student learns from her Mary Poppins landings how to approach the string in such a manner that the string will be activated immediately on drawing an up- or down-bow.

The teacher is aware that often the most effective approach for the first note of a phrase or for an entrance after a rest is actually more like an airplane landing and is seldom made at a 90° angle directly above the string. However, the *Mary Poppins Landings* is a technique on which other skills are built.

Sticky Bubble Gum
SCENE 32

Musical Setting: A melodic phrase requiring a thick, full tone

Teacher: "Picture in your mind's eye some bubble gum mashed all over the hair of your bow. Remember how your shoe sole sticks to the sidewalk after you have accidentally stepped on some gum!

"Now your bow hair will stick to the string! The gooey gum will spread out over every inch of the hair from the frog to the tip! Not a single air pocket will get in between the hair and the string! Listen to that beautiful, pulled tone!"

Cue to Use

1. Whenever the bow hair does not make good contact with the string.
2. Anytime for building a bigger tone.

Inner Drama

The teacher has drawn on a commonplace experience, though an unpleasant one, and used it positively to help the student gain better bow contact. He recognizes that all human beings are linked by a surprising number of similar situations in everyday life. In fact, many professional comedians gain popularity and make a living from dramatizing negative experiences in a humorous manner. The feeling of resistance created by the chewing gum image almost invariably helps a student to achieve a more beautiful, pulled tone and lessens the chance she will tighten the fingers of her bow hand while striving for greater volume.

Pouring Maple Syrup
SCENE 33

Musical Setting: A phrase which requires whole bow strokes

Teacher: "We are seated at the left end of an extraordinary pancake—one that is about an inch wide and two or three feet long! What a mixed-up cook!

"Help yourself to a bottle of imaginary maple syrup. Pour it on the long pancake, moving from the left to the right. Be generous! Use the whole bottle. . . . Good!

"Here is another bottle of syrup! This time watch how you automatically rotate your hand and forearm as you empty the bottle. . . . It is similar to the way we move our right arms during a down-bow. This turning of the forearm is called 'pronation.' It helps focus the supported weight back to the string and makes our tones as big at the tip as at the frog.

"Let's bow some beautiful down-bows. Pour lots of maple syrup!"

Cue to Use

1. When the student's tone at the bow tip lacks volume.
2. Anytime the teacher wants to explain the word *pronation* and its use in bowing technique.

Inner Drama

The analogy of pouring liquid as the bow hand moves away from the body has helped many students. The supported weight of the arm which is directly above the sounding point when playing at the frog naturally produces a big sound. However, as the hand and arm move away from this point of contact between the hair and the string, an effort must be made to channel the energy back to the string. This can be done by making a slight upward curve during the last part of the down-bow and by some pronation of the forearm. Care must be taken not to overdo the rotation of the forearm and hand as this could cause excessive pressure on the first finger.

The maple syrup which is poured on the down-bows may be scooped up on the up-bows.

Hurry Up and Wait!
SCENE 34

Musical Setting: A phrase or passage with martelé bowing and string crossings

Teacher: "HURRY UP AND WAIT was a slogan used by the American servicemen and -women during World War II. They would rush to the mess hall to eat, only to stand in line and wait. They would rush to the quartermasters for clothing issue, then wait.

"In the martelé stroke, the bow rushes across the string in a hurry, stops, and waits. During the waiting period, the player applies pressure on the bow stick with the first finger so the wood almost touches the hair at the place it contacts the string. There is a slight upward pressure of the thumb. Then she releases some of the pressure of both the first finger and the thumb and the bow rushes in the other direction. Again, it stops on the string and waits. Let's practice this on one string. Each stroke will begin with a bite."

The teacher encourages the students to listen carefully to be sure the sound is pleasant. A slight curve upward on the release can help alleviate a crunching sound.

"Now let's play a martelé down-bow on one string and follow it by an up-bow on a different string. There is a special trick for this! Move from the old string to the new string during the last part of the 'rushing' portion of the old stroke but take care that the new string is not heard. The 'wait' will be on the new string. We follow this principle on all successive martelé strokes whether they are up-bows or down-bows."

Cue to Use

1. Whenever the teacher wishes to review or stress various aspects of martelé bowing, particularly in string crossing.
2. Anytime the student fails to cross strings during the action and time value of the old bow stroke.

Inner Drama

The teacher recognizes that young people in the service seem especially gifted at formulating slogans which have a strong wallop in a few words. He borrows this one in order to spotlight the distinctive characteristics of martelé bowing.

The teacher believes that the timing of a string crossing is of special importance and that the bow and arm should be in the optimum position before a new stroke is begun. Since this requires that the move to the new bow and arm level be made *before* the new stroke is begun, the "wait" of the martelé stroke offers an opportunity to feature this timing. The awareness of this order of events can also help the student in string crossings when other types of bowing are used.

In guiding the student to use various lengths of bow in the martelé stroke, the teacher usually starts with the shortest strokes first. He takes care that the contact point remains the same distance from the bridge throughout the stroke and that the weight and speed are adjusted to make the sound pleasing. Some supercooperative students will tend to overdo the "rush." In such a case, the teacher will compliment them on listening to his instructions and responding well, then help them experiment until the most effective ratio of pressure, speed, and distance from the bridge is found.

Suntan Oil and Contact Paper
SCENE 35
(Especially designed for cellists and bassists but could be useful to others)

Musical Setting: A melody which calls for a big, rich full tone as loud as possible

Teacher: "Take a glob of imaginary suntan oil with your right hand and spread it on your bare left arm. Extend your left arm its full length and apply the oil with long sweeping strokes back and forth. . . . Note how flexible and rubbery your fingers feel as they move across the skin. They seem to extend each stroke by continuing in the same direction while the wrist and arm start on back. . . . Do this as heavily as possible. Get the suntan oil deep down into every pore. . . . Good!

"Now let's apply some imaginary contact paper on the top of this desk. Drag your hand across the paper heavily so that every little bubble will be moved out to the edge of the paper and freed. . . . Note the same feeling in your hand. Good!

"We will return now to our instruments. Let's try to keep as much of the same feeling and action in our hands as possible while we draw some long bow strokes. Listen for big, loud but mellow tones!"

Cue to Use

Anytime, except in the very early lessons, to help the student develop a big tone that is not harsh.

Props

A hard flat surface, such as a table, desk, or piano lid.

Inner Drama

Considerable pressure on top of the bow stick is needed to get cello and bass strings to vibrate at their maximum amplitude. The larger the amplitude, the larger the volume. Yet, the quality of pressure is extremely important in order to have a mellowness in the tone.

The teacher's belief is that the more the live energy can flow *through* the fingers and hand—not *from* the fingers and hand—the more beautiful the tone quality. The louder the tone, the more the player needs to let go. Spreading suntan oil and removing air pockets when working with contact paper demonstrate the passivity of the hand, the flexibility of the fingers, and the sequential action of the fingers, hand, and arm. Natu-

rally, the appropriate distance from the bridge and the speed of the bow must be found to compliment the pressure. Also, when playing loudly the vibrato needs to be wider or the tone can sound strident.

Poking Balloons
SCENE 36

Musical Setting: A phrase with two or three articulated notes in one up-bow

The teacher distributes some round balloons to be inflated with air.

"Let's work on our bow arms! Check to be sure you have a good bow hold. Poke your balloon gently with your bow tip. Make it stay up in the air!"

Cue to Use

1. Whenever the class or lesson needs a special lift. It is not recommended for very young children.
2. Anytime for the improvement of the bow arm, especially for playing two or three articulated notes in one up-bow.

Props

Nine-inch round balloons in bright colors. Also plenty of space to move around and a good safe location for the instruments.

Inner Drama

The challenge of keeping a balloon in the air by repeatedly poking on it cannot fail to fascinate string players of all ages. Concentration becomes impenetrable. Poking the balloon is more difficult than it looks but the skill is acquired quickly and pleasantly. It invites a finger action that is most useful for articulation in other bowings, such as collé, as well as the one described in the Musical Setting. Collé is a pinch-and-lift stroke which begins by placing the bow on the string from the air. It is a useful practical bowing as well as a good substitute for spiccato and martelé bowings in some musical passages. It can go faster than martelé and sound more pointed than spiccato.

Ships at Sea
SCENE 37

Musical Setting: A melody or passage requiring very smooth bow changes

The teacher gives the student a cut rubber band to tie around the wooden tip of his bow. The rubber band should run in the same direction as the hair and be drawn very taut. Then the teacher produces a small paper flag to be inserted in the rubber band. If it does not stand straight up, a second rubber band may be added to offer the toothpick-flagpole more support.

"Let's practice changing bow directions slowly near the frog. We will repeat one note many times using only the lower half of the bow. Keep your eyes glued on your flag and make it move back and forth smoothly. No jerks, no bumps, no waving, no rolling! It should glide like a flag on a ship in a calm, peaceful sea!"

Often a student will discover that his flag suggests a turbulent sea from stormy weather. Very soon he will adjust his fingers, hand, and arm motions so the flag moves back and forth undisturbed.

"Now let's repeat a note in the upper half of the bow and watch the flag glide smoothly. This will help you sustain your tones so you can play beautiful legato phrases."

Cue to Use

Anytime the teacher wishes to help the student make smooth bow changes and a sustained sound.

Props

1. Small flags readily available at party shops and some variety stores. These are inexpensive ornamented toothpicks about four inches long, designed to serve as party favors.
2. A cut rubber band for each student.
3. A mirror for violin and viola students.

Inner Drama

The teacher knows that a ship at sea furnishes an attractive mental picture for people of all ages. By erecting a flag she has made any disturbance in the bow change easily discernable. Usually a remedy is quickly found since the goal is so clear. If the problem is not corrected immediately, it undoubtedly will be before the next lesson, provided the flag goes home with the student. With violin and viola students, a mirror should be used so they can see the flag when playing at the frog without straining.

Though *Ships at Sea* has a specific and useful purpose in the development of bowing skills, it is important for the students to realize that not all bow strokes should be smooth. A perpetually calm sea is an invitation to monotony. Monotonous gestures produce monotonous music.

A Lesson from the Students
SCENE 38
(Especially effective for groups)

Teacher: "Would you please teach me how to bounce a ball? Spiccato is called a bouncing bow stroke. I think if I can learn to bounce a ball well, it will help me improve my spiccato bowing!"

The teacher produces a rubber ball and discreetly places a soft object, such as a cushion or a baggy purse, on the floor near her.

She stoops down near the floor and starts throwing the ball upward, catching it on its return. Immediately the students will explain that the ball should go down, not up.

"Oh! This way?"

She then stands erect and drops the ball with a thud on the soft object lying on the floor.

"Hm-m-m."

The students will instruct her to drop the ball on the hard floor. This time she allows the ball to fall nonenergetically to the floor.

"Oh, I had hoped for a bigger bounce than that! Am I doing something wrong?"

The next advice will be that she should throw the ball to the floor—not drop it limply. Success will be immediate and likely be followed by applause.

"Thank you! You are good teachers! So what have we learned that applies to spiccato bowing? Three things! First, we start from above. The bow and hand should feel a bit higher above the string than when we play most other strokes."

The teacher moves her left hand over to her right wrist, takes hold of a fold of skin and lifts the right forearm and hand a little higher.

"Home base for the hand and bow will be here! They will go down to the string and return to this level at the end of each stroke. Second, the spot on the string the bow contacts should not be so close to the fingerboard that the string feels extremely soft and spongy. There is a reason why basketball courts are not carpeted!

"Third, if the bow is to bounce, it must hit the string with an impact! Now, let's experiment with our instruments and bows and apply these principles."

Cue to Use

Anytime to help the students understand some principles of spiccato bowing. It is not intended to be an introduction to spiccato bowing.

Props

A rubber ball, a soft object, such as a cushion or a baggy purse, and a hard floor. All instruments should be placed a safe distance from the scene of action.

Inner Drama

It is the teacher's conviction that most music students have extremely bright and curious minds. Since so much of their early training has focused on modeling and imitation, an activity like the one described in this scene can fascinate the less young students. It offers an opportunity for them to use logic and transfer it to string technique. Anything which brings insight to natural principles cannot be considered a waste of time.

Many conductors and string players prefer that the first stroke of a spiccato passage begin on the string to ensure more precision of ensemble. However, the elevation of the hand and forearm can still be slightly higher than for bow strokes that remain on the string. Thus, beginning with the second note the hand will have the sensation of coming down to the string, just as the ball hit the floor from above. The need for selecting a contact point not too near the fingerboard is more

apparent when playing spiccato bowing on the thick strings of a cello or double bass.

Dear Gabby
SCENE 39

The teacher reads aloud as though from a newspaper:

"DEAR GABBY: I've read your column for many years but never dreamed that someday I, too, would be writing you for advice. It concerns my name—Staccato Bowing.

"For years I have heard musicians, especially pianists and wind players, say 'Play this note staccato.' Or they say, 'See the little dot above this note? It means that the note should be played short. It is staccato.'

"But, alas, to most professional string players staccato is not one note. In their vocabulary staccato bowing is a series of little baby martelé strokes all going in the same direction. Anywhere from two to many notes (even twenty or more) are played in one bow. Not only do the notes have little round dots above or below them but they also have a slur! Sometimes the slur stretches three or four inches across the printed page. The bow hair usually stays right on the string while the first finger and thumb give the bow stick little pinches so every note begins with an attack. Some players are able to play staccato very fast when they give a special impulse to only every few notes. They are really stingy with the bow. Other players deliberately tense their muscles so they tremble. The trembling makes the notes.

"I'm confused about what to do. I'm sick and tired of being misunderstood and am considering changing my name. Do you think that is a good idea?—CONFUSED.

"DEAR CONFUSED: I have consulted some leading string authorities and find what you have written is true. Pianists and wind players use the term staccato one way and many string players another. Several string playing treatises refer to staccato bowing as a series of short notes in one bow direction. However, I learned that some string players and teachers call that bowing combined staccato or slurred staccato. These people use the term staccato to indicate one short note which resembles martelé but does not begin with an accent. If there is more than one short note, each note gets a separate bow stroke and space is left between the notes.

"I have decided to turn this question over to our readers. Readers, please write me whether or not you think that changing her name is the solution to Confused's problem."

Cue to Use

Whenever the teacher wishes to make the students aware of the differences in vocabulary used by various instrumentalists.

Inner Drama

The teacher has noted the striking differences in terminology brought about through the traditions of various musicians. He recognizes that it is not a matter of right or wrong use of words but simply a lack of standardization. While he hopes that in time the terms might become more standardized, during the interim period it is important for the students to be aware of the discrepancies.

Most musicians use the term *staccato* as a generic term. String players tend to use it for a particular style of bowing, but even they do not agree on its usage.

Give It a Heartbeat!
SCENE 40

Musical Setting: A phrase requiring a big full tone

Teacher: "Give your bow stick a heartbeat right above the string while you play some whole bow strokes! Bend the stick down almost to the hair like the throb of each heartbeat. Make several in one bow stroke!"

The teacher guides the students in creating with the first finger a pulsing action which affects the stick above the sounding point.

"Good! Now let's hear you play without the heartbeat. Listen to that big, beautiful tone!"

Cue to Use

1. Anytime, except in the very early training, to help build a full tone.
2. Whenever the student's bow stroke is weak, particularly in certain portions of the bow.

Inner Drama

Louré bowing, which is also called portato, is a wonderful tone builder for home practice. With two or more notes in one bow stroke, the bow is "milked" or "pulsed" so that the impression of

slight separations is given. The separations are caused primarily by a change in volume brought about by the application and release of pressure through the first finger and by slowing down the bow between notes, causing a little swell on each note.

In this scene there is no indication that the whole bow is to be divided into a specific number of individual notes. Thus, the bowing described is not actually louré bowing. Yet, the student's tone will benefit from the same type of pulsing used in louré bowing.

The sound usually is immediately fuller, provided the student is able to produce pulses of equal volume throughout the length of the bow. If she is not successful at doing this, the alignment between the hand and the arm may need to be changed in order to find the power flow. Also, the angle of the bow could require some adjustments. Through the process of doing this, the student will find the optimum position for each part of the bow stroke on the string being played. The discovery will help her bow technique in general. The reader is encouraged to refer to *Kneading Bread Dough*, Scene 130.

Garden Gloves
SCENE 41

Musical Setting: A phrase or passage requiring smooth bow changes

As a surprise move, the teacher wears a brightly colored garden glove on her right hand. Without holding a bow, she mimes a series of paintbrush strokes in the air.

"Watch how the fingers continue to move on in the same direction as the bow stroke approaches the end of the line. The arm starts back on its return trip but the fingers and bow keep moving on a few more inches.

"Notice how the fingers keep changing their shape. They tend to look curved during most of the down-bow and somewhat straighter during the up-bow. Watch how the base knuckles tend to be slightly pointed during the up-bow but flatter during most of the down-bow!

"Here is a glove for you! Try miming the bow strokes in the air. Make super up-bows and super down-bows! . . . Good! Now, without the glove, play some strokes with the same feeling and action. Smooth, flowing motions make smooth, flowing sounds!"

Cue to Use

1. Anytime to help smooth bow changes, finger flexibility, and flowing motions.
2. Whenever the teacher wishes to spotlight the differences between up- and down-bows.

Props

Two brightly colored garden gloves. If the student's hand is too small for a garden glove, any colorful glove will be fine.

Inner Drama

Miming motions without an instrument can help every string player. It offers a wonderful opportunity to watch the natural motions of the hand without it having the responsibility of holding an object. However, observing the motions of bright orange or blue fingers can be twice as effective and three times as much fun!

Although this scene describes the continuous motion which has been termed stroke continuation or sequential action, colored hands can spotlight any bowing style.

Pea Pod
SCENE 42

Musical Setting: A phrase or passage which requires some martelé bow strokes

Teacher: "The beginning of a martelé stroke is like saying 'pea.' Let's hear you say 'pea' as in pea pod. . . . Stop! What is the first thing you did with your lips?"

After some discussion, the teacher summarizes: "First you pressed your lips firmly together, then suddenly you released them. The sound came from the release! You could have held your lips tightly together for two minutes but until the release there would be no sound! Try it. . . .

"Or, you could have pressed your lips firmly together, then very slowly released them. Try that. . . ."

The students soon discover that a slow release results in a different sound.

"Let's practice some martelé strokes. First, press the hair deep into the string. Then suddenly release some of the pressure and the bow will speed on its way. It is only *after* we release the pressure that the sound is produced. Listen carefully to be sure that the tone is pleasant."

Cue to Use

Whenever the teacher wants to help the student improve or review martelé bowing.

Inner Drama

The teacher realizes that, unlike most other bow strokes, martelé bowing requires pressure before the motion begins. He believes that the improvement of martelé bowing technique also can help the improvement of other kinds of bowing. This includes détaché, which is the string player's most useful and basic stroke.

Leaving Fingerprints on the String
SCENE 43

Musical Setting: A phrase in which sensitivity is especially important

The teacher distributes paperback books and keeps one for herself.

"Clutch your book tightly like it is just any old thing! Now touch the chair with it . . . the music stand . . . your clothing. . . . The book is a non-feeling object!

"Now let's hold our books sensitively and lovingly. Mine almost seems like a part of my hand and arm. As the book touches the chair, I can imagine my fingerprints being left there. When I pull it across the chair, I can feel every little bump in the wood. Try this. . . ."

After the students have had time to feel several objects through the book, the teacher says: "Now try feeling through your bow as you pull it across the string. Leave fingerprints on the string!

"If you can feel through a cheap paperback book, just think what you can do with a bow, which has been beautifully designed for this purpose! Remember, the bow is an extension of your hand and arm. If we had been born with long tightly drawn hairs on our fingers, we might not even need a bow!"

Cue to Use

1. Anytime, except in the very early training, the teacher wishes to increase the sensitivity of the tone.
2. Whenever the student clutches the bow tightly.

Props

Paperback books, not too thick. Also any large stable objects, such as a chair, music stand, or desk already in the room.

Inner Drama

The teacher believes that increasing sensitivity is one of the primary justifications for bringing music into the lives of other human beings. Sensitive sensations produce sensitive music, which in turn helps to breed sensitivity in people. At all times the teacher tries to present her subject matter to her students in a gentle, tactful manner. She recognizes that it is most unlikely that sensitivity is born out of insensitivity in any form.

Elastic Pulls
SCENE 44
(Especially designed for groups of two or more students but can be used in a private lesson with the teacher substituting for a student)

Musical Setting: A melodic phrase requiring a big, full tone produced by pulled bow strokes

The teacher distributes a strip of wide elastic to a pair of students. While they face the same direction, each will hold one end of the strip with the right hand shaped somewhat like a bow hold.

"Larry, pull your end, which is on the right side, as though you are pulling a down-bow. Mary, offer some resistance while holding the left end. Watch the elastic stretch!

"Now, Mary, pull an up-bow while Larry holds his end still. Stretch the elastic. . . . Good! Let's hum your piece while Larry pulls the down-bows and Mary the up-bows. . . . Good!"

Later the students will return to their instruments.

"Pull your bows the same way you pulled the elastic! Listen for a big, creamy sound."

Cue to Use

1. Anytime, except in the very early training, to help the student achieve the sensation of pulled bow strokes.
2. Whenever the student plays a melodic passage with a tone that is too small.

Props

Brightly colored elastic about 1½ inches wide cut into strips approximately twelve to fifteen inches long. This elastic, which usually more than doubles its length when stretched, is readily available in fabric stores.

Inner Drama

The teacher is a great believer in beauty of tone being the most important goal for every string instrumentalist. Who wants to listen to a bow cross a string if the resulting sound is not beautiful?

The most beautiful tone produced on a stringed instrument is one achieved by pulling the bow in alternating down- and up-bow directions. The resistance offered through stretching the elastic strip can help the student to discover this feeling.

What, No Hair?
SCENE 45

Musical Setting: A spirited melody which can be played effectively with col legno bowing

Teacher: "Imagine the surprise of a brand new bow when it is used for col legno bowing the first time! The poor thing finds itself landing on the string with the stick, only to spring right up again!

"I can imagine it shouting: 'Help! I'm almost upside down! This guy is all mixed up! I'm supposed to land on my hair!'

"But, if an old bow is around, it would calm the new one with the assurance that all is OK and that the composer indicated this special clicking effect by writing the words *col legno* in the music.

"Let's feel the rhythm together and tap our bows on the string at exactly the same time like a chorus of tap dancers!"

Cue to Use

Anytime after col legno has already been introduced and the teacher desires better ensemble or seeks variety in the lesson. It should not be presented to very young children.

Inner Drama

As in any enterprise, the teacher knows that some students have more difficulty than others in getting the feel for playing in perfect ensemble. By using this bowing, which is exciting and attractive, he motivates them to listen and play exactly together. While col legno is a relatively unimportant technique, its occasional use can serve a pedagogical function and add spice to a music lesson or performance.

Eyes on the Ball

SCENE 46

Teacher: "I've been having trouble with my tennis game! Won't you help me with my serve?"

She pantomimes tossing a ball in the air. While her hand, shaped around the handle of the imaginary tennis racket, swings back in a grand preparatory motion, her head turns to watch the hand in action.

"Whoops! I missed the ball again! It happens every time! What possibly could be wrong? The form of my hand is perfect!"

Undoubtedly, the students will tell the teacher that she should watch the ball instead of the hand. The score improves immediately.

"The same is true with string playing! The form of the bow hand is important, indeed, but, usually, the best place to watch is where the bow touches the string. This is called the 'sounding point.' If we concentrate on that magic spot, most of the time the hand takes care of itself."

Cue to Use

When the student's eyes are focused on the bow hold instead of the sounding point and the bowing technique needs improvement.

Inner Drama

Although the teacher is a great believer in using the eyes in practice and performance, she has discovered that surprisingly often a student will look at the wrong place. On many occasions a student who appears to be preoccupied with his bow hold will find his playing vastly improved when he switches his attention to the sounding point.

Naturally, anyone can cite numerous examples of artists whose eyes are closed during the execution of beautiful phrases. The goal of this scene is to solve a problem if there is one. Should no problem exist and the bow succeeds in its mission, the teacher will not insist on this rule.

Take a Holiday!

SCENE 47

Musical Setting: A fast passage with a separate bow stroke for every note

Teacher: "Give your upper arm a holiday! In this passage, except for string crossings, the upper arm will not get into the act! The fat on the underside

of it will just jiggle sympathetically like cranberry jelly!"

Cue to Use

1. Anytime in fast passages which are played with separate bow strokes.
2. Whenever the student tends to move the elbow and upper arm in the same direction as the hand.

Inner Drama

Knowing when to give certain parts of the body a holiday is all part of learning any manual skill. If the student finds he is unable to move the hand without moving the upper arm in the same direction, or if the elbow is stiff, the height of the elbow should be checked. If it is either too high or too low, taking a holiday would be impossible no matter how strong the mental command.

The level at which the elbow floats will change when strings are crossed. However, in some very fast passages involving a quick change only to return immediately to the original string, the elbow level will change very little or almost not at all.

The "fat" on the underside of a child's arm may be as imaginary as the cranberry jelly itself! Yet, somehow the mental image works like magic with most kids.

Exit the BOW & RIGHT ARM DANCING DUO stage right.

(But they will make a return appearance!)

4 The Fingerboard Theater

The Left Hand is a ham! On a long, slender black stage what a variety of acts it puts on! Constantly expanding its repertoire of character portrayals, this incorrigible showoff can switch in a flash from the cool precision of a heart surgeon to the quivering passion of a prima donna. From upstage to downstage, back and across, it loves to prance, run, glide, and soar. And, what a tap dance routine it will swing into at the drop of a stick!

In the presence of such expressiveness and skill, who would dare to notice the absence of a voice?

The thirty-one Scenes in this chapter may be used in any order to help build better left hand skills. Throughout the text the words "tip" and "pad" have been used interchangeably to refer to the part of the finger which makes contact with the string. Since much depends on the shape of the student's hand, the individual's definition of the terms, and the passage being performed, the choice of words is left up to the reader. For a quick reference as to subject matter and specific needs, the reader is advised to refer to the "Cue Sheets" at the end of the book. *As always, the music itself must play the dominant role.*

SCENES FOR BETTER LEFT HAND SKILLS

A Fuzzy "Pom-pom"
SCENE 48

The teacher tosses a fuzzy "pom-pom" to each student.

"Hold it in the palm of your left hand. Doesn't it feel soft and nice? Notice how the inside of your hand feels. It is as soft as the fuzzy yarn! Now, without the "pom-pom," keep this same feeling in your hand when you play."

Cue to Use

1. Anytime there appears to be tension in the left hand.
2. Whenever the thumb pushes up or grabs the instrument's neck.

Props

A "pom-pom" (pompon) made of soft, fuzzy yarn. These brightly colored balls of fuzz, about three inches in diameter, are readily available in stores where gift wrapping paper is sold. They were designed to adorn gifts.

Inner Drama

Is there a person alive who has not experienced holding a baby frog or baby bird? One instinctively makes his hands as soft and protective as possible for the tiny breath of life trapped in unfamiliar surroundings.

The hand's automatic reaction to a fuzzy "pom-pom" usually is almost identical. Somehow the bones seem to expand and the palm appears to provide a soft and protective nest. When the student carries this feeling over to the instrument, the possibilities for the development of a beautiful vibrato and facile technique seem unlimited.

Rubber Cushions
SCENE 49

Teacher: "Picture a nice rubber cushion at the end of each of your fingers. It will feel soft and springy when it touches the fingerboard."

Cue to Use

1. Whenever the tone is hard and the fingers appear tight, especially in a lyric passage.
2. Anytime to help the student gain this tactile sensation.

Inner Drama

The teacher has found that the mental image of rubber cushions has helped many students discover the tactile sense that aids in producing a beautiful tone. Somehow, magically, all joints in the hand and arm react to the rubbery touch and the perfect combination of strength and flexibility results. An added benefit is the feeling of stickiness between the rubber pad and the wood of the fingerboard. This sensation helps in producing a beautiful vibrato. The player can shake his hand freely without fear of sliding off pitch.

Adam's Apple
SCENE 50

Teacher: "Monkey see, monkey do!"

The teacher places her left thumb on her own Adam's apple. While the students hold their thumbs on this sensitive spot in their necks, the teacher asks friendly questions. These could relate to anything of interest to the students—their families, pets, news events, or a school happening.

"Stop! Notice how tenderly our thumbs are touching our necks. This is exactly the way we should treat the necks of our instruments!

"If you see me touching my Adam's apple while you play, you will know it is a signal to check your thumb. Continue playing but make sure your thumb is soft and gentle."

Cue to Use

Anytime the teacher wants to impress the students of the importance of having a soft, gentle thumb. The signal can be used repeatedly throughout the training.

Inner Drama

The teacher's goal is to call attention to the importance of having a gentle thumb and to introduce a secret signal that can be used without stopping the music making. Such signals are of great importance to a music lesson or class because they do not interrupt the flow. Also, most students take great pride and have enjoyment in responding to silent communication.

Strange Little Animal
SCENE 51

Musical Setting: A passage requiring fast finger action

Gathered around a desk, table, or the lid of a piano, the teacher and students place their left hands on the hard surface somewhat like they are playing the piano or typing. The teacher taps his finger tips on the wood rapidly and audibly in no special sequence. All four fingers move but only one strikes the surface at a time.

"Imagine our hands are strange little animals with four feet lined up in a row. They are running just as fast as they can, yet they don't seem to be going anywhere!

"Let's experiment with different positions to find how they can run nowhere the fastest! Shape your hand several ways—high base knuckles . . . low base knuckles . . . low wrist . . . high wrist . . . straight fingers . . . curved fingers. . . . Search out the way that makes the tapping the clearest and fastest. Faster! Faster! Keep your hand and arm suspended and quiet as your fingers run!

"Good! Remember how this looks and feels. Store it in your memory bank. Let's return to our instruments and play the music using the same action and feeling."

Cue to Use

1. Anytime the student's left hand and arm position appear not to be the most advantageous for playing rapidly.
2. Whenever the fingers need to move faster.

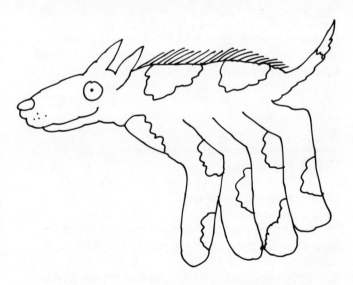

Props

A hard surface, such as the top of a desk, a table, or the lid of a piano. If these are not available, the wood of a stringed instrument can be substituted.

Inner Drama

The teacher believes that many technical problems are solved more readily if the instrument is taken out of the picture. Most students are able to tap their fingers very rapidly on a desk or table. They quickly discover the optimum relationship between the hand and arm, the most advantageous contour of the hand, and the sensation of suspended weight and centered balance.

The Magic Staircase
SCENE 52

Teacher: "Picture a fingerboard floating about eight to twelve inches above your real fingerboard. Tap your fingers on it as fast as you can! Let your hand be the 'strange little animal' running nowhere!

"Now have him run down a magic staircase to your real fingerboard! Run quickly! Keep your fingers running after they land!

"Do this often at home as a checkup for your position."

Cue to Use

Anytime it appears that the student's hand, fingers, and arm are not in the most advantageous position. It should be preceded by *Strange Little Animal*, Scene 51.

Inner Drama

This activity takes only a few seconds yet it can serve as a valuable tool in checking the left hand and arm alignment. It is almost impossible for the hand to run as a strange little animal on the imaginary fingerboard and down the invisible staircase in a bad position. Fourth fingers that have jutted out sideways and wrists that have caved in or bent out disappear as magically as the staircase appeared!

The Magic Staircase may also be used for checking the bow hold to be sure that the hand, wrist, and forearm are in the best alignment. While the bow is held on the string by another person or by the student's own left hand in the case of cellists, the fingers of the right hand can tap on an imaginary bow stick suspended parallel above the real bow. After running down the invis-ible staircase, the hand will slip into the traditional bow hold. This checkup can be made when the bow hair contacts the string in various parts of the bow.

Rattling the Matchbox
SCENE 53

The teacher gives each student a little matchbox emptied of matches. Inside are several small beans, rice grains, or buttons to provide a good rattling sound when shaken. Without instruments the students and teacher shake their individual boxes with their left hands imitating the vibrato action in the neck positions.

"Wrap your fingers loosely around the little box! Now let's check the position of our arms while we shake them. Is there a good straight highway directly from the elbow to the hand? No hills, no valleys, no detours! And certainly no pancake hands! Find out how you can make the matchbox rattle the best. . . . Does the inside of your upper arm feel like jelly? Good!

"Now take your instrument and play a repeated note with a beautiful vibrato. Imagine that you are still shaking the little box with your left hand! Keep your bow moving freely!"

Cue to Use

1. Anytime after the student has a start on vibrato.
2. Whenever the student has a tendency to roll the hand while vibrating.

Props

Little matchboxes, approximately 2 in. × 1 3/8 in. × 1/2 in., readily available in most grocery stores. The matches should be replaced by something that will make a pleasant rattling sound, such as rice grains or beans. Some brightly colored paper may be taped around the boxes if the teacher chooses.

Inner Drama

From experience the teacher knows that no student will have difficulty in rattling the little boxes. In fact, rattling is one of the first skills developed in life. It dates back to the days in the crib! Most students will instantly use cyclic action, the motion will be balanced, and the relaxed upper arm will feel like jelly. As a bonus, the soft, pliable boxes are good for the tactile sensation.

Care should be taken that the student does not use a bye-bye motion because this would vary the pressure on the string instead of changing the pitch, which after all is the purpose of vibrato. Also, a rolling motion of the hand should definitely be avoided.

The statement about pancake hands can be omitted when teaching cello and bass students, for this term traditionally refers to the undesirable trait of some beginning violin and viola students. They allow the left hand to drop so the palm appears as flat as a pancake.

The Alligator's Nose
SCENE 54

Musical Setting: A passage requiring fast finger action

Teacher: "Imagine that the fingerboard is an alligator's nose! Tap your finger on it but get away as fast as you can before he snaps you! Move only from your base knuckles. Faster! He'll get you!"

Cue to Use

1. Whenever the student's fingers need to move faster.
2. Anytime a student's fingers drop quickly to the fingerboard but are sluggish in the lifting motion.
3. Whenever a student's fingers straighten as they are lifted off the fingerboard.

Inner Drama

The teacher believes that in fast passages the quick lift of the fingers is just as important as the drop. However, this is a motor skill in which people have very little experience before playing an instrument. Almost never does an activity in everyday life require this fast lifting action.

In *The Alligator's Nose* it can be helpful to stop between the tap-lift cycles so the student and teacher can observe the finger after the lift. The finger should not move away from the fingerboard in a pulling-type action. Instead it should flip up and immediately drop back a fraction of an inch, then remain suspended in the air. The release is an important part of the technique and makes fast playing possible.

Hidden Double Stops
SCENE 55

Teacher: "There are hidden double stops all over this page! They are a secret from everyone but the player!

"When we cross strings without involving a shift, for one split second our hands are in the shape to play a double stop. Let's look for these secret places in your music."

After the first hidden double stop is discovered, the teacher will lead the student into playing an audible double stop between the two notes of the string crossing. The shape of the left hand and

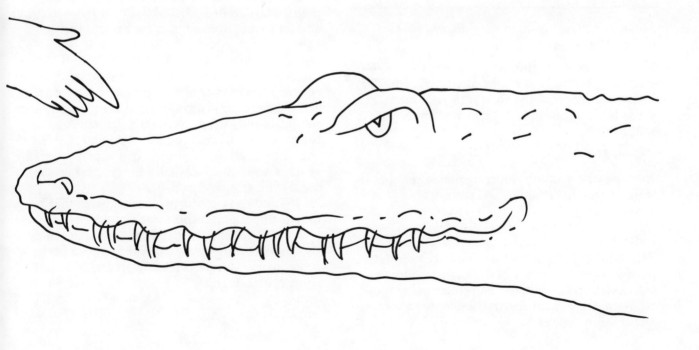

the angle of the bow will be observed. After doing this several times the sound of the double stop will be erased.

Cue to Use

1. Anytime to help bind together notes in the same position on separate strings.
2. Whenever the teacher wishes to highlight the transitory position of the hand and finger in string crossings.

Inner Drama

The teacher believes in balancing on only one finger at a time when vibrating. However, in the process of achieving this, it is possible for the string student to begin using piano technique in her approach to the fingerboard. A pianist must take care not to overlap the depression of keys to avoid the blurring of sounds. In string playing, however, a slight overlap between fingers is needed to ensure legato playing. This is true even for successive notes on the same string.

In finding a good hand shape to play a double stop or chord, generally it helps to position the arch of the hand to favor the note on the string which is the farthest from the palm. If the preceding note is not on the far-away string, the moving of the arch of the hand will take place during the last portion of this note before the real or hidden double stop is executed.

The Optimist
SCENE 56

Musical Setting: A large melodic interval requiring a shift

Teacher: "Be an optimist! While the first note is sounding, picture your hand already playing the next note successfully. Hear it in your mental ear. Then head out for it as though you *know* you will hit it!"

Cue to Use

Anytime the student's shifting needs help but it appears that his position and technical approach are correct.

Inner Drama

The teacher recognizes that fear is the string player's greatest enemy. If the slightest element of self-doubt enters into the picture, causing tension, the odds of hitting the new note in tune are greatly diminished.

The visualizing of success in advance of the event is practiced by many Olympic athletes. While lying relaxed, they picture themselves going through every move of their feat with perfect precision, then being awarded the gold medal in the presence of cheering crowds. The performing musician and the athlete have much in common. Both must be able to perform well in front of an audience or spectators at a designated moment. Neither can allow the wrong attitude to creep into the thinking. Both must "see" and/or "hear" themselves hitting the target successfully before moving into action. This is no place for pessimism.

The Roman Arch
SCENE 57

Teacher: "Why do string players curve their fingers?"

The students will probably answer that the fingers seem stronger when they are curved.

"Right! This is why arches have been built throughout history! Prehistoric people discovered that an arch was the strongest method of spanning an opening. Then the Romans came along and built their beautiful arches and aqueducts. Their enthusiasm for the arch spread to other places and it became an important part of architecture for centuries. In fact, that is why 'arch' is a basic part of the word, architecture.

"But there is another good reason for curving your fingers when you play a stringed instrument! Place your left hand flat on a piece of paper and let's trace around your four fingers with a pencil. . . .

"Look at the difference in the length of your fingers! This is true with everyone, though some people's fingers vary in length more than others. Since a string is always straight and never adjusts to our fingers, we must make our fingers adjust to the string! By arching the hand and curving the fingers, all of the fingers can touch the string at the same time. Naturally the longest one requires the steepest arch.

"If you hear a string player complain that her fourth finger is too short and that she cannot use it without rolling the hand, suggest that she arch the hand and curve the longest fingers a little more. Many wonderful string players have had short fourth fingers!"

Cue to Use

1. Whenever a student tries to play a fast passage with the base knuckles of the fingers sunk in.
2. Anytime a student rolls her hand in order to use the fourth finger or she complains that her fourth finger is too short.

Props

A pencil and paper if readily available. Otherwise they can be imagined.

Inner Drama

In the teacher's long experience he has had many students who seem deaf to the words "curve your fingers," although their hearing seemed quite acute at other times. His goal in this scene is to spotlight in a convincing manner the importance of this advice.

The teacher has had numerous students who had the impression that their fourth fingers were considerably shorter than average. His objective is to make them realize that there is always a way to make efficient use of the hand. In fact, the teacher believes that finding the various adjustments necessary for different students is one reason his work is so fascinating.

The curving of the fingers should not be overdone, especially when using vibrato on the cello and double bass. Many times a finger which appears somewhat straight can produce a beautiful vibrato; however, this finger's first and second knuckles usually must become more curved and its base knuckle flatter during the brief transitory period when moving to a finger with a higher number. For example, a second finger in the optimum position to vibrate may need to change its contour during the last part of the time value of its note if the fourth finger is to play the next note. Since the first finger has a unique role in the playing of extensions, the reader may wish to refer to Scene 78, *The Good Camper*, Scene 153, *Convention Program—Morning*, and Scene 154, *Convention Program—Afternoon*, at this time.

Should a cello or double bass student consistently have trouble with her fourth finger, it is advised that the alignment between the hand and arm be checked. In a good position the fourth finger appears to grow out of the arm and does not jut out sideways. If it juts, the arm should be moved. Naturally the responsibility of adjustment lies with the arm, not the finger, because the pitch has already determined the location of the finger on the fingerboard. Intonation is extremely difficult and unreliable if the back of the hand rolls. Even with practice, who can forecast where the fingers will land?

The Springboard
SCENE 58

Musical Setting: A melodic interval requiring a shift

Teacher: "Think of the last note before the shift as a springboard! Unless this note is of long duration, approach it in such a way that your hand and arm will want to spring up to the next note. The bigger the shift, the greater the spring!
   "Give them a nice boost as a send-off!"

Cue to Use

1. Anytime, except in the very early training, to improve a student's skill in shifting.
2. Whenever a student's shifting seems heavy or inaccurate.

Inner Drama

The teacher's goal is to help the student execute shifts with as much agility and confidence as possible. She realizes that two of the greatest enemies of a shift are the feeling of stickiness in the fingers and a heaviness in the hand and arm. The springboard image immediately counteracts such tendencies and the student will cover the distance with ease, yet without a feeling of haste.

The high jumper uses the last step of his run to spring his body over the rod. The success is largely determined by the approach to that last step. If the note before the shift is one of long duration, the teacher suggests that the springy boost be given during the last part of its time value rather than relying on the initial approach to provide the springing action. Naturally the finger will contact the string throughout the shift. The sensation of stickiness, so helpful in making a beautiful vibrato, must magically vanish while the hand is en route.

For the sake of variety the hand may be viewed as a frog or grasshopper springing from one location to another.

The Traveling Sequin
SCENE 59

Musical Setting: A fast run on one string

Teacher: "Paste an imaginary sequin on the back of your left hand. Play the run again and this time keep the sequin traveling all the time! It will never stand still!"

Cue to Use

1. When the student is playing a fast run up or down the fingerboard and it requires several shifts in position.
2. Anytime the left hand looks jerky when playing such runs.

Inner Drama

When a student examines a run involving several shifts up or down one string, it would be most logical for him to think that he should hold his hand still in one position, finger the two to four notes in that position, shift quickly to the next landing spot, finger those notes, then shift again. This works for a slow passage, so why not a fast one?

The teacher believes that this stop-and-go method is ineffective for most fast runs. Because of the speed required, the shifts between the landing spots would be quite jerky. Each shift would have to stop as suddenly as it started. Thus, tension in the player's muscles could be created and the desired characteristics of ease and agility would not be communicated. The teacher recognizes that fast technique requires a different approach than slow technique. A person running down a road uses a different approach than when he walks.

Doorbells and Doorknobs
SCENE 60

Teacher: "Imagine that we are standing in front of a door. Ring the doorbell!"

Before the student's hand reaches the button the teacher says: "Freeze! Note the shape of your hand. Your index finger is pointing, ready to push the little button. Good! It is preshaped for the task it is to perform.

"Drop your arms to your sides again. Now open the door." When the student's hand almost reaches the doorknob, the teacher calls: "Freeze! Look at your hand! It has already assumed the shape of the round doorknob.

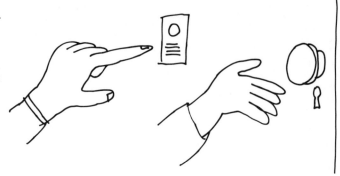

"Now let's check the timing. Drop your arms to your sides again. Watch your hand to see *when* it prepares its shape. Push the doorbell button. . . . Again drop your arms to your sides. Now reach for the doorknob. . . ."

The student will discover that during the initial few inches the hand has prepared its new shape in anticipation of the job required. Almost immediately after its point of departure the hand was preshaped.

"This same principle applies to string playing. Long before the hand reaches the fingerboard it should be in the position to play the first notes! Let's try that now."

Cue to Use

1. Whenever the student shapes her hand after touching the fingerboard instead of preshaping it.
2. Anytime the teacher wishes to stress hand preparation.

Inner Drama

The teacher recognizes that universal principles underlie the motions of the human body in most everyday activities. If this were not so, there would not be nearly so many similarities among people from all parts of the world.

Yet, the teacher has observed that frequently a person learning to play a musical instrument will somehow abandon many of these natural principles. In fact, the student who accidently applies them to her instrumental technique usually is labeled "talented." Ensuring that more people will be accredited with this positive label is the goal.

As a four-star variation of this scene, the student's attention can be drawn to the impulses felt in the hand as it reaches for the doorknob. Racing through the nerves directly from the brain, the message is instantly delivered to the fingertips! Not only does the arm transport the hand to its destination; it also serves as the hand's communication conduit. To assist the hand appears to be the arm's primary function.

Take a Lesson from a Dog
SCENE 61

Musical Setting: A melodic interval requiring a shift

Teacher: "Take a lesson from a hunting dog! Watch his ears when he moves in a hurry!

"Do they flop in the breeze as he runs? No! He pastes them back against his head so the wind against them will not slow him down.

"Make your hand sleek and compact before this shift. Traveling will be easier!"

Cue to Use

When a student has difficulty with a shift and for no apparent reason has some fingers stretched or raised high in the air while en route.

Inner Drama

Designers of high-speed vehicles are keenly aware of nature's marvelous designs and make their cars, airplanes, and boats sleek and without unnecessary projections. The teacher's goal is to help the student apply the principle of aerodynamics to string playing. He takes care, of course, that the student does not gain the idea that all shifts should be extremely fast or that the hand must always be compact during shifting.

In some situations a string player finds it to his advantage not to use a compact hand in shifting. One example is when the note following an ascending shift is to be played by a finger which has a larger number than the old and the travel is to be done on the old finger. The new finger may be held rather high and pointed toward its destination. It feels alert and ready to drop into the new note.

An extreme example of compactness occurs in an ascending shift if the traveling is to be done on the old finger, which has a larger number than the new finger. The new finger appears to shove the old finger out of the way in order to drop into its note. The traveling finger lifts quickly just at the moment the new finger seems to shout, "Get out of my way! This is my note!" This situation occurs in a descending shift if the new note is played by a finger with a larger number than the old note.

The old adage which advises against fixing something that doesn't need fixing also applies to string technique. If a student's shift is reliable and sounds good, and the following notes are played with ease, his method is probably good.

The Light Show
SCENE 62
(Especially designed for groups)

Equipped with flashlights, three or four students stand with the teacher facing a blank wall. The room lights are dimmed.

"Line up your balls of light so they suggest the length of the fingerboard when the player is viewed from the side. The lights will form a straight line. Don't worry about the dark spaces between the lights. Just give us an outline—our imaginations will do the rest! Hold your lights very still."

The teacher may wish to quickly draw a line on the wall with her flashlight—a diagonal line for cello/bass or a horizontal line for violin/viola—to serve as a guide until the students' lights are in position.

"Good! Now we have a fingerboard profile! My light will represent the vibrato action. Watch how it moves in relation to the fingerboard. It moves like an eraser!"

The teacher shakes her spotlight in short, straight, nonstop cycles just above and parallel to the fingerboard line created by the students' lights.

"The vibrato moves in this direction . . . not in little arcs like this. . . . The rolling of the hand in little dome-shaped arcs would make it almost impossible to link notes with the vibrato motion. . . . But watch how easy it is for me to shift my ball of light to any part of the fingerboard if I keep the vibrato moving like an eraser. . . .

"Now let's switch roles. Anne Marie, you provide the vibrato motion with your flashlight.

Erna, you take her position as part of the fingerboard."

After each student has had the opportunity to direct the moving light, the teacher adds: "Without your instrument, use your right arm or hand as a substitute for a fingerboard. Try to hold it in about the same location as your instrument's fingerboard and vibrate on it with your left hand. Sink a finger into the flesh and watch the profile of your whole hand. Shake it like the moving spotlight."

Cue to Use

1. Anytime after the student already has a start on the vibrato technique.
2. Whenever the student has a tendency to roll her hand when vibrating or to stop the vibrato motion before a shift.

Props

Four or five flashlights and a room that can be dimmed.

Inner Drama

The vibrato action is only one of many techniques that can be dramatized by lights. The possibilities are limited only by the imagination of the teacher, which is another way of saying that there are no limits. In fact, the teacher has a profound belief that creativity flows most freely when the need for a solution to a problem presents itself. Thus she deliberately seeks out situations in which needs are apt to arise. She has no desire to fill her schedule with problem-free students.

Leaving for an Appointment
SCENE 63

Musical Setting: A large melodic interval that requires a long shift, for example B up to A

Teacher: "I can imagine the hand saying to B, 'I must leave now. I have an appointment with A on the fourth beat.'

"The farther the distance, the sooner the hand and the arm will start on their trip!"

Cue to Use

1. Whenever the student shifts so quickly that the shift sounds abrupt and/or the action looks jerky.
2. Anytime the student shifts late and the second note is delayed.

Inner Drama

The teacher believes that confidence in shifting is greatly related to the timing of the departure from the first note. Some students' anxiety about the shift will cause them to leave too early, thus increasing their apprehension when the anchor of good, solid rhythm is removed. Other students also have tension problems for a different reason: they are overly conscientious about holding the note before a long shift for its full value. This scene is designed for them.

Any motion takes some time. The wise player recognizes this and designs a plan with a built-in time allowance. If the rhythm is to be accurate and without a rubato, the travel time must be taken from the first note. No one should feel guilty for leaving one place in order to meet an appointment at another place punctually!

A Speck of Lint
SCENE 64

Musical Setting: A melodic interval requiring a shift

Teacher: "Move your finger on the string like a speck of lint! When it reaches its destination, drop with a snap into an imaginary hole. Let some weight sink into the fingerboard and swing into a beautiful vibrato!"

Cue to Use

1. Anytime the student has a good start on vibrato and shifting.
2. When the shifting tends to be heavy and awkward.
3. Whenever the last note of a shift is not well defined.

Inner Drama

Three basic shifting principles are highlighted in this scene: the suspension of weight during a shift, the sudden release of weight into the new pitch on arrival, and the importance of using vibrato on the destination note. If the teacher has not yet introduced vibrato, the last point can be postponed until the appropriate time.

Another Lesson from a Dog
SCENE 65

Teacher: "Our dog loves to stretch after a nice nap! Stand up and stretch!"

While the students stretch, the teacher calls, "Freeze!

"Look at your hands! All of you have your fingers spread far apart just like our dog does her toes. Yet, I'm sure none of you were thinking of your hands. You were just stretching out from your back. Now pantomime a good form for playing in first position. Note how easy it is to have your fingers spread far enough apart.

"Let's try something different. Squeeze your fingers close together and line up their tips on the edge of this desk. Naturally you will need to curve your fingers so your fingertips can form a straight line. Now try to spread them apart. . . . Does your hand feel tight? For most of us, this is the difficult way to spread our fingers!

"How does this apply to your playing? When you practice a passage which makes you wish your hand were larger, stretch it first, before touching the fingerboard, then curve your fingers. The reverse can cause tension in your hand. And when you stretch, think from your back out. That makes stretching easy!"

Cue to Use

1. Anytime a student has difficulty reaching the notes.
2. Whenever a student's hand appears tense from stretching.

Props

A desk, music stand, chair, or anything with a straight edge.

Inner Drama

The teacher first became aware of the stretching-from-the-back principle when he watched his dog stretch. Then he observed that no one yawned and stretched her arms with her fingers close together. Naturally a musician cannot stop a performance to stretch, but, when this approach is used in the initial practice of a passage, the hand usually falls in proper alignment with ease.

The teacher is also aware that two other points warrant checking if a student has difficulty in spreading her fingers far enough apart when playing. First, a hand which shows a very high profile above the fingerboard can be restrictive; second, too square a hand position (more likely to happen in the case of cellists and bassists) can make the second and third fingers feel bound together.

Though in this scene the stretch is incorporated to demonstrate a technique, the teacher also uses it on other occasions. He has found that

standing up and stretching can offer a quick rest break, especially when the class has been sitting. Concentration immediately following a stretch is usually improved.

The Man on the Flying Trapeze
SCENE 66

Teacher: "Think of your left hand as a trapeze artist! Picture how fluid and graceful his motions are as he lets go of one swing to reach for another. Not a jerky motion in his act!

"The music may call for sudden starts and stops or accents and releases in the bow arm but keep the left hand as graceful as the man on the flying trapeze!"

Cue to Use

1. Anytime the bowing action requires accents, jerky motions, or sudden starts and stops.
2. Whenever the student tends to use jerky motions in the left hand.

Inner Drama

The teacher has witnessed much improvement in left hand technical facility with many students when they learned to divorce the actions of one hand from the other. The natural tendency of any person is for the mood and style of one hand's motions to be reflected in the other. This inclination is particularly revealed in music making because of the mood created by the music itself. Though helpful at times, it can cause tension.

The drama of music demands that the bow arm move in a variety of ways including sudden starts and stops. However, the transferral of these styles to the left hand can make the music ugly and can harm the technique and tone of the student. The virtuoso's left hand, of course, complements her right hand, but the variety of left hand motions is mostly concentrated in varying styles and speeds of vibrato, different points of contact in the finger tips or pads with the string, various hand elevations, the differences in the balance and action of slow and fast techniques, various styles of shifting, and the different placement of impulses. Almost never is a jerky motion allowed to creep into her left hand technique.

Guiltless
SCENE 67

The teacher reads aloud as though from a newspaper:

"DEAR JAN SANDERS: I am sick and tired of being blamed for something that is not my fault. I am the arrival note of a shift on a stringed instrument. Time and again players will blame me for being out of tune!

"Please advise the readers of your column to give this some thought. Most of the success of the second note of a shift depends on the energy of the boost off from the first note. If the hand overshoots, the energy should be reduced. If the hand undershoots, energy should be added. Please sign me—GUILTLESS.

"DEAR GUILTLESS: You are absolutely right in not accepting unfair criticism. String players, take note!"

Cue to Use

Anytime the second note of a shift is persistently out of tune yet the position of the hand and arm appears correct.

Inner Drama

The teacher has observed that almost never does a basketball player blame the basket or the golfer blame the hole for miscalculated shots. Although their disappointment and possible anger may be evident and even misdirected, they seldom accuse the target. The goal of this scene is to help the student focus on the source of the problem so it can be corrected. If the position is correct, the motion is free, and the ear alert, the probability of hitting the second note in tune is predetermined from the moment of the send-off.

Shock Absorbers
SCENE 68

Teacher: "Let's do some research! Stand up on this chair. Now jump off!"

After the student has jumped off the chair the teacher remarks: "I notice that when your feet landed on the floor, your knees bent. Why did they do that?"

The student will undoubtedly explain that, if he had not flexed his knees, he would have hurt himself.

"You are absolutely right! Your knees serve as shock absorbers. Our bodies seem to know just what to do for survival.

"This principle can be applied to string playing. When a finger drops on the fingerboard, all of its joints should serve as shock absorbers. They should be flexible and ready to swing into a gorgeous vibrato. Practice dropping a finger now. Check to be sure that it approaches the fingerboard at an angle which allows the joints to flex."

Cue to Use

Anytime the teacher notices that the student's finger joints appear stiff or the vibrato needs improving.

Inner Drama

Most students are experienced jumpers and will enthusiastically participate in a demonstration. On another day the teacher may wish to point out that anyone who hits a punching bag instinctively knows to use her wrists, elbows, and shoulders as shock absorbers.

Although an occasional dropping of a finger with tight joints on the fingerboard would likely not injure the finger, it is impossible to have a beautiful vibrato with any stiff joint in the left hand or arm. The "natural" player instinctively uses the body's shock absorbers. Others may be taught.

The initial approach of the finger to the fingerboard is a great determiner as to the workability of the finger. A 90° angle restricts the flexing of the joints, especially the first joint (nearest the fingernail), which is so vital in making a beautiful vibrato.

Pitching the Tent
SCENE 69
(Especially for cellists' and bassists' left hands but adaptable to the bow hands of all string players)

Teacher: "My hand is a tent collapsed on the ground ready to be pitched. Slowly the crown of the tent rises and it is ready for use!"

As the teacher starts talking, his left hand rests on a desk or the top of a piano. The extreme finger tips, the heel of the hand, and the entire side of the thumb touch the surface. The first and second knuckles are curved but the base knuckles, which connect the fingers to the hand, are sunk in.

Slowly the base knuckles of the four fingers rise to their maximum height. The finger tips, the entire side of the thumb, and part of the heel of the hand still contact the hard surface.

"Try this. Your finger tips will act like tent stakes and be firmly anchored to the ground. Push them down hard. Your base knuckles will point to the sky. . . . Good! Keep the tent raised while we count to ten. One, two, three, . . .

"Do this many times while you watch TV or ride in the car or bus. It will strengthen the arch of your hand so your fingers can work well in thumb position."

Cue to Use

1. Whenever a cellist or bassist collapses her base knuckles while playing in thumb position, unless the music demands an extremely wide interval between the thumb and third finger.
2. Anytime to strengthen cellists' and bassists' hands for thumb position.

Inner Drama

The teacher recognizes that the first step toward developing a technique in thumb position is to strengthen the arch of the hand. Many students tend to collapse the base knuckles when they first play with the side of the thumb on top of the fingerboard. This awkward shape puts the fingers out of commission and no facility will be developed.

It is suggested that in practicing this isometric exercise away from the instrument, the student push her fingers and thumb down with excess pressure. This will hasten building a strong arch. Naturally, excessive pressure should never be used on the fingerboard and probably the arch will not be raised quite so high when playing. Later, after strength is developed, this scene can be modified. All of the finger tips will be lifted off the hard surface by the base knuckles. The tent then will be anchored only by the thumb. The student will find new freedom and agility in her fingers because the supporting muscles in the arch of her hand are now doing their job. *Pitching the Tent* can also help strengthen the joints of all string students' bow hands.

Rattling the Bones
SCENE 70

Teacher: "Rattle every bone in your hand when you vibrate on that note! Think of a Halloween skeleton with plastic bones strung together with a cord. Even the bones in your thumb will shake!

"Now shake your hand in the vibrato motion high above the fingerboard. Don't touch the instrument. Just rattle every bone in your hand!

"Good! Keep shaking the bones as you lower your arm. Bring your hand right down to the fingerboard!"

Cue to Use

1. Anytime to help the vibrato motion and free it of tension.
2. Whenever the teacher wishes to check the left hand and arm position to be sure that it is workable for the vibrato motion.

Inner Drama

From working with many students the teacher has learned the importance of every joint being loose when vibrating. Even one tight spot can sabotage the whole system of springs in the joints. Most students react positively when their attention is drawn to a Halloween skeleton instead of their own arms and hands. Who could have a flicker of inhibition when rattling those cheap plastic bones?

A common fault among cello students asked to shake their bones in the vibrato motion without touching the instrument is for the hand to fall. This produces a sharp bend in the wrist, which makes a good vibrato impossible. The advice, "Support your hand so there is a direct line

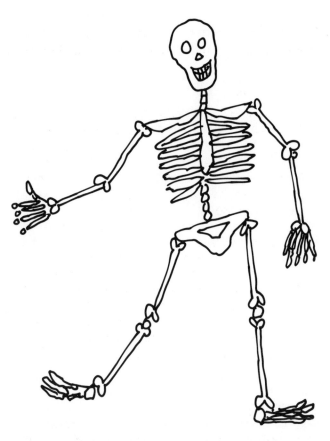

from your elbow to the back of your hand," usually offers an immediate solution. In playing a stringed instrument the supporting muscles are as important as those that move.

A Homing Pigeon
SCENE 71

The teacher and student identify a problem note which is repeatedly off-pitch.

"Let's isolate that note . . . Good! Now it is perfectly in tune! Remember how your hand looks and feels. Memorize its location and shape.

"While holding your hand in the same form, touch the tailpiece, then play the note. . . . Touch your head, play the note. . . . Touch the scroll, play the note. . . . Touch the back of your neck, play the note. . . . Touch your leg, play the note. . . .

"The homing pigeon returns to the same place on the fingerboard every time! Now practice returning home after you play the preceding note."

Cue to Use

Anytime a note is frequently out of tune or the form of the hand is not consistent when playing a specific note or double stop.

Inner Drama

The teacher is convinced that memorizing kinesthetic sensations is a major part of home practice. Scientists believe that there is a part of the brain which specializes in this fascinating aspect of developing manual skills. Along with repeated success in playing a note after the hand has been in such far off locations as the instrument's tailpiece and the player's leg comes an almost guaranteed confidence. In this scene it is essential for the hand to keep the same form throughout its travels. *A Homing Pigeon* is especially helpful for double stops.

Match Mates
SCENE 72

Teacher: "Let's team up and play one instrument! I'll provide the left hand work. Anne, you provide the right hand. Let your bow sink into the D string so the tone is big and full. We'll listen carefully to one note while I find the vibrato that matches your bowing. Change the bow direction as often as needed to keep the tone loud."

When the teacher finds the vibrato that both she and the student agree sounds beautiful, she says: "Now, I will keep vibrating exactly the same way, but you change your part. Bow lightly so the tone is soft."

The beautiful tone will suddenly be transformed into an ugly one. Although the teacher has not changed her vibrato, it will sound wobbly and strange.

"The width of the vibrato should match the width of the vibration of the string. A large vibration requires a large vibrato. A narrow vibration requires a narrow vibrato. Listen carefully as I make my vibrato smaller. . . . There! I like that tone. Do you? Let's experiment with another dynamic level. . . . Remember: if we listen carefully to the string, it will tell us how to vibrate."

Cue to Use

1. Anytime after a good vibrato suited for a loud tone is well established and the teacher feels the time is right to vary its size.
2. Whenever the vibrato is not beautiful although it seems balanced and rhythmically even.

Inner Drama

Active participation in any kind of venture almost always helps to arouse a person's interest in the subject. Although the teacher could easily have demonstrated this basic principle with her own two hands, the student would have been relegated to the role of spectator. Whenever possible, active participation is desirable in the learning process.

In this scene the teacher may prefer to have two students play one instrument rather than the teacher-student team. If so, she will be sure to choose a student with a beautifully developed vibrato to take the left hand role.

When the vibrato is made smaller to match the small amplitude of the string vibrations for the soft notes, it will also sound faster. Although the speed of the motion could remain exactly the same, the shorter distance will be covered in less time; thus, more cycles will be completed per second.

The Dance of the Double Stops
SCENE 73

Musical Setting: A passage with successive double stops or chords

With his hands on his hips, the teacher performs a little foot dance. He hops to a new foot position. Both feet land on the floor at the same time and have equal balance. He moves from one foot pattern to another and at times may choose to cross his feet.

"Join me! The only rule is that both feet should land at the same instant."

After the dance is under way the teacher calls attention to the timing of the change in foot position. From the moment the feet begin the spring up from the floor, they start moving into a new pattern.

"Take your instrument and let's practice this double stop passage. Play the first double stop. With your fingers still pointing to the fingerboard and your thumb still touching the neck, flip your fingers up to the shape required for the second double stop. Hold them there in the air a second. Look at them! Notice how relaxed they are. Now drop them to the fingerboard. Let's hear it. . . . Flip up to the shape of the third double stop. . . .

"Now play the passage as written and make a little hop from one finger pattern to the next. At times some of your fingers will remain very close to or on the strings but it helps to feel your hand snap into position."

Cue to Use

Anytime in the study of consecutive double stops or chords.

Inner Drama

Double stop passages can cause tension in the player's hand. With each flip in this scene, tension is released. The action will come from the base knuckles, which are the large knuckles joining the fingers to the hand. The teacher has chosen to begin with the foot dance because it is easier to see and to feel. Through experience he has discovered that most students instantly grasp a technique which is demonstrable with legs and feet. An added benefit of a foot dance is that almost never does a student have a fear of failure.

Since it is not possible to demonstrate with the feet and legs the brief suspension in the air after each fast flip, the teacher may choose to suggest an imaginary videotape which is halted momentarily after each flip. The still picture will show the feet in the new position.

Walking Forward
SCENE 74
(Especially designed for the larger instruments, but helpful to others)

As the teacher walks slowly around the room, she remarks:

"Moving from a finger on the first finger side of the hand toward a finger on the fourth finger side is like walking! Watch how the knee of the 'old' leg bends so my weight can shift to the 'new' leg. In fact, the balance is already there before the 'new' foot hits the floor. My weight precedes my foot.

"This is the way we 'walk' with our fingers in slow technique. At the very end of a note, the base knuckle of the playing finger will bend inward to make it possible for the weight of the hand to stay ahead of the next finger. This way you can move from one finger to another and vibrate beautifully without rolling the hand!"

Cue to Use

Anytime to help the student transfer the balance from one playing finger to another in slow technique. It is designed for moving from a finger with a smaller number to one with a larger number on the same string.

Inner Drama

Most people are virtuosi at walking. Transferring this skill, which is already well developed, to string playing can give an enormous head start. There are only six possible combinations for the student to master: 1 to 2, 2 to 3, 3 to 4, 1 to 3, 1 to 4, 2 to 4.

In relation to the crossing of strings the reader is advised to see *Hidden Double Stops*, Scene 55, and *Walking Backward*, Scene 75, at this time. A definition of slow technique may be found in *Learning to Race*, Scene 109.

Naturally, the term *weight* is not as meaningful to violinists and violists as to cellists and bassists, but the term *balance* always carries a mighty punch.

Walking Backward
SCENE 75
(Especially designed for the larger instruments, but helpful to others)

This time the teacher walks around the room backward! She explains:

"Moving from a finger on the fourth finger side of the hand toward a finger on the first finger side of the hand is like walking backward! Watch how my foot goes first and touches the floor with the toe of the shoe. Then my weight follows! As the heel lands on the floor, my weight is balanced on the 'new' leg. The timing is exactly the reverse of walking forward!

"Now try walking backward with your fingers from the fourth finger toward the first. The finger tip will lead and the weight will come later. As the 'old' finger lifts, the 'new' finger will pop into a shape that allows the balance on it to be perfect. Watch how the base knuckle slips farther away from the instrument neck as your vibrato begins its swing."

Cue to Use

Anytime to help the student learn to transfer from one optimum position to another for a beautiful vibrato. It is designed for moving from a finger with a larger number to one with a smaller number on the same string. It should be preceded by *Walking Forward*, Scene 74.

Inner Drama

The principal difference between *Walking Forward*, Scene 74, and *Walking Backward* is the timing of the change of balance. In walking forward with the fingers, the balance shifts before the new note is played but the note does not sound until the finger lands. In walking backward, the balance shifts at the exact moment the note is to sound, but the tip of the finger will have arrived early. It is this timing and the reshaping of the playing finger that make all the difference in producing a beautifully balanced vibrato.

There are only six combinations for the student to master in walking backward: 4 to 3, 3 to 2, 2 to 1, 4 to 1, 4 to 2, and 3 to 1. However, in the case of string crossings, a new element enters the picture. The hidden double stop between the notes generally requires that the arch of the hand be shaped to favor the string which is the farthest from the palm of the hand. No finger should feel terribly stretched. Thus, the relocation of the arch of the hand might also need to take place during the time value of the last portion of the old note. The teacher has found that in such instances it can be helpful for the student to first practice the transfer of the balance between the same two fingers on one string, then add the element of changing strings. Breaking down technical problems to two or three isolated components can be most advantageous and, in the long run, timesaving.

The reader is advised to consult *Hidden Double Stops*, Scene 55, and *Learning to Race*, Scene 109, at this time.

Stepping over a Mud Puddle
SCENE 76
(Designed especially for the larger instruments, but helpful to others)

Teacher: "Stand over here please. . . . Now suppose there is a big mud puddle directly in front of you. How would you step over it? Don't jump."

After the student has stepped over the imaginary mud puddle, the teacher reports her observations:

"I see that the knee of the 'old' leg bent so that your weight was in line with the 'new' foot long before it landed on the other side of the puddle. . . . Let's see you do that again.

"Good! This is the way we move from the first to the fourth finger in slow technique. As we balance on the first finger, the base knuckle will stick out and be closer to the scroll than its tip. Then the base knuckle starts to sink in, the finger and hand reshape, and the fourth finger lands on the other side of the imaginary mud puddle on the fingerboard! It will already be in a perfect position to vibrate!"

Cue to Use

Anytime to help the student learn to transfer the balance from the first to the fourth finger on one string in slow technique.

Inner Drama

Practicing the giant step between the first and fourth fingers helps the student to achieve the kinesthetic sensation of transferring weight. The goal is to achieve the same beautiful vibrato on both fingers because each has found a perfect balance. This Scene as well as *Stepping Back over a Mud Puddle*, Scene 77, can be adapted to string crossings.

Stepping Back over a Mud Puddle
SCENE 77
(Designed especially for the larger instruments, but helpful to others)

Teacher: "Suppose there is a big mud puddle behind you! Let's see you step back over it!"

The student will automatically extend one leg back over the imaginary puddle until his toe touches dry land. His balance will remain on the "old" foot until the toe has reached its destination. Then the "old" foot lifts, the body weight shifts to the new side of the puddle, and the "new" leg reshapes.

"Good! You have just demonstrated how to step from the fourth to the first finger in slow technique! The first finger tip is like the toe that paved the way, then the whole finger reshapes after you snap up the fourth finger and the hand shifts its balance to the first finger. You will be ready to swing into a beautiful vibrato!"

Cue to Use

Anytime to help the student learn to move from the fourth finger to the first finger on one string with a beautiful vibrato on each finger.

Inner Drama

Shifting the balance is one of the most fascinating aspects of playing and teaching a stringed instrument. Mud puddles in the middle of a studio and fingerboard can keep the student alert and tune up what some scientists believe to be the very special right side of the brain.

The Good Camper
SCENE 78
(Especially designed for cellists)

Musical Setting: A melodic pattern of two consecutive whole steps requiring an extension, for example, G# F# E F# G# played with the fingering 42124 on the D string at a moderate or slow tempo requiring vibrato

Teacher: "Let's look in on a camping trip! First, find a good position to vibrate on 4. Then 2. Now, while holding your second finger down, tilt your wrist slightly as though you plan to look at your wristwatch and move your first finger tip back to E by making a tiny arc above the string. The first finger is a good camper going ahead to find a suitable campsite! When he touches E, he calls, 'Hey, you guys, I've found a good spot. Come quickly!'

"Flip the second finger up and move the hand and forearm to the new location while the thumb slides back along the neck about a half step. Now balance on the first finger and vibrate beautifully. Its base knuckle will stick out and slightly back toward the scroll. The other fingers will stay close to it and enjoy the ride! They will all swing together!

"Now it is time to break camp. The tip of the first finger says, 'You guys go on. I'll stay here a little longer to finish things up. My base knuckle will travel with you.'

"And sure enough, the base knuckle of the first finger, the thumb, the hand, and the forearm all move toward their original location. For a split second the first finger is straight, or almost straight, and its base knuckle is collapsed and low. The second, third, and fourth fingers are suspended in the air. As the second finger drops to its place on the fingerboard and vibrates, the first finger tip leaves the campsite with a snap to join the other fingers for a ride in the air. Then the second finger springs up when the fourth finger drops into place and begins its vibrato swing.

"Whenever you use vibrato, balance perfectly on the playing finger! Pretend that you are going to rock away on it for the rest of your life!"

Cue to Use

Anytime after the cello student can vibrate well on isolated notes and on melodic fragments not involving extensions.

Inner Drama

The teacher believes that no vibrato should be used when the hand is in an awkward or stretched position. She considers that each finger has an optimum position for vibrato and that the shape and location of the thumb, hand, forearm, and the nonplaying fingers are very important in making the vibrato of the playing finger effective. It is impossible to balance on the playing finger if the other fingers do not cooperate.

The teacher is convinced that the trick is to move the hand and forearm from one optimum position to another with as much ease as possible. The hand should not roll and the elbow should remain rather quiet. Measuring distances is extremely difficult if there is no constant factor.

Later the goal will be to move to the new hand shape on one of the vibrato swings but there is no hurry in learning this skill. Beauty of each individual tone is the primary goal in this scene.

The LEFT HAND exits stage left.
(*But it will make a return appearance!*)

5　The Variety Show

The vaudeville stars wait in the wings. Their routines are sharpened and ready to go! The hoofers' straw hats are on, the magician's bunny is up his sleeve, and the ventriloquist's dummy tests his voice. The acrobats loosen their knees as the mime stands quietly alone. Who could say who rates top billing?

The Emcee strides on stage. Let the music begin!

The thirty-two Scenes in "The Variety Show" are designed for better understanding and are intended to be interspersed with the music. *As always, the music itself must play the dominant role throughout every lesson.*

SCENES FOR BETTER UNDERSTANDING

Panther Pink

SCENE 79
(Especially for groups)

The teacher explains that she is going to tell a fictitious story.

"I just moved to the United States and learned to speak English. I thought I was doing OK but people don't seem to understand me. Perhaps you can advise me about what I'm doing wrong.

"For example, the other day I was telling some friends about Panther Pink. They didn't know what I was talking about. But, I know you have Panther Pinks because I saw one on television!"

The students will advise that it is a Pink Panther.

"Oh! But that is not all. I told them about seeing some jay blues and they said there are no jay blues in America. Yet I saw a whole flock of jay blues in my backyard! What is wrong?"

After the students explain that they are blue jays, the teacher will say quietly as though thinking aloud: "I see. The *color* goes before the main word.

"OK. Here is my story. Yesterday I saw a blue jay and a [*pause*] red cardinal walking toward each other. I thought they were going to say hello but suddenly I realized that they both had their eyes on the same supper—a caterpillar fuzzy!"

When the students correct the storyteller, the teacher exclaims: "But 'fuzzy' is not a color!"

Quickly the teacher moves from her storytelling style to a more serious vein. "What are we talking about? In English classes we have learned the principle: *An adjective precedes the noun it modifies.* In music we also have hundreds of principles.

"We all know that the very young learn by imitation. Of course, we don't discuss these principles with the children any more than we would tell a three-year-old that the adjective precedes the noun it modifies. However, when we reach a certain age, it can help much to acknowledge basic principles.

"So, from time to time, including today's class, we will examine principles related to string playing."

Cue to Use

When the teacher wants to present ideas from this book, but wants to be sure that the teenage students, or those approaching teenage, realize that they are based on serious concepts and are not child's play.

Inner Drama

The teacher acknowledges that the process of learning to play music appears to be similar to the process of learning a native language. Both start with imitation but soon branch out to something far more than imitation. The adult who listens to a child say, "I kicked and hollered and he sticked his tongue out at me!" realizes that this was not learned through imitation. Nor was the sentence, "We walked through a park and goed to a store." The teacher views both such remarks not as bad English but as something remarkably phenomenal. Each demonstrates that the child is actively engaged in making structural sense out of the language. Many linguists are fascinated by the compelling question of how people learn their native tongues and note the striking similarities of the process throughout the world, however diverse the languages.

The teacher is convinced that many music students try to package together the material presented to them just as a child tries to find the underlying structure of his language. She believes that at some point it helps to discuss basic principles. Through her own personal experience she knows that some of the concepts arrived at by the student on his own can be erroneous or, at least, only partially accurate. Her immediate objective is to introduce principles in a fun, light-hearted manner that sparks insight rather than present them as dull facts to be learned and memorized. Her ultimate goal is to help the student gain transferrable knowledge and skills so he will eventually become his own teacher.

TV Game Show
SCENE 80
(Especially designed for groups)

The teacher asks for three fearless volunteers, then seats them in a row facing the class. Without explanation he starts speaking in the style of a TV game show host.

"Ladies and Gentlemen: Today we have with us three distinguished guests! One has been so busy with his important work that he has not eaten for twenty-four hours! He is ravenously hungry! Another is a robot. The third is a high society lady who thought she was invited to a tea. In Australia she is called 'Lady Muck.'"

The volunteers draw papers assigning roles.

Pointing to the "audience," the teacher advises: "Your job is to determine who is who!"

Gesturing to the "distinguished guests" he says: "Your job is to demonstrate the proper way to peel a banana! There is only one rule: no talking. If you wish, you may eat the banana."

From a hiding place the teacher produces a grocery bag containing three bananas.

"Guest X: Are you ready? Please step forward."

Guest X peels her banana. The teacher leads the applause.

After Guests Y and Z perform and the laughter and applause subside, the teacher drops his TV role and says: "Of course, you know who played each part. But, how did you know? How does this relate to string playing?"

After discussion the teacher summarizes:

"A banana does not get peeled without motion on the part of the peeler. A stringed instrument produces no sound without motion on the part of the player. You were able to distinguish among our three guests because of the expressiveness of their motions. They had nothing else—no costumes, no backdrops. Much of the expressiveness of our string playing depends on the expressiveness of our motions, especially in the bow arm. The characteristic of a tone reflects the same characteristic of the physical motion that generates it!

"Remember: It is impossible to have a dramatic tone without a dramatic gesture!"

Cue to Use

1. Anytime an icebreaker with a meaty message is appropriate.
2. Whenever the students' playing lacks expression.

Props

Three bananas in a brown paper grocery bag. Also three empty chairs lined up conspicuously in front of the class.

Inner Drama

The teacher knows that nothing brings a group together or reduces tension as quickly as laughter. His primary goal is to create an emotional climate which will nurture learning. Most assuredly the teacher who dares to schedule such an unexpected activity as banana peeling will capture the interest of his students.

A winning variation of this TV game show is to have hidden cameras in three kitchens. They are focused on people cooking breakfast: a French chef preparing an omelet, a person cooking for the first time, and a school orchestra director who has overslept and is rushing to meet an eight o'clock class. The presentations are made one at a time. A few cooking utensils and a small table may serve as props.

Though great fun, this scene, or its variation, carries a powerful punch. Who possibly could fail to get its important message?

Reprogram
SCENE 81

Teacher: "Suppose that you are an actor playing the part of a timid, fearful person at a party. Show me your body language . . . Good!

"Notice how you've folded up your arms and drawn them in closer to your body. And your shoulders are hunched. I wonder why people tend to do that when they feel uneasy in a situation?"

Together it is evolved that all living creatures have been given defense mechanisms. If unable to flee, fight, or use other means of protection, they try to make themselves smaller and become a part of the surroundings. Their appendages draw in. The turtle becomes a rock, the rabbit a blob of fuzz, and the insect a speck on the floor. Nature also has programmed human beings for self-preservation.

"So, what do we do if we feel ourselves 'drawing in' during a public performance? We instantly reprogram! First, we remind ourselves that our bodies are not in danger. A recital hall is a place where people gather to enjoy music. Its reported mortality rate is actually quite low!

"Second, watch those elbows! Free them! Send them a mental command to move where needed so the hands can do their important work!"

Cue to Use

1. When a student's gestures appear fearful.
2. If a student introduces the subject of performance anxiety or stage fright.

Inner Drama

Performance anxiety is seldom a music teacher's favorite topic. Some believe that the subject should be avoided. Others stress that the key to confidence is thorough preparation.

The hiding instinct of some students, however, is obvious and their playing is harmed by it. For example, a cellist may draw her bow much closer to the fingerboard in a public performance than in a lesson; or she may approach the higher registers of the fingerboard apologetically. Both char-

acteristics signal that nature's protective instinct is dominating.

Humans have been given not only the priceless instinct for survival but also a mind with the capability to reprogram itself. Without this, civilization would never have been born.

Putty Hands
SCENE 82

Teacher: "Imagine that our hands are made of silly putty. Let's mold them into five different shapes. . . .

"Why there is no limit! Look at what we are doing! We could go on and on. I bet we could make a thousand different shapes! What a miracle the human hand is! Can you think of anything else that can do this?"

The students possibly will point out that silly putty, mud, clay, dough, cake icing, and other materials can be shaped in many ways.

"You are right! But there is one huge difference. It takes hands or machines to shape those other materials! They can't do it by themselves. Even our wonderful animal friends don't have anything equivalent to the human hand. Imagine what an intelligent dog could do if he had even one hand! And what about an elephant or a porpoise?

"We each have been given a marvelous gift! Two in fact! A concert artist molds her hands into many shapes when she plays but her hands are probably no better than ours. Some concert artists have skinny hands—others fat. Some have long fingers—others short. They have simply learned how to use their hands in the very best way and to send them mental commands.

"Let's make our hands and fingers like putty when we play and let every joint be flexible but strong. They will obey our commands and move from one shape to another as the technique demands. Play your piece again with this in mind."

Cue to Use

Anytime, except in the early training, when the student's hands look rigid or stiff.

Inner Drama

The teacher recognizes that the close relationship between the music teacher and his students gives him the unique opportunity to influence them in many positive ways. This scene, in addition to helping with technique, reflects an attitude of gratitude and appreciation.

If the teacher chooses, he might extend this scene to point out that nature considers the human hand so important that nearly 90 percent of the cerebellum, the part of the brain responsible for the regulation and coordination of complex voluntary muscular movement, is set aside to assist in the control of the movement of the hands and fingers.

Elbow Watchers
SCENE 83

The teacher produces an "elbow watcher" to be placed on a knee of the seated student.

"The elbow watcher is going to make sure that your elbow _____."

The teacher fills in any description she chooses. In some short, fast bow strokes, such as rapid

détaché and sautillé, the elbow will float in one place if the notes are all on one string. During a whole bow stroke in the up-bow direction, the elbow watcher can make sure that the elbow moves closer to the body as the hand and frog approach the string. The elbow watcher can also keep a sharp eye on the left elbow to be sure it is not tight.

Cue to Use

Anytime the teacher wishes to call attention to an instruction regarding either elbow.

Props

A little fuzzy, colorful ball with eyes, antennae, and paper feet. These inexpensive personalities are readily available in most drugstores near the checkout counter.

Inner Drama

This scene is obviously designed for the younger child. Any elbow problem is soon corrected under the watchful eyes of such an appealing helper.

A Green Rainbow
SCENE 84

Teacher: "Everyone loves a rainbow! I wonder why?"

After a brief discussion, the teacher adds: "Yes, we love the mixture of colors. Suppose a rainbow were solid green? Or imagine a yellow rainbow. They might be beautiful but not nearly as special as a combination of many colors.

"Let's treat our music the same way. With a stringed instrument, a bow, and an imagination, we can learn to make tones with a large variety of colors. Some will be brilliant, others pastel, still others dark.

"Let's try now to match in sound these color samples from the paint store!"

Cue to Use

Whenever the teacher feels the time is right to add more variety to the student's playing. He should already have a well-developed, pleasing vibrato and a good bow arm.

Props

Several color samples from a paint store.

Inner Drama

The teacher's goal is to motivate the student to seek a variety of tonal colors in his playing and to make him aware that this is a desirable goal. Often, when a person is growing up or learning to do anything new, he does not have clearly defined goals. For example, he may want very badly to learn to play an instrument beautifully but cannot distinguish which characteristics are to be sought out and which are to be avoided.

The teacher recalls instances in which she was surprised when a student had deliberately adopted an undesirable characteristic. Sometimes he had picked up from a fellow student the very trait the teacher had been trying to eliminate.

To the professional, certain qualities are so clearly labeled in her mind as desirable or undesirable that she assumes they are equally obvious to all people. Teaching discrimination, though in a gentle and kind manner, is an essential part of the profession.

Straight Lines from Arcs?
SCENE 85

Teacher: "Monkey see, monkey do!"

Without holding an instrument or bow the teacher moves his right forearm up and down using only his elbow joint.

"Hm-m. If a pencil were attached to my fingers, it would be drawing an arc! Let's try moving the forearm sideways using only the elbow. . . . Again, it is drawing an arc!"

The teacher and students try moving only the shoulder joint, then only the wrist, then only the base knuckle of a finger.

"It appears that our bodies are designed to draw arcs and circles! Then, how is it possible for us to draw straight lines? I know it is possible because I've done it!"

Together it is discovered that drawing a straight line requires moving more than one joint.

"While sitting quietly, let's trace the edge of this desk with a hand. It is one long straight line! Look how fluid your motions are as the finger joints, wrist, elbow, and shoulder all get into the act!

"Now let's return to our instruments and make our motions just as fluid. Not one single locked joint!"

Cue to Use

Anytime the teacher wishes to stress fluidity of motions, especially in whole bow strokes and shifting.

Props

A desk if readily available. If not, the edge of a piano keyboard lid, a window sill, or any other straight line will suffice.

Inner Drama

The teacher's goal is to make the student aware of the miraculous design of the human skeleton. Through a series of joints a person is able to move almost any way in order to meet his needs, including the technical mastery of a musical instrument.

The teacher looks for every opportunity to stress the fluidity of motion and to make the student aware that this is a desirable and attainable goal. Just one locked joint can throw the whole system off!

First Note of the Piece
SCENE 86

Teacher: "Play this note as though it is the first note of the piece! You have just walked out on the stage and tuned. Let's hear it. . . .

"Beautiful! It shows what you and your instrument can do! Now play the preceding note and go directly to this beautiful note."

Any differences will quickly be detected.

"Play the note again as though it is the first note of the piece. . . . Good! Remember the position and the feeling in your hands and arms. Also note the angle of the bow. The trick is to move to this same position *before* you begin to play the note. Make it sound beautiful from the start!"

Cue to Use

Anytime the tone quality of a note does not sound good to the teacher although the student may find it acceptable.

Inner Drama

It has been the teacher's observation that almost everyone plays the first note of a piece well. The student is able to take plenty of time and usually approaches it from above. Moving to the same note, however, from another note, particularly one on a different string, is quite a different matter. Once a student hears herself play a note well it is not just proof of what she and her instrument can do. A new aural standard has been provided by the student herself.

Many undesirable sounds can slip past unnoticed by the player because they are sandwiched between other notes. Built into this scene is the training of a discriminating ear, which will become the student's teacher in home practice.

The Tireless Arm
SCENE 87

Teacher: "Your arm is tired from playing? This could be a signal that you are doing something wrong."

The teacher places the fingers of his left hand on top of his own right shoulder about where the seam joins the sleeve and the shirt.

"Put your hand here on my shirt seam. As I raise my arm, feel where my muscles start getting very tight and hard. The secret is *not* to raise the upper arm this high and hold it there.

"Feel your own shoulder. Raise your upper arm so it is almost level with it. This position can hurt! If you hold your elbow this high for very long, it probably will feel like breaking off!

"Drop the elbow just a few inches so it rests on some imaginary foam rubber. Good! You could easily play in this position for a longer time without your arm feeling brittle."

Cue to Use

Whenever a student complains that an arm or shoulder is tired or hurts.

Inner Drama

The musical passage most likely to bring about a complaint of tired arms from cello students is one that has repeated short strokes played in the upper part of the bow on the A string for an extended period of time. A similar passage on the G string can tire the arm of a French bow bassist. Playing in the lower part of the bow on the G string of the violin or the C string of the viola is more tiring. For this reason it is recommended that strokes in various parts of the bow and on various strings be interspersed during the practice of such a passage.

In the case of cello and bass students, the position of the instrument or the length of the endpin may possibly need a slight adjustment so the student can bow without raising her upper arm to an

undesirable height. This requires reexamination periodically as the student grows. If there is pain present, the teacher will encourage his student to seek medical advice.

The Seeds of Today
SCENE 88

Teacher: "Sometimes we practice a passage for hours and it doesn't seem to improve. Then suddenly we play it with confidence!

"This is true in other fields also. Think of the months that Dr. Jonas Salk and his associates must have worked before their announcement of the polio vaccine!

"Look at the gardener! She can spend hours hoeing, shoveling, and planting and not a flower will be in sight. Much later her garden will burst into bloom!

"We plant seeds when we practice. As the Chinese proverb says, 'The seeds of today are the flowers of tomorrow.' Let's look at some new ways to plant and nurture those seeds."

Cue to Use

Whenever the student appears discouraged or needs new ways to practice.

Inner Drama

As in any worthwhile enterprise, encouragement is important. The teacher is in a position to offer either encouragement or discouragement at every lesson. From her own experience she knows what a boost even a few words can give.

An additional goal is to give the student new ways to practice a troublesome passage not only to help him learn it faster but also to give new life to practice sessions.

A firm believer in the success-breeds-success theory, the teacher carefully gauges the sequence of music and activities so that one success is stacked on another. Each performance is well prepared; contests are not entered unless there is a reasonable expectation of winning some kind of approval. She considers that the statement "I knew I didn't stand a chance of winning but I did it for the experience" is based on falacious reasoning. Experience is better gained another way. No matter how fine a salesperson, the conscious brain appears not always to convince the subconscious. A failure continues to be labeled a failure. If repeated too many times, the confidence shrinks and losing becomes a habit and an expectation.

A generally known fact is that the experienced trainer of boxers carefully selects his young future champ's opponents to provide a ladder of victories. Gradually both skill and confidence are built as the opponents get tougher.

Boxing is not reputed for its sensitivity. If the boxing trainer handles his student this carefully, doesn't it make sense to give the music student at least equal treatment? Finding a good balance between challenge and risk of failure for each individual student is the trick.

7:05 A.M.
SCENE 89

The teacher places an alarm clock on a desk or chair about an arm's length from the student.

"It is six o'clock in the morning and you are awakened by an alarm clock. Oh, surely you can save fifteen minutes by eating breakfast faster, so why not reset the alarm clock to ring again at 6:15?"

The student reaches for the clock and carefully turns the knob to reset the alarm.

"Watch how you are doing this. You are making very small motions with only your fingers. Good!

"Reach for the clock again. . . . Notice how big your motions are. If they were not big and you did not use your whole arm, your hand could not reach it! Now I would like for you to try something different. Move your arm and elbow in big motions while you reset the alarm for exactly 7:05."

Undoubtedly the student will have great difficulty in achieving the goal because of the excessive motion.

"You have proven a very important point. Too much motion can be just as harmful as too little motion. Setting an alarm clock is only one example. If you watch, you will discover many things require small motions and involve only the fingers or hand.

"Some string techniques require only limited motion. Take a trill, for example. We need only to lift and drop the finger(s), moving from the base knuckles. The rolling of the hand and arm would make the trill much more difficult and slow it down. Let's practice trills now. Keep the hand and arm quiet."

Cue to Use

1. Whenever the student uses excessive motion.
2. Anytime the teacher wishes to emphasize the finger action of a trill.

Props

An alarm clock, if possible. An imaginary clock would be OK in a pinch but not as effective. In either case it should not be a digital clock.

Inner Drama

The teacher is a great believer in free, flowing motions. However, he recognizes that some students tend to use much more motion than necessary. Such a student usually feels very uncomfortable with any form of restriction and must be convinced that too much motion is harmful to her technique. Since setting an alarm clock requires meticulous, refined motions, the scene dramatizes the complications that can arise if gross motor action is employed at the wrong moment.

Another factor to be considered is the direction of the motion which is not immediately necessary for the task at hand. For example, some violinists and violists unconsciously move their instruments down and up while playing. This can disturb the bowing, particularly during a bow change. Moving targets are generally recognized as being more difficult to hit than stationary ones. However, a swaying, horizontal motion of the body and instrument can often free the player and improve the sound without disturbing the skill. The vertical motion, on the other hand, can make the degree of contact between the bow hair and the string more difficult to measure. This contact is what largely controls the amount of energy flowing from the player's body into the instrument.

Some musicians with a vivid aural dream and a gigantic will can play beautifully despite their motion habits, not *because* of them. Sorting out which characteristics to imitate can be tricky at times.

Imagination, Inc.
SCENE 90

Teacher: "I think we could use a little more imagination in our approach to this music. "Let's see where we can buy some. . . . Oh, yes, here is a place listed in the Yellow Pages. 'IMAGINATION, INCORPORATED. We stock a wide variety of imaginations suitable for every occasion.'"

After the teacher dials an imaginary telephone, she listens, then questions: "Health Food Store? I must have dialed the wrong number. I was trying to call Imagination, Incorporated. . . . It did? . . . I'm sorry to have bothered you. Thank you very much."

The teacher explains: "That was strange. The man said that Imagination, Incorporated closed down because of lack of business. It turns out that everyone is born with the power of imagination and that all a person has to do is have the courage to use it!

"Well, let's get back to the music and dare to use our imaginations. Let's bring this music to life!"

Cue to Use

When the students are playing in a lifeless, mechanical manner.

Props

A telephone directory if readily available. Otherwise it can be imagined.

Inner Drama

The teacher believes that anytime a person stimulates the imagination of another human being in a positive manner a noble act is performed. She recognizes that the music teacher is in a unique position to help in this way because of the nature of the subject and the climate created in the classroom or studio brought about by the very presence of music. She believes that creative living depends on a well-developed and freely expressed imagination nurtured in youth and that this quality can carry over into adulthood

even if the person does not continue to play his instrument.

Through this scene the teacher calls attention to the marvelous truth that all human beings are born with the gift of imagination. She knows that teachers and parents can either encourage or squelch it. By doing something as preposterous as trying to telephone a store where imaginations are sold, the teacher demonstrates her own fearless approach to the generous use of this quality; thereby, she helps to free those in her presence. She takes particular care throughout every class of every day that no youngster feels inhibited in his use of his imaginative powers because of the fear of being jeered at by the teacher or his peers.

Who could possibly deny the importance of imagination in a field that exists only because of the creative mind?

The Dark Window
SCENE 91

Teacher: "Picture yourself walking down the street with some friends after dark. Suddenly a light in the front room of a house is turned on. What looked like a dark wall is transformed into a brilliantly lit window!

"Think about this. To the people walking on the street, this appeared to be a sudden thing. However, to the person in the house, there was nothing sudden about it. He decided he needed light, walked to the electric switch, and turned it on.

"The same thing happens in string playing! When we watch a musician move swiftly from one type of technique to another, it doesn't look possible! Yet, in actuality the musician sent alert signals to her body several moments before the change in technique took place.

"Learn the last part of a passage so well that you can put it on automatic pilot, while you think ahead to the next. You, too, will surprise people!"

Cue to Use

Anytime, except in the very early training, a student has difficulty moving from one type of technical passage to another.

Inner Drama

The teacher recognizes that a student who has practiced a technical passage well can be disappointed with the results when moving from one type of technique to another. A student who can perform etudes and exercises with great facility does not always show up well on a piece. Usually a piece requires a greater variety of techniques within a shorter time span. The teacher's goal is to help the student learn to focus her mind on the forthcoming passage while she completes the passage at hand.

Supermarket
SCENE 92

Teacher: "Suppose we were able to go to a self-service supermarket that caters to musicians. It has a special shelf of fine qualities that string players like to have in their playing. Let's think of what qualities we would like to stock up on."

With the teacher's guidance the students will shop for such items as good intonation, rhythmic vitality, a beautiful tone, and expressive phrasing.

Finally the teacher concludes: "Knowing what you want is half of it! If you clearly mark any or all of these qualities as your goal, there is no reason you can't have them. Focus your thoughts, time, and energy on the qualities you want most. You will be surprised how possible they are!"

Cue to Use

Anytime a student needs a special lift or help in setting a goal.

Inner Drama

In the teacher's opinion the teaching of skills in string playing is only one aspect of his profession. He considers that his job also is to help the student set her sights on worthy goals and believe that they are attainable. He recognizes that most students are not sure about their abilities and a few words expressing the teacher's faith in their potential can provide much assurance and inspiration. Many youngsters look on champions and artists as being of a completely different species and have no concept of their own innate abilities that can be developed. Frequently, the adults in their homes or other teachers have helped to impose imaginary limitations.

The teacher is convinced that the starting point for attaining any goal is to acknowledge the existence of the goal and to believe that it is possible to achieve it.

Ask the Expert
SCENE 93

The teacher will be on the lookout for any activity that a student appears to do better than anyone else. For example, one student's instrument may consistently look very clean.

"Mike, I notice that your instrument is always so clean and shiny. Tell us how you keep it so nice." The student shares his technique.

On another day the teacher may ask, "Claire, I've noticed that you are usually the first to have your instrument unpacked and ready to go. How do you do that so efficiently? Won't you demonstrate?"

Cue to Use

1. Anytime the teacher spots an "expert" of anything.
2. Whenever the teacher feels a certain student needs special recognition.

Inner Drama

Almost everyone has something in which she excels. The teacher is aware that calling attention to a special skill can help everyone to learn and will give a great boost in confidence to the person cited. This scene offers the opportunity to recognize nontechnical and nonmusical skills as well and is a useful tool to help build the self-esteem of the youngster who does not stand out in music making. Naturally the teacher will be very careful that at one time or another every student will have recognition as an expert.

Building self-esteem is considered one of the highest of all priorities by the teacher. He believes the success and happiness of every human being greatly depends on this quality and that the young person's opinion of herself largely mirrors the opinions of people with whom she has interactions. The teacher welcomes the opportunity for the youngster to experience honestly earned success and believes it will carry over positively to other areas of her life.

Besides, learning from everyone makes living more fun. Recognizing another person's ability is half the trick. Asking is the other half. Most people are eager to share.

The Houselights Are Dimmed
SCENE 94

Teacher: "Suppose you are a great concert artist! The houselights are dimmed . . . the New York Philharmonic is on stage . . . the audience waits breathlessly. From the wings you make your entrance with the conductor. This is the moment we have waited for!

"Bring out your solo part above the orchestra! Let's *watch* you as you play! How confidently you send out your beautiful message!"

Without the instrument and bow, the student mimes playing while she and her teacher sing or hum.

"Good! Now, as you play your instrument, continue acting the role! Use the same style of gestures. Your tone will soar above the famed 106-piece orchestra!"

Cue to Use

Whenever the student knows the notes of a composition well but plays it shyly.

Inner Drama

Acting the part of someone else can do phenomenal things. Even the most introverted of persons can adopt a courageous and outgoing manner if the role assigned requires those characteristics.

Inside many a shy music student is a big ham! If she has practiced well and knows the music, sometimes all she needs is a casting director and the appropriate imaginary backdrop. Who wouldn't be inspired for a performance with the New York Philharmonic?

The Xerox Machine
SCENE 95
(Designed for groups, but adjustable to the private lesson)

The teacher announces that something new has been installed in the classroom—an imaginary Xerox machine!

"Elliott's performance will be the original. Carey, Eva Marie, Caroline, Carissa, Charles, and Carolyn will be the copies. Since the machine was serviced yesterday every copy should be exactly like the original.

"I will set the machine for three copies. This is a high-speed machine. One copy comes out right after another!"

After the original is heard the teacher presses the imaginary PRINT button and the copies come nonstop.

Cue to Use

1. When the teacher wishes to stress good listening and/or the ability to imitate.
2. Whenever she desires to hear each student play alone in a very short amount of time.

Inner Drama

This scene offers the opportunity for unlimited variations. The original can be one or more notes, a phrase, or even a sound effect. It can be designated by the teacher or originated by a student.

The imitation of sounds is a necessary skill for musicians. Though all distinguished musical performances depend on originality in interpretation, chamber music requires the ability to create on-the-spot copies of nuances and to make quick adjustments in order to capture the spirit of the other players. The entry of one part relies on what has gone before. Yet the other musicians' interpretation of the phrase today may be slightly different than yesterday's or tomorrow's. This is one of the main reasons that musicians are fascinated and challenged by chamber music.

One method used by motor behaviorists to classify motor skills is by the predictability of the environment. For example, in bowling and in signing one's name to a check, the environment is predictable. By contrast, the skills of the football player about to return a punt, the wrestler, and the fencer require rapid adaptation to a changing environment. The chamber musician's skills frequently fall into the second category.

Keen listening to one's own performance, as well as to others', is the starting point. In fact, it is the most basic and essential ingredient of all music making.

The Plastic Gobbler
SCENE 96

The teacher distributes a large plastic bag to each student. She exclaims, "Suppose the hand is a plastic gobbler!"

She places a plastic bag and the underside of her wrist on a hard surface. With one hand she crumples the plastic into a ball. As it vanishes into her palm, the hand appears to have eaten it.

"Do this often and you will be surprised how strong your hand will become!"

Cue to Use

Anytime for the strengthening of the fingers and hand, but most especially when a student has joints which tend to collapse. It is not designed for the very young student.

Props

A large piece of plastic for each student. The plastic bag used by dry cleaners to protect freshly cleaned jackets is especially good. This is about 2' × 3'. Also, it is desirable for each student to have a hard surface, such as a piano lid or desk, on which to work. If not available, they can use their laps.

Inner Drama

Quite a few string students, particularly those who study the cello or double bass, do not have strong enough hands to play their instruments with ease. A hand that is able to support itself so that the knuckles and joints have no tendency to collapse when live energy flows from the player's back to the fingerboard and bow is in a far better position to develop an agile technique and a beautiful vibrato.

The exercise of crumpling newspapers has been used in hospitals for many years to help patients strengthen their forearm muscles and hand grips. The plastic bag is cleaner and is reusable. However, it is dangerous and should not be near any child too young to realize the danger of suffocation.

In geographical areas where the videogame character who gobbles up everything in sight is popular, the teacher may wish to rename this scene. The exercise builds strength quickly in either hand and can easily be done while conversing or watching television. The teacher prefers, when possible, to develop strength away from the instrument.

Self-Correcting Ears
SCENE 97

The teacher announces that she would like the students to critique her storytelling. She explains that she enjoys sharing stories but people don't seem to listen to her. Perhaps, if she told them a tale, the students could give her advice.

"Kangaroos come in a variety of sizes, shapes, and colors but one of the largest is the gray kangaroo, which lives in eastern Australia, you know. She is about six feet tall and has powerful hind legs and a muscular tail that acts as a balance when she travels. She goes places by series of leaps, you know. When ambling along on a lazy day, she moves in six-foot jumps. But, if in a hurry, they become thirty-foot jumps, you know. At times a gray kangaroo can travel up to thirty miles an hour!

"But what seems like the longest, hardest journey of his lifetime is the one a baby kangaroo makes shortly after birth when he is only about one inch long, you know. With his little front feet he starts crawling up to his mother's pouch, which seems like miles away, you know. She helps him by putting saliva on his body and scratching little roadways in her fur, pointing the right direction, you know. We can almost picture road signs saying INTERSTATE 35 NORTH TO POUCH.

"On arrival he finds a nice warm supper waiting for him, you know. He puts the faucet in his mouth, and, low and behold, it swells and locks him in, you know! So, there he stays attached to the supper faucet until nature gives the OK for him to explore his surroundings, you know. Later the joey will take an occasional little side trip outside his mother's pouch but he always hops right back in when his mother signals that they are going on a trip, you know. At the end of six or seven months the free ride is over!"

After the students generously offer their critique, the teacher adds:

"At times we develop self-correcting ears! Perhaps we make a little crunch in a certain part of the bow or lift the bow at every bow change near the frog. Our ears soon learn to erase a repeated annoyance the same as the storyteller overlooked the extra words. That is why many professionals record their own playing periodically or ask a colleague to critique. But, of course, in lessons it is the teacher's job to report anything that can mar the beauty of the music."

Cue to Use

Anytime the teacher feels it is appropriate but most especially if there is a persistent habit that needs correcting.

Inner Drama

The teacher knows that the musician can be so involved in the music making process that he can miss hearing the product objectively. However, certain persistent habits can be most evident to even the layperson who has had no musical training. Students easily identify with the storyteller's problem because almost everyone has known someone who accidently stumbled into repeating one phrase or word too frequently in speech.

Marble Statues
SCENE 98

Teacher: "Be a marble statue! Select any pose you like—a discus thrower, an orator, a violinist, or a flag bearer. . . . Ready? Freeze!"

Surrounded by statues the teacher does something productive so the students' time will not be wasted. Perhaps he reads aloud a story about a musician, a composition, or an instrument. When he senses that the students are getting tired, he exclaims: "OK. Come to life. You are made of flesh and blood!"

The students probably will have much to say after being immobile. When things have quieted down, he asks: "What can we learn from this? . . . Yes, a static position is the most tiring of all. The Statue of Liberty would feel like her poor arm was breaking off if she were alive. Ten minutes of holding that torch would be far more tiring than swimming to Manhattan Island! It appears that our bodies were designed for motion!

"In your practice don't let any part of the body be a statue. It may at times appear that a concert artist moves only her hands and arms but don't be fooled! No part of her body is completely still for long!"

Cue to Use

Anytime the teacher wishes to stress mobility, particularly if a student appears stiff.

Inner Drama

Although the teacher is aware that he could have told the students in one sentence not to make their muscles static, he has chosen to take the heuristic approach. He respects the innate desire of most human beings to discover things for themselves and understands why many people will touch wet paint to verify the sign.

He also demonstrates respect for the students by allowing them to choose their posture. Such autonomy brings a feeling of goodwill to a studio or classroom.

This scene allows the possibility of many variations. The teacher might choose to point out that the guards of the royal palaces in Europe are trained to keep their bodies moving continuously at a very slow rate. Their apparent immobility is only an illusion.

Rusty Knees, Rusty Elbows
SCENE 99

Teacher: "Monkey see, monkey do."

While standing the teacher traces in the air a giant figure 8 lying on its side. Her right arm moves freely and rhythmically as she repeats it over and over nonstop.

"Let your whole body feel loose and free! Gently bend your knees. Watch your right arm move in beautiful flowing motions. Every joint feels freshly oiled!"

While the students continue to trace the lazy 8's, the teacher says: "When I call out 'Lock your knees!' make your knees as tight and rigid as possible but keep your right arm moving freely. . . ."

To the students' surprise, when the knees lock, the arm motions instantly change from flowing to labored. What once was easy has become difficult.

"Rusty knees mean rusty elbows! In your practice, check your knees often by moving or bending them. If rusty, mentally apply a drop of WD-40!"

Cue to Use

Anytime the teacher wishes to emphasize the fluidity of motion or suspects a student's knees are too tight.

Inner Drama

In this scene the teacher not only has conveyed an important, easily understood message but also has provided a welcome change in pace. She is well aware, however, that oiled knees do not guarantee oiled elbows; a problem could exist elsewhere. For example, if a cellist fails to lower her right elbow slightly as the frog and the bow hand approach the string during the last portion of an up-bow, the resulting motion could lack fluidity. Even tight fingers can cause a tight elbow.

The name of any oil product can be substituted for the WD-40.

Building Materials
SCENE 100

Teacher: "Complete the sentences!

"The house builder has his wood, bricks, cement, pipes, roofing, and hundreds of other materials, including _____.

"The baker has her flour, eggs, milk, and dozens of other products, including _____.

"The automobile maker has steel, chrome, and glass plus _____.

"The music maker's ONLY building material is her _____."

After the students complete the final sentence, the teacher adds:

"Yes, the musician's only building material is her TONE. She places it at different pitches and in various rhythms and sometimes in harmonies. She colors it, shades it, and molds it into music.

"Strive for the biggest and most beautiful tone you can bring from your instrument! Then you will have lots of material to work with when you make music!"

Cue to Use

Anytime to help inspire the goal of developing a big, beautiful tone.

Inner Drama

The teacher has inherited many intermediate and advanced students with well-developed techniques but small, soft tones. From these experiences he has learned of the extreme limitations in expression if the only building material is scanty. Often, when the tone is small, tension was built into the technique. The flow of energy from the player's body was restricted or misdirected.

Since playing with a big, full sound that has a beautiful quality is a technique in itself, the teacher wishes to stress its importance and help the student to prize it highly. The listener does. Whoever heard of an audience at intermission raving over the "wonderfully small and restricted tone" the performer draws from his instrument?

Ready—Set—HOLD!
SCENE 101

Teacher: "Let's have a race! Shall we make our starting line over here?"

After the students and teacher are lined up, the teacher says: "Get ready—set—HOLD! Look at the position of our bodies! The shape of our legs, shoulders, and arms—all look pretty much alike! Why are we doing this?"

The students will explain that they are getting ready to be off the second the signal is given. With the teacher's guidance they will notice that even their muscles tingle with excitement.

"Now let's try it another way. Stay as loose and floppy as a rag doll while I say 'get ready—set—

GO!' Now wouldn't that be ridiculous?

"Let's try a third method. Stand as stiff as a board! OK, get ready—set—GO!"

After some discussion the students evolve the principle that all runners send signals to their bodies to get ready for action. Their muscles anticipate the motion and their bodies assume a shape that will boost them into the race. They lean in the direction they will go.

"We string players also get ready! Let's play now some very fast notes and find how we can get off to the best possible start!"

Cue to Use

1. Anytime the student gets off to a slow start in a fast passage.
2. Whenever the teacher wants to help the student improve his fast technique.

Inner Drama

The teacher recognizes that the ready-set-go principle is familiar to every person. Although the student has experienced this firsthand, the possibility exists that he has not related it to string playing.

Superior technique is largely a matter of timing. Many players can play fast but the person who has worked out perfect timing is called a virtuoso.

Catching the Beat
SCENE 102

The teacher tosses a rubber ball into the air, then catches it when it returns to the original starting point.

"Bow an open D. Make the tone sound the instant the ball lands in my hand. . . . Good!"

As the students gain skill in sounding their open strings in perfect ensemble, the teacher will use the ball to conduct scales and simple unison pieces already memorized.

"My ball signals the beginning of each note. The conductor's baton signals the beginning of each beat. She will like having you in her orchestra because you will soon be a virtuoso at catching the beat!"

Cue to Use

Anytime for the emphasis of watching the conductor's baton.

Props

A rubber ball that is not too heavy. Also, enough space in the room so the ball will not be dangerously close to the instruments.

Inner Drama

The teacher is aware that all young people enjoy balls. If a ball appears in a music class for such purposes, a guarantee can be made that it will magnetize the students' eyes. Who would possibly be so callous as to look anywhere else?

Unless the teacher has a well-developed ball technique, probably the music should be kept rather simple and at not too brisk a tempo.

What's the Difference?
SCENE 103

Teacher: "Let's sit in front of the mirror while we play this together. I think I'm doing something a little different than you. If we both watch carefully, perhaps we can detect what it is."

Cue to Use

When there is a technical problem and the teacher has difficulty in identifying the reason.

Props

A large mirror. If not available, perhaps the teacher can invite a third person to help determine the difference between the teacher's and the student's approach.

Inner Drama

The identification of a problem and the discovery of a solution may occasionally elude the finest of teachers. Yet, by putting two examples side-by-side and looking for the differences, even a non-musician can help.

A mirror in the studio can be a real mystery solver. If it is too narrow for two people to stand or sit side-by-side, they can position themselves as though they are sitting on the aisle seats on a bus with the teacher sitting in the second row slightly to one side.

Through his request that the student help identify the difference, the teacher invites the sharing of responsibility. With most students the reaction is very positive. Self-esteem and general awareness are increased.

Garage Sale

SCENE 104

Teacher: "It is time for a garage sale to get rid of all the ugly tones we have no use for! Let's prepare an ad for the newspaper. How about something like this?

"GARAGE SALE. Wide assortment of ugly tones including those made by bowing too fast near the bridge, bowing too heavily near the fingerboard and . . .'"

After the students have contributed to the ad preparation, the teacher adds: "We might like to close it with 'For the benefit of a worthy cause.'

"I would like each of you to bring in two or three ugly tones to our next class for donation to the sale. Be ready to explain exactly how you produce them and what you would change to make them beautiful. In fact, be prepared to teach us how to duplicate your garage sale sounds, then transform them into beauty."

Cue to Use

1. Anytime for review of the technique of producing beautiful tones.
2. Whenever there are some unpleasant sounds that need to be eliminated.

Inner Drama

While such an approach might sound dangerous to a new teacher, the experienced teacher recognizes that nothing highlights the positive more than placing it beside a negative. She has learned that such an episode, if used very rarely, can be

highly educational, motivating, and fun. However, the teacher will need to tighten her control of the class to be sure it does not get out of bounds. Time is a precious commodity in any lesson and the teacher is the only person responsible for its judicious use.

The TV Store

SCENE 105
(Designed for groups)

The teacher asks for four volunteers to leave their instruments and form a line facing the class. Each selects a paper from those the teacher has previously prepared.

"I have decided to buy a new color TV and would like your help! We are in a television store and [*turning to the volunteers*] you are the new TV sets! Have you noticed how in stores usually several sets are turned on so the customers can compare the pictures? Yet, none of them has sound.

"It just happens that today the same piece as ours is being performed on four different channels! But, each musician is playing it in a different mood and style. Let's look at Channel 9 on this 25-inch Zenith."

The volunteer who drew the Channel 9 paper pantomimes playing the piece in the manner described on her secret paper. After she has completed a phrase or two, the teacher says, "Let's turn on the sound." He dramatically turns an imaginary knob in front of the volunteer actor and signals the remaining students with instruments to produce the sound.

"Now let's take a look at this 19-inch Sony tuned to Channel 7."

After each channel has been viewed and listened to, the teacher asks the sound producers to guess what the picture makers were thinking. Usually the transfer from the written words to the silent picture to sound is amazingly accurate.

"This game demonstrates three important principles. One, the characteristic of the tone reflects the same characteristic as the physical motion that generates it. Two, everything starts with the attitude. Three, a mental picture helps!"

Cue to Use

1. Anytime the teacher wishes to dramatize some important principles regarding motion and the use of mental imagery.
2. Whenever a class needs livening up.

Props

Four small pieces of paper. On one is written "Channel 24—a military general." Others are "Channel 7—a mother holding a sleeping baby," "Channel 36—playful puppies," and "Channel 9—pompous kings in a procession."

Inner Drama

The teacher believes that the mental image is a powerful tool. He advocates its generous use in the teaching and playing of a musical instrument. He also strongly believes that everything in life starts with the attitude.

In order to make the game more relevant to the youngsters, he selects numbers of the television channels in the community and the makes of the TV sets popular in the country in which the students reside. If the class is large, the teacher may prefer to have two or three students represent each channel. This provides an opportunity to involve the less outgoing youngsters. Should the students get off to a false start and have to begin again, the teacher can announce: "Stand by, we are experiencing technical difficulties!" It also can be fun to have the volume of some TV sets operated by remote control.

No Owner's Manual
SCENE 106

Teacher: "What terrific motion machines our bodies are! Though they did not come with an Owner's Manual, somehow nature helps us find out just how far a group of muscles should move to do a job well. Take walking, for example. If we don't lift our feet, it is difficult. If we lift them too high, it appears we are wading! And, how wonderful it is that we can talk so well!"

Suddenly the teacher starts talking with very restricted motion in her lips and face. After mumbling several sentences she quickly switches to very large exaggerated motions for each syllable. When it is evident that the student understands what she is doing and why, the teacher resumes speaking in a normal manner.

"The principle of finding just the right amount of motion also applies to string playing! Too much motion can be as bad as too little. Most professionals experiment in playing a passage several ways and then decide what works best. Which passage would you like to try first?"

Cue to Use

Anytime, except in the very early training, the student uses either restricted or excessive motion.

Inner Drama

The teacher recognizes the importance of experimenting with varying degrees of motion to find the most effective way to perform a passage. In general, she wants to encourage freedom of motion. However, she realizes that not infrequently a student with much innate musicality will incorporate too much motion and that this can be detrimental to the technique. Naturally the teacher will take precautions so that in no way will a student feel sensitive or self-conscious. Usually, in the case of excessive motion, the student is so completely involved in the music that he is unaware of a problem. In a sense he may be dancing to the music.

At the end of this scene the teacher deliberately offers the student some independence by letting him decide which passage to play. Such granting of autonomy communicates respect for students as individuals and helps to ensure future cooperation.

A Letter to the Editor
SCENE 107

As though discovering an item of interest in the LETTERS TO THE EDITOR section of the newspaper, the teacher reads aloud:

"Dear Editor:
"We have noted with interest two recent articles in your fine newspaper. The first cautioned dog owners to be extremely careful about leaving their pets in a closed-up automobile during hot weather. It explained that the interior temperature can build up rapidly to intolerable levels. Within a short span of time the animal can become sick and die.

"We of the Stringed Instrument Family would like to advise your readers that the same care applies to members of our family. Extreme temperatures, either hot or cold, can be harmful to us. It is also essential that we never rest on our bridges. As there is already so much tension on us from the tightened strings, any extra weight or force can be damaging. A blow on the bridge can crack the entire top of an instrument.

"The second article reported that a Stradivarius violin was sold for an enormous price at a recent auction in London. We believe that your readers should be cautioned not to assume that all instruments which have Stradivarius labels were truly made by him. Usually they are copies modeled after a Strad and were made in a factory or a shop where there is a production line. These violins are referred to as 'Attic Strads' since they are usually discovered in attics. Experts believe that Signor Stradivarius, who lived from about 1644 to 1737 and worked in Cremona, Italy, made around 1,100 instruments. However, many times that number have Stradivarius labels!

"If a reader is considering buying an expensive instrument, we strongly advise that it be accompanied by papers documenting its authenticity and be appraised by an expert. A highly trained expert knows every characteristic of a specific maker's style and can often identify his name, the geographical region in which he worked, and the approximate date the instrument was made without peering through the F holes at the label pasted inside. Labels are not to be trusted.

"In closing, we would like to say that some modern instruments are very fine and that we consider all members of our family valuable whether they were made by famous makers or not. Every instrument can be precious to someone. We are a long-lived family and hope that each of us will be treated with love and respect.

"The Stringed Instrument Family"

Cue to Use

Anytime the teacher wishes to emphasize the importance of guarding an instrument from extreme temperatures and from stress on the bridge and of using caution in the purchase of expensive instruments.

Inner Drama

Many bits of knowledge which are picked up in most informal ways can influence people's thinking. This time the teacher has chosen an unusual method which adds variety to her day as well as the students'.

A Prisoner of One Tight Joint
SCENE 108

The teacher shakes out one of her hands in the air, then gently taps each finger and thumb with her other hand.

"Monkey see, monkey do! Tap each of your fingers and thumb. They should each spring back to

their original position. . . . Good!

"Now try something different. Make the thumb tense and hard but keep your fingers soft and flexible. Test them by tapping. . . . What is this? It's not working! Try again!"

To the students' surprise no one will be able to demonstrate springy fingers while holding the thumb tense.

"Now let's try the reverse. Tighten your fingers but keep your thumb loose and relaxed . . . Why, this doesn't work either! My thumb is stiff as a board!

"One tight joint affects all joints of the hand! We become a prisoner of one tight joint!"

Cue to Use

1. Anytime the teacher wants to stress flexibility of the joints in either hand.
2. Whenever she suspects tension in a thumb or finger.

Inner Drama

The teacher knows that no concept is as meaningful as one discovered by a person himself. Even 'discovering' a famous painting, such as the Mona Lisa, in a museum meant more to the teacher than being led to it by a guide lecturing on the life of Leonardo da Vinci.

The goal of this scene is to help the student discover a characteristic of the human hand. It is impossible to have a facile left hand technique or to draw beautiful tones from a stringed instrument without flexibility in every finger and thumb.

Learning to Race
SCENE 109

Teacher: "I've decided to become a fast runner! I plan to go about it very systematically—starting rather slowly, then gradually building up speed."

The teacher sets his metronome at 100 and walks across the room and back in step to the beat.

"Good! Now I'll try 108."

Again he walks across the room and back. He resets the metronome at 116 and once more walks to the beat.

"Something must be wrong! Things just don't feel right!"

The students undoubtedly will point out that he is walking—not running.

"But I will get there eventually! No?"

Together they evolve that running is an entirely different technique than walking. The body feels centered and lifted, the leg action changes, and the foot strikes the pavement in a different manner.

"We do not learn to run by walking! They require two distinctly different techniques! This is also true in string playing! Slow technique, when we use vibrato, is entirely different than fast technique."

Together the students and teacher work out a list of differences between fast and slow technique.

"Naturally the first steps toward mastering a fast passage is to learn to play the right notes in tune. But soon we move into the feeling and action of fast technique."

Cue to Use

Anytime, not too early in training, the student needs a lesson or review concerning the differences between fast and slow technique.

Props

A metronome, if readily available. If not, an imaginary metronome and clapping hands can substitute.

Inner Drama

The teacher is aware that he himself wasted much time in practice because he was not aware of this truth. He now realizes that careful, conscientious practice does not guarantee results unless the technique is founded on natural principles which are sometimes so obvious they go unnoticed.

In fast technique the weight of the left hand and arm is suspended; the fingers are curved so their tips, not their pads, land on the string; the balance remains in one place, probably near the third finger for most players; the action comes from the base knuckles of the fingers; and lifting is emphasized more than dropping.

In slow technique the weight of the hand and arm help the fingers "sink" into the fingerboard (particularly with cellos and basses); the fingers are not so curved and may contact the string with their pads; the balance is centered on the playing finger; the transfer of weight from one finger to another is similar to walking; and the emphasis is on a beautifully balanced vibrato.

In this use of terms, slow technique refers to any time vibrato is used. It does not refer to the tempo of a piece. Within a single phrase there can be some places requiring slow technique and other places fast technique.

The reader is advised to read *Walking Forward*, Scene 74, and *Walking Backward*, Scene 75, at this time.

The Mystery Words
SCENE 110

Teacher: "These people have something in common. So much, in fact, that I could use the same words to complete each sentence!

1. John F. Kennedy became president of the United States because _____.
2. Ms. X is wonderfully organized because _____.
3. Signor Stradivarius made beautiful stringed instruments because _____.
4. Mr. R. is kind and thoughtful because _____.
5. Madame Curie made milestone discoveries in radioactivity because _____.
6. Henry Ford built his automobile because _____.
7. Ms. Z. won a mile race because _____.
8. Margaret Thatcher became prime minister of Great Britain because _____.

"What are the mystery words?"

After the answer "because he/she had the desire" is derived, the teacher continues: "Yes! The first step toward any achievement is to have the desire—a burning desire, not a lukewarm desire! Remember! There is nothing accidental about quality!

"Now try this:

1. Donald has a rich, warm tone because _____.
2. Deirdre's intonation is almost perfect because _____.
3. Richard has a facile technique because _____.
4. Mary Eleanor has an expressive bow arm because _____.
5. Alan's sautillé bowing is terrific because _____.
6. Linda's playing has great vitality because _____."

Cue to Use

Anytime the teacher chooses. It probably should be reserved for students not too young.

Inner Drama

The teacher recognizes that one of the most important aspects of good teaching is to spark the student's ambition. She believes that nothing great was ever achieved by a person with this ingredient missing. The goal of *The Mystery Words* is to affirm this fact and make it an integral part of the student's thinking. It can trigger an awareness in the student of his own personal responsibility. In no example was the sentence completed with the words, "because he had a great teacher!"

INTERMISSION

6   The Children's Theater

Ah, the enchantment of the Children's Theater—where asparagus stalks dance and prairie dogs steal! So why shouldn't a bow hair talk? Here rules and limitations vanish with a puff and anything goes! Let the gateway to fantasy land be flung open to the wonderment of all!

The forty-four Scenes in this chapter are designed for older children of various ages—approximately ten to seventy-eight. They may be used for constructive rest breaks in music lessons, classes, and practice periods. Doesn't every play have an intermission? It is suggested that the scripts be read aloud.

SCENES FOR BETTER REST BREAKS

Campaign Promises
SCENE III

TV Reporter: Here at the Convention Center this has been an exciting day! Many promises have been made by the candidates for the office of Chief Bow Holder.

Thumb promises never to grab and squeeze and to always remain flexible and gentle. However, he assures us that he will give the bow stick a little pinch when needed. Fourth Finger has pledged that, if elected, she will help keep the bow in balance, particularly when playing at the frog. She believes that she is the *only* member of the party that can work without strain, along with the assistance of the Third Finger, to keep the tip from falling.

Second Finger considers himself the true running mate of Thumb and stresses that the balance of the hand is centered in them. He promises that together they will assume positive leadership and will take particular care in guiding the bow at the most advantageous sounding point. Earlier today First Finger reminded us that she is the most expressive voice of the party. She promised greater richness, more variety, and striking accents if elected.

By far the most modest candidate on the slate is Third Finger. He has made no personal claims. In fact, he has said very little about himself and at times appears to be riding along with the other candidates. Yet he is winning delegate support through what is considered to be a sensible, broadminded approach. His campaign speeches are riddled with such phrases as "party unity," "greater teamwork," and "working together for the cause." He declares that *all* candidates are vital and are speaking the truth. He frowns on grabbing and pushing and stresses the need for constant change to meet the mood of the moment. The slogan from the Third Finger Headquarters is "Let us pull together!"

Down on the floor rumors abound that through his influence the candidates may decide to withdraw their individual candidacies and draw up a new party platform.

This is Steve Baldwin reporting from the Convention Center.

Traffic Violation
SCENE 112

Traffic Officer: Pull over to the side of the road.
Bow: What is it? Did I do something wrong?
Traffic Officer: Yes. You are traveling too slowly

with too heavy a load. You should have been in the lane near the bridge—not near the fingerboard. Didn't you see the sign?
Bow: What sign?
Traffic Officer: The one that says SLOW HEAVY TRAFFIC STAY NEAR BRIDGE.
Bow: Oh?
Traffic Officer: The lane nearest the fingerboard is reserved for light fast traffic like motorcycles or sports cars. Slow heavy traffic, like heavy dump trucks, belongs in the lane closest to the bridge. The in-between traffic should use one of the middle lanes.
Bow: But, officer, I weigh the same whether I'm traveling, lying on the piano, or resting in the instrument case! Since I'm a violin bow, I weigh in at about two ounces. Even a cello bow weighs only about three ounces!
Traffic Officer: Sure. But what counts is your load. That guy who does your steering also adds to your load. He either lets his live weight sink in or he suspends it. Because of that, the string thinks of you as heavy or light and vibrates accordingly. This helps to give dynamics to music.
Bow: So the problem is not me—it's my driver. Right?
Traffic Officer: I guess so. I'll let you off easy this time. But tell your driver to obey the laws.
Bow: By the way, whose laws are they? New York's? California's?
Traffic Officer: No, the Universal Law of String Acoustics. Listen to the tone. If something doesn't sound beautiful, you are breaking a law. Make a change! My ears told me something was wrong. Getting just the right combination of speed and weight for a specific distance from the bridge can be tricky sometimes. Experiment until you find just the tone you like. I must move on now. I see another bow changing lanes carelessly. So long!

Eight Coats
SCENE 113

Piece of Spruce: Hi! I'm glad to meet you. I think we are going to be a part of a team!
Piece of Maple: How's that?
Spruce: We are going to be made into a stringed instrument! I'll be carved to be the front and you will be the back, sides, and neck. That is why we are here in the violin maker's shop.
Maple: Violin maker? Oh, I had dreamed of being

a cello—not a little violin. Look at my nice long lines! Not a knot hole or insect mark on the whole length of me! It would be a crime to cut me shorter!

Spruce: Be calm! We *are* going to be a cello! They refer to all people who make stringed instruments as violin makers. I've never heard of someone being called a cello maker. A cabinet-maker isn't called a "drawermaker" when he makes drawers!

Maple: I see.

Spruce: The violin maker said we will have eight to ten coats.

Maple: Coats! Man, where does he think we are going? Alaska? Who knows, we may live in Sarasota, Florida, where there are palm trees!

Spruce: Calm down now. Our coats will be of varnish! We will have a lovely, transparent finish. The violin maker will sand each coat lightly before applying the next. I feel honored to have been especially chosen.

Maple: Especially chosen?

Spruce: Yes. I was just one piece in a large stack of wood. The violin maker said that he liked my resonance.

Maple: What makes him think you are resonant?

Spruce: When he thumped me, I yelled! If I had said "thud," I might have ended up being a boat or a barrel.

Maple: Why a boat or a barrel?

Spruce: Because in my family we are soft and elastic but strong. I understand you maples are hard. Right?

Maple: Yes. I could have been a floor.

Spruce: The violin maker said that we will still be able to expand and contract under varying weather conditions after we are varnished. I worried for a while. Another guy had me drying out for what seemed like ages. It must have been five or ten years. But I will always take in big gulps of moisture on rainy or humid days the rest of my life.

Maple: Me, too! But not as much. In our family we are not big drinkers.

Spruce: Well, we better be getting some rest now because tomorrow is the big day! The violin maker will cut us into our beautiful new shape.

Maple: Great! See you at dawn tomorrow!

The String and I
SCENE 114

TV Talk Show Host: We have a great show for you tonight! Our first guest is a singer, dancer, and gymnast! He is the author of a new book which will soon be in bookstores throughout the country. Good evening, Bow.

Author: Good evening. I am delighted to be here. I just slipped away from a rehearsal in another studio to be with you for a few minutes.

TV Host: I see your hair is still tightened and that you are wearing freshly applied rosin. Let's talk about your new book. What is its name?

Author: The String and I.

TV Host: What prompted you to write it?

Author: Well, it was this way. I trust you know my line of work is to get the string to vibrate. When it vibrates beautifully, the air is filled with music. One night I was lying in my case with my hair loose and I began to think about my long relationship with the string. I decided to share it with others.

TV Host: I see. You wrote a lovely dedication. I would like to read it to our viewers: "Dedicated to the String, without which I would have no reason to exist." Beautiful. . . . There is only one string in your life?

Author: Uh . . . no. Actually there are four.

TV Host (embarrassed): I see. Let's move on to other points. How do you get a string to vibrate?

Author: I have several methods worked out with my assistant, the Player. Sometimes she pulls

me across the string. That is one of my favorite methods. I do nothing but just cling to the string as she pulls me in up-strokes and down-strokes. When I really cling to the string and resist her motions, the sounds are big, round, and gorgeous. If I don't resist so much, the tones are softer.

TV Host: What are other methods you use to get the string to vibrate?

Author: First, you have to remember that, before I come along, the string just lies there stretched out over the bridge doing absolutely nothing! Sometimes I have to work hard to convince it to vibrate. I do lots of different things! At times I shoot across the string; other times I bounce up and down on it. I've coaxed it, pinched it, whipped it, and rubbed it! Occasionally I skip across it.

TV Host: The skipping sounds fun! What is that called?

Author: Ricochet. The player drops me on the string and I go skipping across it like a tennis ball. Usually I land in the middle of the bow and skip toward the tip.

TV Host: I note that Chapter 3 is headed "On the String" and Chapter 4, "Off the String." How can you get a string to respond to you if you are off of it?

Author: Oh, those two phrases have been around for a long time. Conductors will say, "Play this on the string." In another section of the music, they will say, "Play it off the string." If they say, "off the string," it means that I won't touch the string the full value of the note. I'll land on the string just a fraction of the time, then spend some time in the air before touching the string, or another string, again. It is kinda like bouncing or springing up and down in down- and up-strokes. It is fun, too!

TV Host: But why didn't the composer decide whether something should be on or off the string?

Author: The trouble is they use the same symbol for short notes played either on or off the string. They put a little dot above or below the head of the note. Unless they write in a word, such as "spiccato," the musician must make a decision. Of course, in an orchestra the conductor makes the decisions for the whole group.

TV Host: Name several "off the string" bowings.

Author: Spiccato and sautillé are the two most popular. But there is also ricochet, flying staccato, and flying spiccato.

TV Host: And "on the string" bowings?

Author: Legato strokes, slurs, détaché, louré, martelé, and tremolo are used the most.

TV Host: They never go off the string?

Author: Oh, yes, for a special reason lots of times the player lifts his bow and resets it on the string.

TV Host: A special reason?

Author: Yes. For example, if an up-bow of a martelé stroke ends very near the frog, the player may lift the bow slightly and reset it. That way he avoids a scratch.

TV Host: Oh. One last question. Who is this François Tourte you mention in the acknowledgments? You expressed gratitude to him. I haven't met him.

Author: Oh, he is the Frenchman who perfected the design of the modern bow. He lived about two hundred years ago. I'm modeled after his design, so, because of him, I'm able to do so many exciting things!

TV Host: Well, we thank you for coming past and wish your book, *The String and I*, much success! I hope it will be translated into several languages!

Three Cheers for Leftie!
SCENE 115

At a testimonial dinner given by the left hand, arm, and their joints.

Toastmaster: Friends, we are brought here together to pay tribute to Left Thumb. We believe he is the unsung hero of the string player's left hand and arm. His dedication, unselfish devotion, and cooperative spirit have made it possible for each of us to do our work. For the most part he has stayed out of the limelight but is always there when needed. There are many times that no one is aware he exists.

In the past we have known other left thumbs that have pushed up, grabbed, or insisted on getting into the act. Their tension restricted the motion and flexibility of all joints—the wrist and knuckles especially. But, our friend and honoree, Left Thumb, has given freedom to all of us by remaining calm and flexible throughout. Let us join in saying "Three cheers for Leftie!"

Friends: THREE CHEERS FOR LEFTIE!

Obedience School
SCENE 116

Instrument: Have you heard the rumor?

Bow Tip: What rumor?

Instrument: They are planning to send you to Obedience School.

Bow Tip: Obedience School! I thought that was for dogs! Isn't that where they teach them to heel, sit, and do other things on command? Surely they know I'm not a canine!

Instrument: Of course. They are sending you anyway.

Bow Tip: But, I'll be lonely!

Instrument: No problem. Your master will go with you.

Bow Tip: Master! I don't have a master! Haven't you noticed that I'm my own person? I'm free to do anything I want to.

Instrument: That's one reason we don't always sound so good! You swing and roll around as you please. They feel you should be under the control of your master—our player. At Obedience School you will learn to respond to her command.

Bow Tip: But I'm the active type. I love to move around.

Instrument: Oh, you will move OK. You will go in the direction and manner the player desires.

Bow Tip (sobbing): My carefree days are over. What will our player and I do at the school?

Instrument: First, she will be instructed to concentrate on you.

Bow Tip: That sounds nice.

Instrument: Then the instructor will give lots of exercises and gymnastics. While holding the bow with a good bow hold, the player will use it to stir some imaginary witches brew, draw paintings in the air, and skywrite names and words. In other gymnastics the player will hold the bow parallel to the floor and move it up and down like an elevator. There is no end to the

number of things they can do to get our player to manage you, the bow tip.

Bow Tip: Is this what they mean when they speak of bow control?

Instrument: Yes. They want the whole bow to be under the control of the player just as though it is a part of her own arm. In fact, I heard of a great concert artist who said that, on placing his bow in the instrument case after a practice session, he felt as though he had put away a third of his arm!

Bow Tip: This will help our music?

Instrument: Definitely! Every fine string player can control the tip of her bow. If the tip is in her control so are all other parts of the bow. That way the player is better able to match her actual performance with the ideal one she "hears" in her mind's ear.

Bow Tip: Will I get a diploma on graduation?

Instrument: I'm sure you will. You will probably graduate *magna cum laude* and our player will be declared Master of the Tip!

Go on a Diet
SCENE 117

Thick String: I think I'll go on a diet. I dream of being as slender and suave as you.

Thin String: Hold it! We need you to be on the plump side.

Thick String: Why?

Thin String: Because of your gorgeous low notes. We thin strings can't sing in the low range.

Thick String: Couldn't our player just loosen you with your tuning peg so your pitch will sound lower?

Thin String: Oh, mercy no! I would flap around all over the place. We strings have to be drawn very taut. "Relax" is an ugly word to a string! We all need tension in order to vibrate.

Thick String: But I vibrate so much slower than you. I think it is because I'm so fat. If I were thinner, I just know I could move faster.

Thin String: Sure you could. But that is the whole point! Because you vibrate slower, you make fewer vibrations per second. Fewer vibrations per second mean lower pitches! Besides, you go farther when you vibrate. They say you have a wider amplitude than I do.

Thick String: But they treat us big strings differently.

Thin String: How's that?

Thick String: Well, for one thing, a player tends to steer his bow a little closer to the finger-board than with you slender guys. I'd like to know what it feels like to have a bow travel across me in the lane nearest the bridge.

Thin String: Oh, they do that because you bigger guys sound better when the bow isn't so close to the bridge. No one thinks a thin string is better. It is just that our requirements are different. In general, I need the bow to use one of the lanes a bit closer to the bridge than you do—especially in brilliant passages and in those where the player moves his left hand high up the fingerboard, shortening the string length.

Thick String: That brings up another point. Our player seldom moves his left hand to my higher pitches. I'd like to try being a soprano.

Thin String: We don't need you to play so high. Your higher pitches can also be found on your neighboring string. The player can decide which tone quality is most suited to the mood of the phrase. Or, sometimes, the composer specifies by writing in the score the words *sur une corde*, which in English means "on one string." Since I'm the highest string, lots of time the player has no choice. The only place he can find extremely high pitches is on me. Frankly, I like the way the player approaches you with his bow. I wish he treated me that nicely.

Thick String: How is that?

Thin String: He seems to have a way of coaxing you to sing. It is as though he is saying, "Come on now, Honey. Won't you please vibrate for me?"

Thick String: That's because I hiss at him if he

doesn't treat me nicely. Just let him slap his bow down the way I've seen him do with you sometimes! I fix that! If I don't hiss, I whistle or make gruff sounds. After a few ugly noises he soon learns that it is better to use persuasion. I don't like being rushed. I prefer to take a little time to respond.

Thin String: So there! It is not at all bad to be a fat string. Stay as you are and let the player make the adjustments. I may have more fun with my fast vibrations but you have trained him to treat you with great respect.

The Good Trillers
SCENE 118

Kid: Fingerboard, you've been around for a long time. Can you tell me why some string players' trills sound so much better than others'?

Fingerboard: Sure, I can give some pointers. First, the good triller puts her left hand in a balance that favors the top note of the trill. In fact, I don't feel much weight from the finger that plays the lower note. Second, she shapes her hand so the tips, not the pads, of the fingers strike the string. Third, she emphasizes the lifting motion of the finger while trilling. The not-so-good trillers pound me so hard I ache all over!

Neck: Talk about suffering! Some trills are a pain in the neck!

Bow: I thought trills were made by tapping on the fingerboard—not the neck.

Neck: Yeah, you are right! But, the not-so-good trillers grab and push me with their thumbs. While I'm gasping for life, they wonder why their trills are so sluggish and slow! The artist's thumb treats me kindly. It is soft and gentle.

Fingerboard: I can always tell when the thumb is grabbing and pushing you. But any player can correct that if she wants to badly enough. She just has to command her thumb to ease up.

Bow: I have my problems, too. I find it hard to do my work when the string bumps up and down.

Fingerboard: Oh, yes, that has given other bows worries too. Try to avoid bowing too close to the fingerboard where the string is looser. Also, don't press as hard during a trill as when playing a solid note.

Kid: I surely do thank all of you for your help. It is good to hear things from another viewpoint. So long, now!

A True Marcel Marceau
SCENE 119

Bow: I like being a mime! A true Marcel Marceau!

String: What do you mean? I thought a mime made no sound! Between the two of us we make lots of sound! Music, in fact!

Bow: Oh! Haven't you noticed that sometimes I move silently? The main sound comes while I'm touching you. Often when there is a short rest or a separation between notes, I stop touching you. But I usually keep right on moving in the air above you. I stay with my act! A true mime!

String: Yeah, I've seen you do it. But, that doesn't stop me! I keep right on vibrating!

Bow: Exactly! That is the main reason I do it. Those vibrations you let off while I'm in the air add a beautiful ring to the music. Have you ever noticed how our player's left hand, except during open strings, keeps you mashed down to the fingerboard as I glide off the string? He does that to help you continue to ring! Even the other strings may keep on vibrating sympathetically. This gives warmth to our tone. In fact, the little hum after the main body of the tone ceases is one of our special traits. You can really hear this in an orchestra. When a band cuts off, the sound stops almost instantly.

String: I hate to stop cold. I like to keep spinning just a little longer. I guess I prefer to wind down.

Bow: I know. If my hair stopped on you for the rest, you couldn't continue to spin. It would kill the vibrations and our music would sound dry.

String: You do that in martelé bowing.

Bow: Yes, that is a characteristic of martelé. Of course, another string can continue to vibrate sympathetically if you are playing a note found in its harmonic series, so the music is not all that dry. But there are also other times I stay on you. For example, when the player and I make a diminuendo at the end of a piece, I often stop for a moment to rest. But, of course, you are barely moving by that time anyway and the other strings have lost their enthusiasm for vibrating sympathetically.

String: How does the player feel about your miming during a short rest?

Bow: He likes it! It makes his motions natural and easy. People do this sort of thing all the time in everyday life. Watch a person sweep the floor. Part of the time the broom doesn't touch the floor but the arms and broom move right along in the same manner. They change directions in midair and start swinging back. That is how I often do down- and up-strokes when the notes are supposed to sound separated.

String: Oh.

Bow: And hair brushing! Watch how the brush goes beyond the hair, circles around, and starts all over again. The player's arm and I do this in consecutive down-strokes. The motion is non-stop. It continues in one flow. Watch a person brush some bread crumbs off the dining room table. Same thing! The mood and style of the motion never change during the act.

String: So that's the rule?

Bow: Absolutely! My player and I try to move in the air exactly the same way we would move if I were touching you the whole time. If you feel me moving with vigor, we mime in the air with vigor. If I feel silky to you, I make silky motions in the air. I stay in character! I'm a true actor—sound or no sound!

The Life of a Soundpost
SCENE 120

Cave Explorer: Hey! Is anyone down there?

Soundpost: Sure! I live here.

Cave Explorer: What are you? A hermit living down there in the dark all by yourself?

Soundpost: Oh, I have one neighbor—the bass bar. I live here because this is where my job is!

Cave Explorer: What do you do?

Soundpost: I have a position of great responsibility! I get the instrument to vibrate!

Cave Explorer: *You* do that? I thought that was the player's job. Isn't that how a string player makes music?

Soundpost: Yes, you are right. We work together. The string is his responsibility. He energizes it. Once he gets it spinning, I take over.

Cave Explorer: But what does the bridge do?

Soundpost: It is the go-between. It passes the vibrations from the string to the front of the instrument. Then I carry the vibrations from the front to the back of the instrument. I give resonance. Without me the instrument would have no voice! Even a million dollar Strad without a soundpost could only whisper! I have a position of status and power.

Cave Explorer: You are important! Don't you ever move from this spot?

Soundpost: Yes, the violin repairman will move me occasionally if the player thinks the instru-

ment's tone can be improved. When they speak of "adjusting the soundpost," that is a cue that I will be moved around slightly until they find a better location for me.

Cave Explorer: So you are not glued in?

Soundpost: Oh, mercy no! I'm held in place by the force on the bridge caused by the tension in the strings. This squeezes me. That is why it is so important for the player never to loosen more than one string at a time.

Cave Explorer: What happens if all the strings are loosened?

Soundpost: I can topple over like a tree! Then I have to rattle around in the cave all the way to the violin repair shop. The instrument can't be played until I'm set upright again.

Cave Explorer: So you have lived in this general area most of your life?

Soundpost: Yes, in the same neighborhood. I keep fairly close to the foot of the bridge.

Cave Explorer: On the side nearest the string with the highest pitch?

Soundpost: Yes. However, in my early days I lived in a forest as part of a tree. I must get back to work now. I hope to see you again someday. Happy exploring!

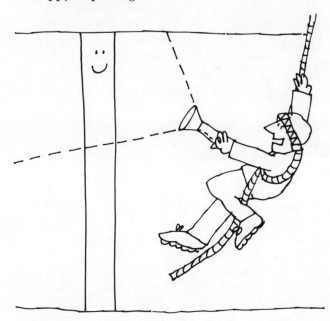

Going to Pieces?
SCENE 121

New String: Help! What is happening to me? I thought I was doing just fine. Then all of a sudden I feel I'm vibrating in little pieces!

Old Neighboring String: Be calm. Everything is OK. The musician is playing a harmonic. You are exactly right! You *are* vibrating in little pieces—four to be exact!

New String: How do you know?

Old Neighboring String: First, you are not sounding your open string pitch, yet no part of you is down on the fingerboard. The player's finger is touching you so lightly that you are still suspended in the air. Second, listen to that unusual tone quality. The color is quite different than when the string is "stopped." In this case you are sounding two octaves above the open string because the finger is exactly on a spot one-fourth the length of the string. When measuring the string length they only count the distance from the nut to the bridge. WOW! It is quite a view from here! You are vibrating in four equal segments. Beautiful!

New String: I'm beginning to enjoy the feeling now. Can I do this on every note?

Old Neighboring String: Oh, no! Just on certain notes. This is why string players memorize what is called the harmonic series. They learn that the half string harmonic sounds an octave above the open string; the third of a string harmonic sounds an octave and a fifth above the open string; the fourth of a string sounds two octaves above the open string; the fifth of a string sounds two octaves and a major third. . . .

New String: I can't wait to try them all! I think I'm going to like this music job!

Sur Meets Sul

SCENE 122

Sur la Touche: Hello! I don't think we have met. I'm Sur la Touche.

Sul Tasto: I'm delighted to meet you! I'm Sul Tasto. I assume you are French.

Sur la Touche: Yes. And you? Italian?

Sul Tasto: Si. How did you know?

Sur la Touche: I met another guy down the road named Sul. Sul Ponticello, I believe. He was Italian.

Sul Tasto: Yes, I know him. Sul isn't really a typical first name in Italian. It means "on the." They use my name in music.

Sur la Touche: No kidding! My name is used in music also! Sur la means "on the." Touche means "fingerboard." A composer writes my name on her music when she wants a string player to bow over the end of the fingerboard.

Sul Tasto: I don't believe this! My name means "on the fingerboard" in Italian. So we do the same work! Or, rather, we let our names be used for the same worthy cause. In Italian there is a bow stroke called flautando or flautato, which means flute-like tone. Some composers prefer to write one of those words in the music. It is a light, airy bow stroke played over the end of the fingerboard.

Sur la Touche: The player needs to draw the bow a bit faster and lighter whenever one of our names is used. Isn't that right?

Sul Tasto: You bet! That is the secret for making the tone beautiful and special whenever the bow gets near the fingerboard, no matter what name is used. Another name is Sulla Tastiera. By the way, our names are not capitalized when written in the music.

Sur la Touche: Mine isn't either. It surely was good meeting you. We have a lot in common. I feel I have known you for years!

Investigation of Spiccato

SCENE 123

Anchor Man: We will now go directly to the bow site for a report regarding today's work of the Investigating Committee of Spiccato, which is in its sixth month.

Reporter: Standing with me is the five-member committee called ICS, which just flew in from a field investigation. The distinguished senators look windblown but exhilarated. Tell us about your experience, Senator.

Senator: Well, after months of testimonies regarding spiccato bowing, the committee decided to come right down here to this location about halfway between the bridge and fingerboard to look into these rumors.

Reporter: You mean to say that you rode on the bow?

Senator: Indeed! Right on top of the bow stick! Our pilot, the string player, explained to us that in this thing called spiccato it helps to approach the string from above. She usually starts by moving in the direction of what is traditionally called a down-bow. Then she allows the bow to hit the string with enough impact that it bounces right up to the other side.

Reporter: Bounce! Have you been bouncing all afternoon?

Senator: Right! It was a fascinating experience! The pilot's hand and bow swung in little arcs—

much like a pendulum—with the bow glancing off the string at the bottom of the arc. We would go in one direction only to immediately swing back to our starting point. It went on this way all afternoon.

Reporter: Tell me, Senator, what started this congressional investigation of spiccato bowing?

Senator: Rumors of irregularity. Also, there was some talk of an energy waste and noise pollution.

Reporter: Do you believe that there was basis for the charge of irregularity?

Senator: Absolutely not! It is certainly one of the most regular of all bowings. Naturally, sometimes the composer will write varying rhythms but a series of notes of the same durational value played with spiccato bowing is highly regular!

Reporter: And what about the rumors of wasted energy?

Senator: Not true! One swing made the next! The pilot said that she could have gone on all day. Her right arm might have become a little tired from being suspended above the string, however.

Reporter: And noise pollution?

Senator: There is a possibility of this if the pilot makes the arc very deep so the bow bounces too high off the string. This seldom happens with an experienced string player.

Reporter: When do you and your committee anticipate that your investigation will be complete?

Senator: If all goes well, we expect to wind it up and have our final written report completed in six or seven more months. The investigation will require several more trips to various locations. We need to make a study of the spiccato bowing in Paris, Honolulu, Tokyo, and Bermuda to verify our findings.

Reporter: Thank you, Senator! We will return now to our anchorman.

From the Heart of a Tree
SCENE 124

Scroll: What's on your mind?

Tuning Peg: I'm planning my autobiography.

Scroll: Oh?

Tuning Peg: The opening chapter will focus on a tropical forest in South Asia where I was born. You see, I'm made of ebony, a wood treasured by ancient kings!

Scroll: Wow! You are solid black! Was your whole tree black?

Tuning Peg: No, only the bark and the part called the heartwood, which is the older, inactive central part of the tree. They made me from that.

Scroll: Let's get back to those ancient kings. Why did they like ebony so much? Because of your beautiful dark color?

Tuning Peg: Yes, partly. But also ebony is extremely hard and durable. It is the favorite wood for tuning pegs and the black keys of a piano. Have you noticed that the fingerboard and tailpiece of our instrument are also made of black ebony?

Scroll: I see that now. Do you enjoy your work?

Tuning Peg: Oh, yes! I plan to write several chapters about it and close with some advice to string players.

Scroll: Such as?

Tuning Peg: I will point out the proper way to put on a new string. After pushing the end of the string through my hole, the player should guide the string so it crosses over its end at least one time. He needs to be sure that the string is anchored down so it won't slip when I'm turned.

Scroll: Any other tips?

Tuning Peg: Yes, wind the string over me—not under me—and wind it from my hole to the side of the scroll box where the largest part of me lives. This keeps me from slipping and I can better hold the string in tune.

Scroll: And?

Tuning Peg: I'll advise players, when they have difficulty in turning me, to spread a little peg compound on the parts of me that touch the peg box. This can be purchased at the violin maker's shop or through the catalog of a musical supply house. It surely makes my work smoother!

Scroll: Is your work quite heavy?

Tuning Peg: It was when I first started my career. But in recent years more players have used steel strings, which require the use of fine tuners attached to the tailpiece. Some people call these little gadgets string adjusters. This has relieved me of considerable work. I do the big jobs in tuning but let the little guy at the other end of the string take care of the lighter, detailed work. I must stop talking now. My player wants me to help him tune. This is the first thing we do before any practice session or concert.

League of Bow Hairs
SCENE 125

TV Reporter: We have with us today Bow Hair, a spokesperson for the League of Bow Hairs. Bow Hair, tell us about your association.

Bow Hair: Our newly formed organization is made up of bow hairs from around the world. Our goal is to make musicians conscious of our needs. Unfortunately, often through misuse and neglect, we are handicapped in our work.

TV Reporter: What is your work?

Bow Hair: Our job is to get the string to vibrate freely so that beautiful tones flow from a musical instrument.

TV Reporter: How do you do this?

Bow Hair: Take a look at me up close through this microscope. See those little barbs? When I'm drawn taut, covered with rosin, and pulled across a string, *I* can set the string in motion! The word for that is vibrating. Before I come along, the string just sits there doing nothing—unless, of course, someone plucks it with a finger. But, in my opinion, a plucked tone has limited expressive value. I'm the first step toward those beautiful tones drawn by a bow.

TV Reporter: What a responsibility! Please tell us about your concerns.

Bow Hair: Our league makes three demands. One, we insist on the use of good quality rosin. Two, we don't like to be touched by fingers, no matter how clean they look. Those natural body oils, as essential as they are to human beings, defeat our goal. They make us greasy and then we slide across the string rather than gripping it. The string stands still, the sound vanishes, and the musical phrase is destroyed. Three, we insist on not being tightened too much. If we are too taut, the flexibility of the bow stick vanishes. It likely will lose its inward curve and eventually become warped. The same thing happens if the player forgets to slacken us after use. Then, the talk begins about replacement!

TV Reporter: Replacement!

Bow Hair: Yes! They say we are no good! Unfortunately this neglect has put many a bow and bow hair out of business. Of course, we bow hairs recognize that normally we will have to be replaced many times during the life of a bow. However, we don't want to be forced into early retirement.

TV Reporter: Of course not! Tell me, BH, what did you do before you went into music?

Bow Hair: I spent my early years in Siberia as a horse's fly swatter. That is how most of us got our start. My horse was very nice but my present employment is much more gratifying. Members of the League and I feel highly honored to have been selected to help musicians in their worthy cause. We ask only that they be aware of our needs.

TV Reporter: We wish your association much success. Thank you for stopping by today. Stay tuned—we'll be back in a moment after we hear how to make your dog's mealtime happier!

Roots
SCENE 126

Détaché: Hi there, Sautillé, what have you been up to?

Sautillé: I've been studying my family tree. I decided I wanted to know my roots!

Détaché: Roots? What do you mean?

Sautillé: My ancestors! I've got a surprise for you. We are related!

Détaché: No kidding! How could this be? I thought you were related to the Spiccato family.

Sautillé: Lots of people think that. It is because we have the same jumpy characteristics. We both like to jump up and down on a taut string. But, a Sautillé can go a lot faster than a Spiccato! The Sautillé ancestry traces to Détaché.

Détaché: Tell me more.

Sautillé: Here is a good way for a string player to practice a passage that is to be played sautillé bowing. Learn the notes at a rather slow tempo using détaché strokes near the middle of the bow. It helps to be very exact rhythmically and to use flat hair. Gradually practice the passage faster. As the tempo speeds up, the strokes will become shorter and the action will appear to center more in the hand. The fingers will feel rather loose, especially the second, third, and fourth, and they will remain curved for both the down- and up-bows. One impulse will make several notes. The motion looks and feels like erasing a pencil mark. Then, finally, an oblique motion is added to give the jumpy sound.

Détaché: Oblique motion! What does that mean?

Sautillé: About halfway between a vertical motion and a horizontal motion.

Détaché: Is there anything that a player can relate this to in everyday life?

Sautillé: Sure. Have you ever watched a basketball player "dribble" a ball? He waves his hand up and down to get the ball to "dribble." Try that. Now imagine that he dribbles the ball near a wall. The ball will hit the floor *and* the wall. The player's hand now is moving obliquely.

Détaché: Great! How does a string player do this?

Sautillé: The same way except her starting point is more horizontal than vertical. Then, while she is playing the fast eraser-type strokes, she directs her hand so it goes in this oblique direction. When she does this, the balance of the bow is thrown off just a little bit and the bow hair cannot hug the string. So, the bow starts jumping off the string slightly and we have that wonderful effect called sautillé bowing!

Détaché: You really like yourself, don't you, Sautillé?

Sautillé: How right you are! I give a lot of spice and zest to the music. I've developed a brilliant, exciting style. If the composer has me in mind when he writes a fast, virtuosic passage, there is no substitute!

Détaché: I agree! You help all of us by giving more variety to the music. Because of our differences, you even make me feel special when I appear in the music right after you. Thank you, Sautillé!

My Security Guard
SCENE 127

Scroll: I wonder what we sounded like when you were smaller.

Instrument Front: Smaller? What do you mean?

Scroll: I wonder what we sounded like before you got extended.

Instrument Front: Extended?

Scroll: Sure. Haven't you ever noticed that line around the edge of you? There is also one around the edge of the back. It looks like someone thought you should be a little larger so he added to you.

Instrument Front: Oh! That's not an extension! It is my purfling!

Scroll: Purfling?

Instrument Front: Yes. My security guard! It is an inlay that helps to prevent cracks that could result if something bumped the edge of me. When the violin maker made us, he put in my purfling before he ever attached you. He carved a little groove, then filled it with some other wood. It follows the outline of my lovely curves.

Scroll: I want to ask you about those curves. Why did he give you such a slim waist?

Instrument Front: Oh, you noticed! Think about it for a minute. That bow has to have some space in which to travel. How could a musician move the bow on our outside strings if I didn't have a trim waistline?

Scroll: Oh. Tell me about those two long holes in you. What are they for?

Instrument Front: Those are my F holes. That is where the air which is moved around inside the instrument while it is played comes out. An F hole is like a mouth of a person speaking. I have two mouths. But I would like to know about you. You have your own beautiful curves! Do we sound better because you look so fancy?

Scroll: No, I have nothing to do with the sound. I'm just up here as part of the peg box. My job is to look pretty! In fact, one time I heard our violin maker say that he enjoyed making me more than any single part of the instrument. He said something about my not affecting the "acoustical properties" of the instrument so he could just concentrate on making me look beautiful.

Instrument Front: He succeeded! I had better get back to work now. Looking nice is only a tiny part of my job! I have lots of physical activity in my work! Every inch of me is supposed to vibrate and resonate. Take care! I enjoyed talking with you.

Call the Authority
SCENE 128

Radio Announcer: Today our vibrato authority is in the studio to answer your questions. Local listeners, dial 471-7766. The number for our out-of-town callers is 512-471-3434. Let us hear from you!

First Caller: Hello. I play the cello. I've always had trouble with my hand feeling tight when I vibrate and people tell me that my vibrato sounds tense. Could you possibly help me?

Authority: Sure! That is a common complaint and lots of people who have had tense vibratos have changed them into beautiful ones.

First Caller: It is possible to change?

Authority: Of course! Anything is possible. Is your thumb tight?

First Caller: I don't know. I'm real careful not to move it.

Authority: Oh, that's probably the root of your problem!

First Caller: What do you mean?

Authority: Try this. Hold up your left hand as though you are playing an invisible instrument. Now shake your hand in the same direction as the line formed by the base knuckles.

First Caller: Base knuckles?

Authority: Yes, the big knuckles where the fingers join the hand. Shake vigorously! Imagine that your hand is attached to your arm with only a string. But don't drop the hand. Support it. Watch your hand and fingers move! Does everything feel loose?

First Caller: It sure does!

Authority: Look at your thumb. Is it shaking with the rest of the hand?

First Caller: It is! My forearm is moving, too, but not so far.

Authority: Good! Now continue to shake vigorously but this time hold your thumb perfectly still. Just shake all the other parts of your hand.

First Caller: Help! I can't get anything to move!

Authority: Exactly! It is impossible to shake your hand if your thumb is held still. Loosen that thumb! Let it move!

First Caller: Move when I play?

Authority: Yes. But first I want to tell you a little trick. Put your instrument in playing position now. Place your thumb in its usual location but make the touch very gentle. Let no other part of your hand touch the instrument. Now shake your hand vigorously—just like you did a minute ago. Watch the base knuckle of your thumb move along with the rest of the hand and fingers. Your skin will stick to the cello neck but the bones will move! The finger pads will be suspended well above the fingerboard. Your fingers will be gently curved. Look at them move!

First Caller: My hand feels free!

Authority: Yes. Do this often. You can even substitute your other arm for the instrument's neck when you are riding on a bus or watching television. Soon you will get the knack of it and can transfer it to your cello playing. Remember: balance on only one finger at a time when vibrating. The other fingers will just go along for the ride. I'm sure your tone will be much more beautiful. At times you may want to remove your thumb from the neck. Thank you for calling. . . . Hello, line two.

Second Caller: Hello. I want you to know how much I look forward to Thursdays, when you are on the show.

Authority: I'm glad to hear that. What's on your mind today?

Second Caller: I heard you talking about shaking the hand in the same direction as the line formed by the base knuckles. I, too, play the cello. Which direction should I shake first?

Authority: How many choices do you have?

Second Caller: I can make the first thrust either away from my body or toward my body.

Authority: Exactly! Now pantomime shaking something. Shake a dust mop. . . . Shake a bell. . . . Shake some dice. . . . Shake a gift-wrapped box. . . . Shake some car keys on a key ring. . . . Was the first burst of energy toward your body or away from it?

Second Caller: Away!

Authority: Exactly! That must be the way nature intended because most people do it instinctively. Try it the other way. Shake those things toward your body.

Second Caller: Oh! My hand and arm feel tight!

Authority: Right! But, remember we are talking about cello vibrato. For violin and viola it can feel very different because your hand is not in the position in which you normally shake things. Some wonderful violinists make the first shake toward the body, others away. Sorry, our time is running short. I suggest that you locate a copy of the book called *Playing the String Game*. It is full of ideas designed to help players and teachers. Two chapters deal with vibrato.

Second Caller: Who publishes it?

Authority: The University of Texas Press, *Austin*. The author is Phyllis Young. Time for one more quick question. Line One.

Third Caller: Hello. People tell me that my vibrato makes them nervous. I don't feel nervous.

Authority: Try moving farther on each cycle. That should slow it down. A longer trip takes more time. That's all for today. I'll be back next Thursday. Meanwhile, string players, keep the springs in every joint well oiled and imagine beautiful tones! Experiment until your real tone matches the one of your dreams!

Radio Announcer: Thank you for listening. Tomorrow's guest on *Call the Authority* will be an organic gardener, who will answer questions about mulching, potting soil, and insect control through ladybugs. Remember: When you don't know, *Call the Authority*!

Born at the Blacksmith's
SCENE 129

Cello Endpin: My favorite people are blacksmiths.

Bow: Blacksmiths? The people who make horseshoes?

Endpin: Right.

Bow: I think my hair must have been in a blacksmith's shop at least once. You know, of course, that it came from a horse's tail and that horse must have had shoes. But what connection have you had with a blacksmith?

Endpin: My earliest ancestor was born in a blacksmith's shop.

Bow: You've got to be kidding!

Endpin: No. That is the story I've heard.

Bow: Tell me about it.

Endpin: You see, for many years cellos had no endpins.

Bow: How did a player hold his instrument? Did he prop it up on a stack of telephone directories?

Endpin: Mercy, no! The telephone hadn't been invented yet either! He held it up with his knees.

Bow: Cellists still use their knees.

Endpin: That's right. But now the legs kinda cradle the cello. I'm the one who holds the instrument up off the floor. I do all the work so the player is free to make music.

Bow: That's nice.

Endpin: As I understand it, there was a famous Belgian cellist named Adrien François Servais, who lived in the middle 1800s. They say that he played very beautifully and had a brilliant concert career. But, how he loved to eat! As a result his tummy started sticking out so far that he had trouble holding his cello! He took it to the blacksmith's shop and explained his terrible problem. The blacksmith made and installed a rod at the bottom of the cello. Presto! The endpin was invented!

Bow: Wow!

Endpin: I can picture it now. When the job was finished, Servais probably asked the blacksmith how much money he owed. "That will be five francs and one song, Monsieur Servais." I bet Servais sat down on a work bench and played one of his own compositions with his famous glorious tone. What a joy his new endpin must have given him!

Bow: I bet all of the cellists rushed to the blacksmiths' shops with their cellos! If the great Servais could do it, they could too!

Endpin: No, I don't think so. The opera cellists were the first to add endpins to their instruments but the other cellists were slower. It takes time for any new invention to become popular, particularly in the days before radio and television.

Bow: What a great TV commercial could have been written showing Servais playing his cello in the blacksmith's shop! The camera could zoom in on the new endpin. "Dial our toll free number—1-800-471-7644. Major credit cards accepted. Cellists, don't delay! Order this new indispensable product today! If you are not completely satisfied, return it within thirty days and your money will be cheerfully refunded."

Endpin: Yes, I'm truly indispensable to modern cellists. I like to think that in my own quiet way I help people express through music the beauty in their hearts.

Kneading Bread Dough
SCENE 130

Bow Stick: I don't believe this!

Bow Hair: You don't believe what?

Bow Stick: Our player must not like my shape! At first I thought she had decided to make my curve deeper. But now it appears she plans to reshape me! She keeps pushing down her first finger so different parts of me bend. I think she can't decide just where she wants the bottom of my curve!

Bow Hair: So that is what is happening! I thought she was encouraging you, the string, and me to be friendlier! She makes you snuggle up close to me right where I'm tugging on the string. I thought it was kinda nice.

Bow Grip: Ask the expert! I can tell you exactly what is going on! We are doing louré bowing! Some people call it the portato stroke.

Bow Stick: How come a bow grip knows so much about this?

Bow Grip: I'm right where the action starts! The player applies pressure through her first finger to pulse a note, then she releases it, then she applies pressure again, and so on. Each note has a little swell, then a decrease in sound. I feel like I'm getting a massage! Sometimes I wonder if she thinks I'm bread dough and she is trying to knead me!

Bow Stick: You say the pressure is from her first finger?

Bow Grip: No! The pressure flows *through* her first finger. That is an entirely different matter! I bet you can feel her thumb gently pulsing on the underside of you, Bow Stick. If she just pushed her finger down, the tone might sound hard.

Bow Hair: I like the sound of louré bowing. It is sweet and songlike.

Bow Stick: Yes, I do, too. How does our player know when to use portato or louré bowing? Just anytime she is in the mood to give you a massage?

Bow Grip: Oh, no! The composer marks little lines above or below the notes she wants pulsed and then puts a slur over or below them. She wants the notes to sound slightly separated through the pulsing action. Often the arm and bow keep moving but slow up slightly during the separations. Sometimes we even stop between notes. We can lift up gently so the string will keep right on vibrating. It feels like we are drawing little waves or scallops. By the way, a composer will occasionally use dots rather than lines above or below the notes.

Bow Stick: Sounds kinda vague to me. Don't they use dots and lines for other kinds of bowing also?

Bow Grip: Yes, composers can only suggest how they want their music to be played. It is up to the musicians to interpret the little lines and dots. They study and "feel" the music and finally give their interpretation. Maybe someday someone will invent a perfect alphabet of symbols so one little line or dot isn't used so many different ways.

Bow Stick: Listen to that sound! The vibrato is extra beautiful.

Bow Grip: Yes, vibrato is especially important in louré bowing. Expressiveness is the goal!

Bondage
SCENE 131

Bridge (groaning): Oh, here it comes again!

F Hole: What?

Bridge: That mute!

F Hole: The Italians call it Sordino; the Germans, Dämpfer; the French, Sourdine.

Bridge: I don't care what they call it! How can I do my work of carrying those beautiful vibrations from the string down to the box if I can't move! Everything depends on me! That thing is like a straitjacket. It puts me in bondage.

F Hole: That is the whole point. The "thing" is a clamp and it is supposed to restrict you. It makes our tone a different color.

Bridge: Sounds nasal to me.

F Hole: Sometimes I think it does too. Other times it sounds sweet. Composers like it for contrast. That is when they write in the music *Con sordino, Mit Dämpfer,* or *Avec les sourdines.* Patience. It won't last long.

Bridge: Who determines when I'm freed? Our player?

F Hole: No, the composer. When he wants the player to remove the mute, he writes in the music *Senza sordino, Ohne Dämpfer,* or *Otez les sourdines.*

Bridge: Oh, well, I will be going on my summer vacation before long.

F Hole: How come you get those long holidays? None of the rest of us do!

Bridge: I was designed to be a winter bridge in a cold climate. I'm taller than my sub, who is considered a summer bridge.

F Hole: Do you have a label that says "Winter"?

Bridge: Oh, no. Some instruments are more sensitive to weather conditions than others. Our instrument is one of those. When the instrument expands, it makes me lift the strings farther off the fingerboard. The musician finds it too difficult to play so he calls in my sub and gets out his little bridge jack. After loosening the strings to a lower pitch he jacks up the strings, takes me off, sets up my substitute, removes the jack, and retunes. You realize, of course, that we bridges are individually fitted to the instrument. Our feet are shaped to snuggle up against the top plate and our height is carefully gauged.

F Hole: Have you noticed my notches?

Bridge: Yes, what are they for?

F Hole: They point to where you are to stand. The violin maker cut them when she made the instrument so people would know just where to put the bridge.

Bridge: Good deal! That shows how important bridges are! And it is very important for me to be straightened every time the player notices that I'm leaning. It is easy for me to become warped into a bad shape. Then I would lose my effectiveness.

F Hole: Oh, here comes the player's hand to remove the mute!

Bridge: Ah, freedom at last!

Ricochet
SCENE 132

Writer: Hello! I'm a freelance writer. *Individuals* magazine has asked me to write a feature story this week. I wondered if you, as a bow, have done anything interesting recently.

Bow: Have I! I ricocheted yesterday!

Writer: What is that? When someone speaks of a rock ricocheting, it hits something then bounces off.

Bow: Exactly. I ricocheted across the string!

Writer: Oh?

Bow: Have you ever thrown a rock across the top of a pond? It skips right across the water.

Writer: Sure. It's fun!

Bow: That's what I do—only I skip across a string.

Writer: How does your player do that?

Bow: That's the funny part! She does very little. This is one bowing she lets me do my thing.

Writer: Bowing? Is this an official bowing?

Bow: Yes. It is called ricochet bowing.

Writer: Back to the player. She lets you do what you want to?

Bow: Yes. She throws or drops me on the string and then lets me jump.

Writer: You mean your player doesn't hold you?

Bow: Of course, she does—but not too tightly. After that first impulse I go skipping across the string. Or, if you prefer, you may say in your article that I bounce across the string or strings.

Writer: Strings?

Bow: Sure. I love to ricochet across strings. Four-string arpeggios are especially fun!

Writer: What makes ricochet different from spiccato and sautillé? I understand these are bouncy types.

Bow: There is a big difference! In spiccato and sautillé I move in the direction of a down-bow for one note, then the next note is an up-bow. I go back and forth and only one small area of my hair touches the string. But in ricochet I play two or more notes while going in one direction. I prefer down-bows but in either an up- or down-bow my player's arm and I just keep moving right along. By the way, it helps when the player angles my stick so it is just a little lower than usual at my frog end. It makes me a little closer to the neighboring string on that side. It also is easier for me to ricochet when my hair is very flat and I'm working in my upper half.

Writer: How does the player know when to let you ricochet?

Bow: That is a tough question. The composer writes some notes of equal length, usually eighth notes or sixteenths. Then he puts dots above or below each note and adds a slur above or below them. There are at least two notes inside the slur but usually more. The problem is staccato and flying spiccato are marked the same way! The conductor or player has to choose which to use. When I ricochet, I make a sputtering type sound.

Writer: You do this in rhythm?

Bow: Yes, the player has to experiment at home by throwing me against the string at various parts of my hair to find where I can best do the rhythm. I like to bounce faster near the tip and slower near the middle. Also, the higher I bounce, the slower the notes.

Writer: Ricochet must be a very important bowing.

Bow: No, not really. It is rarely used, but from my viewpoint it is the most fun!

Writer: Talking about it has been fun, too. It should make a great story! Thank you for your help.

Long Distance
SCENE 133

Long Distance Operator: I have a collect call for Bridge from Fingerboard Nut.

Bridge: Go ahead.

Fingerboard Nut: Hi! How are things at your end? What are you doing these days?

Bridge: Fine. I just sit here shivering. You know, of course, that during my working hours I transmit vibrations from the strings to the top of the instrument. Other times I get in a little rest but I just stay right here on the job site supporting the strings. Between the two of us we make those strings workable. Right? How are things at your end?

Fingerboard Nut: OK, but no one pays much attention to me except when a string is changed. Then people notice my lovely smooth grooves.

Bridge: Smooth grooves?

Fingerboard Nut: Yes, I have four grooves—one for each string. It is very important for them to be smooth because the strings slide through them every time they are tuned.

Bridge: What happens if they are not smooth?

Fingerboard Nut: It makes it rough on the strings!

That is why an experienced string player sometimes runs graphite in a groove when he changes a string.

Bridge: Graphite? Where do you get it?

Fingerboard Nut: Handiest stuff available! That is the lead of an ordinary pencil.

Bridge: I wish our player would notice *me* more often!

Fingerboard Nut: You mean that our player has failed to keep you real straight and your feet solid?

Bridge: Oh, no, that part is OK. He keeps me in good shape. I'm not getting bent over toward the fingerboard and my feet are snug against the top of the instrument. But our player doesn't seem to know the importance of my curves. If he would study my curves and angles I could tell him how to angle the bow on each string to make the best sounds. And everyone knows a string sounds best when the bow crosses it at a contact point that stays the same distance from me throughout the stroke, unless there is a musical reason to change it. It helps for the player to look at me!

Fingerboard Nut: Well, I hope our player starts noticing you soon because you are reputed to be a great guide. He is missing a good thing if he doesn't use you as one.

Bridge: I must stop talking now and get back to work. The whole crew depends on me. Without me the string vibrations would never get to the front of the instrument, through the soundpost, and down to the back. Everything would come to a halt! Goodbye. Thanks for calling!

Lost Slur
SCENE 134

Note with a Line: What is this? I've lost my slur!

Staff: Oh! The reason you don't have your slur is that the composer did not intend for you to be played louré bowing. This time you are to be played as détaché porté.

Note with a Line: No kidding! What is that?

Staff: You will sound similar to one note of a group of notes played with louré bowing, but one bow stroke is devoted to you alone. Louré has at least two or three notes in one bow direction. Sometimes there are more.

Note with a Line: So that is what the line above me means? But sometimes it is below me.

Staff: Yes, both ways have the same meaning. The composer wants you to stand out in an expressive way. She is saying, "Make them notice this guy." The player gives a slight swell in volume at the beginning of the note, then lightens the sound at the end. Sometimes there is space between the notes but often there is not. The inflections make you stand out.

Note with a Line: I sound important!

Staff: Exactly! You are more important than the other notes around you and the player is supposed to acknowledge this.

Note with a Line: But what if several of us have lines and there is still no slur?

Staff: The player will make each one of you sound important. When he sees a line, he will dip the hair deeper into the string soon after the start of each stroke. That is when we hear the little swell.

Note with a Line: How does the player do this?

Staff: By varying both the pressure and the speed of the bow. He "milks" the tone.

Note with a Line: Détaché porté is a beautiful bow stroke. Right?

Staff: Yes, this is one way to bring out a special note without accenting it. That is why some people call it expressive détaché.

Note with a Line: But I'm sure I've heard other notes that don't have lines above them played that way.

Staff: You are absolutely correct. The musician has the right to stress certain notes although they have no special markings. Remember, a composer expects the musician to interpret her music!

Fortune Teller
SCENE 135

Bow Grip: Did you know that I'm a fortune teller? I can forecast events!

Bow Tip: You can? I don't see any tea leaves or a crystal ball down there.

Bow Grip: I don't need them! But the bow stick and I often can predict what kind of bowing we are going to use.

Bow Tip: You can? How?

Bow Grip: By the way the player's hand touches us.

Bow Tip: Oh?

Bow Grip: Yes, if he holds us lovingly—almost like his fingers are made of soft rubber—I know the chances are good that we are going to play big, beautiful, full tones. He will sink his live, supported weight into me. Sometimes it feels as though his fingers spread a bit farther apart. He pulls me in either an up-bow or a down-bow direction.

Bow Tip: H-m-m.

Bow Grip: If he holds me very loosely, I predict that we may be going to play ponticello or, possibly, tremolo.

Bow Tip: And, if he holds you a bit tighter?

Bow Grip: The chances are good that we may play softly.

Bow Tip: Any other predictions?

Bow Grip: If I can hardly feel the player's fourth finger, I know that possibly we will play tremolo or sautillé bowing. Then, there are times the bow stick and I get pinched.

Bow Tip: Pinched?

Bow Grip: Yes! If the player gives me a little pinch by pressing down with the side of his first finger and up with his thumb, I know we are going to articulate.

Bow Tip: Articulate?

Bow Grip: Yes, we will start the tone with a bite. Usually a pinch is the first sign that we are going to play a martelé stroke or possibly a big accent. Of course, martelé strokes always start with some kind of accent. Sometimes a pinch is a sign we are going to play staccato bowing. Then the first pinch is only a starter! It may be followed by many throughout a long bow stroke!

Bow Tip: Does it hurt?

Bow Grip: Oh, no! Each pinch lasts only a split second.

Bow Tip: What is your favorite bowing?

Bow Grip: I love louré. It makes me feel like I'm being caressed. But, louré bowing is difficult to predict. Sometimes the player doesn't seem to give any signs until after the tone has started. Then he sinks some weight in me so the hair dips into the string deeper and moves a bit faster. The tone swells at the beginning of each note, then lightens.

Bow Tip: It must be great to be able to forecast events. You lead an exciting life! On the other hand, predictions eliminate surprises. My life is exciting because it is filled with surprises and that is fun, too. Thanks for sharing with me.

Mail Order Accents
SCENE 136

Clerk (answering the telephone): MAIL ORDER HOUSE FOR MUSICIANS. May I help you?

Customer: Hello. I've heard that you carry a wide assortment of accented notes but I can't find them in your catalog.

Clerk: I'm sorry. We recently discontinued listing this item. It has been moved to the do-it-yourself department.

Customer: Oh?

Clerk: We had too many complaints that our accented notes, although they were of the finest quality, did not fit into our customer's phrases. We discovered that most of the effectiveness of an accented note depends on the notes that go before and after it.

Customer: I just want a dynamic accent.

Clerk: I understand. It is, by far, the most popular variety. But, suppose I mailed you one of the pitch and duration of your choice and it happened to be the same dynamic level as the preceding note in your phrase. You would have no accent at all!

Customer: I hadn't thought of it that way.

Clerk: Remember, the term accent means a stress of one note over others.

Customer: I suppose it would be safer to buy only accented notes that are forte.

Clerk: That doesn't work either. You see, generally an accent should be only one degree louder than the passage in which it occurs. A forte accent would sound terribly out of place in a passage marked piano or pianissimo. By the way, what instrument do you play?

Customer: I'm a string player.

Clerk: Good! You string players have all kinds of wonderful possibilities for great accents. You can approach them so many different ways.

Customer: Tell me more.

Clerk: First of all, you have the martelé stroke, which always starts with an accent even if there is no accent marked. You begin by applying pressure into the string through the bow. Then the pressure lets up and the bow immediately shoots across the string. The timing is quite different for an accented détaché.

Customer: Oh?

Clerk: Yes, in accented détaché the pressure and motion usually start at the same moment. The bow can move from the instant the string feels the pressure. Both the pressure and the speed let up a little after the note starts sounding. The volume drops off some.

Customer: A diminuendo?

Clerk: Yes, every dynamic accent has some kind of diminuendo. Otherwise the note has not been accented.

Customer: Is the bow usually on the string before an accented note is played?

Clerk: Most teachers recommend this until a student becomes quite advanced. Later one can learn the whipped stroke, or fouetté. In this bowing one barely lifts the bow off the string, then slams it back down on the string in a hurry. It gives a nice snap to the sound, especially near the tip of the bow.

Customer: Suppose I play several accented notes in a row. Does each one need a diminuendo?

Clerk: You bet! An accent or a sforzando is like a head on a nail. If there is no head, there is no accent or sforzando.

Customer: I know that an accent mark is a little v turned sideways and placed above or below the head of a note. How is a sforzando indicated? I understand that it is a sudden and strong accent.

Clerk: By *sf* or *sfz*. If you see an *sfp* or *fp* (fortepiano), the accent should be followed immediately by a piano. Earlier I mentioned that a martelé stroke begins with an accent although one might not be indicated. There are other accents with no markings at all! For example, a syncopated note is traditionally accented. The player usually makes a diminuendo on the note preceding it or lifts his bow. He takes care that there is not a swell during the syncopated note. By the way, vibrato is an important part of any good accent.

Customer: So we should vibrate on accented notes?

Clerk: Yes, if there is time to get a good balance on the playing finger. The vibrato should be larger at the beginning of an accented note since the tone is louder. In fact, sometimes, especially in a singing melody, a string player will prefer to make an accent by adding energy to the vibrato instead of having an attack with the bow. People refer to this as a vibrato accent.

Customer: How does one know which kind of accent to use?

Clerk: I think the best method is to sing the phrase several ways. You can try out such words as toe, dough, mow, go, and low on the accented note. After you decide which sound suits the music the best, then imitate it on the instrument.

Customer: Do you also have agogic accents in your do-it-yourself department?

Clerk: Yes, the agogic accent is not done through a dynamic change. Instead, the note is held a little longer than the time value marked in the music.

Customer: I've used those. I play the note as though I love it so much that I can't bear to leave it. I linger on it a moment longer.

Clerk: Yes, agogic accents can be very expressive if the vibrato is beautiful.

Customer: Thank you very much for your help today.

The All Star Bowing Team
SCENE 137

Sports Announcer (*speaking fast and enthusiastically*): The members of the ALL STAR BOWING TEAM have been warming up in the Green Room and will soon make their appearance! We hear that they are in great shape today! HERE THEY COME NOW! LADIES AND GENTLEMEN: The ALL STAR BOWING TEAM! (*Cheers*) Rapid Détaché—the Eraser! Legato—the Puller! Martelé—the Shooter! Col legno—the Tapper! Sul Tasto—the Floater! Spiccato—the Bouncer! Ricochet—the Skipper! Staccato—the Biter! Sautillé—the Jumper! Ponticello—the Squeaker! Simple Détaché—the Smoothie! Détaché Porté—the Sweller! Louré—the Pulser! Collé—the Pincher-Lifter! Détaché Lancé—the Darter! Fouetté—the Whipper! Tremolo—the Shaker!

Fans: (*More cheers*)

Sports Announcer: Sitting next to me here in the lookout booth is the world authority on bowing! Tell us, Sam, how did the All Star Team members choose their nicknames?

Bowing Authority: First, I must stress that the nicknames for today's performance are entirely unofficial.

Sports Announcer: Oh?

Bowing Authority: Each member of the All Star Team selected a name that describes one single characteristic that distinguishes him or her from most of the others. Another day they might choose other names to describe other traits of the bowing styles.

Sports Announcer: Why are they doing this?

Bowing Authority: They want string students to

realize that the bowing terms were made up by people just like us! Picture an Italian violinist practicing some three or four hundred years ago. He could have been experimenting with his bow and out came some short notes. Perhaps he said in Italian: "I like these short notes. They are spiccato."

Sports Announcer: Why would he have made up such a name?

Bowing Authority: That's the point! Spiccato is a form of the Italian verb, *spiccare*, which means to detach. The notes were separated from each other. We have no idea how! As time moved on, the term was passed along from one musician to another. For some years now spiccato has referred to one specific type of bow stroke. The player swings his bow in little arc-like motions. It starts in the air, hits the string at the bottom of the arc, and bounces back up in the air to complete the arc. Spiccato bowing is never terribly fast. It usually is played near the middle of the bow and can vary from a crisp, percussive sound to a singing sound. The quality mostly depends on the depth of the arc, the shallower arc producing a more singing sound. If spiccato is played near the frog, it can become very dramatic and forceful.

Sports Announcer: Why are there so many different kinds of bowings?

Bowing Authority: To make music as expressive as possible! Actually there are more bowings than are represented by the Team today and each has variations. We must remember that the terms are not completely standardized. Some musicians use different names for the

same bowing. Saltato is an example. That term can refer to any number of bowings that bounce.

Sports Announcer: Say, what is the Green Room? I understand that is where the All Star Bowing Team members hung out before they made their appearance.

Bowing Authority: The Green Room is the room behind the stage where musicians wait before a concert. People call it the Green Room even if it is lavender.

Sports Announcer: I believe they are about ready to start playing now so we better listen. Thank you, Sam, for sharing your expertise with us today.

Cloned
SCENE 138

String: Hey, kid, treat my harmonics with a little more respect! I consider them to be my most miraculous feature!

Kid: How is that?

String: Look what I can do! Touch me lightly halfway down the road between the nut and fingerboard. Don't push the string down to the fingerboard—leave air space. Now bow carefully. . . . Do you realize what I've done? I transformed myself into two equal shorter strings. Both are vibrating nicely! Cloned!

Kid: Wow! Is that what you are doing? I hear a pitch an octave above your open string.

String: Right! Try me a third of the way down the road. . . . Presto! I'm cloned into three parts now. Listen to that exceptional sound! It is an octave and a fifth above my lowest possible pitch. Now touch me lightly two-thirds of the way down the road. . . . Listen! We have the same lovely pitch because I'm still cloned into three parts. How many people do you know who can clone themselves into three identical people? I can move on to four, five, six . . .

Kid: Can I do anything to help?

String: Sure. Always bow very carefully but not too lightly when I'm in this magical state. If you get rough, you could jar me back to my original self. And, don't ever touch me at any other place with your fingers, nose, or whatever while I'm cloned. Any such interference sends my whole anatomical system into a tizzy and my distinguished tone becomes an ugly noise.

Kid: Oh! Anything else?

String: Yes, I prefer that you draw your bow a

little closer to the bridge and faster than usual. Listen to that clear bell-like sound we are making.

Kid: It sounds great but isn't the pitch a bit flat? I'll move my finger a little higher. Whoops! Where did your harmonic go?

String: I forgot to tell you about that special feature. In my natural harmonics, some pitches always sound flat and there is nothing your finger can do to make the pitch higher. This is one time that no one can justly criticize the player if a note is out of tune, provided I've been tuned properly. Just find the spot where my tone rings the best and let nature take care of the intonation!

Call EMS?
SCENE 139

String: Ouch! You are too heavy! I hate it when you bear down on me there!

Bow: Where?

String: Anywhere near the fingerboard! It goes against my principles and I get all choked up. (*Cough*) Help! I can't breathe!

Bow: Shall I call the EMS (Emergency Medical Service) for oxygen?

String: No! Lighten up and move faster! Or stay slow and heavy but move down closer to the bridge.

Bow: OK. . . . Do you feel better now?

String: Yes. Now I can breathe. Why do you do that?

Bow: Talk to my player. She is the pilot and navigator.

String: You don't have any say about where you travel?

Bow: Not much. But, if my navigator-pilot starts daydreaming, I love to drift up near the fingerboard.

String: How come?

Bow: Haven't you noticed how much more soft and flexible you are up there? You are nice and spongy like a pillow. Near the bridge you feel hard.

String: Yes. I appear much tougher near the bridge. Ask your player to feel me both places so she will understand why you like to drift up near the fingerboard.

Bow: So you prefer that I cross you nearer the bridge?

String: No, in my job I can't afford to have favorite places. To make music live we must have lots of variety with many different colors and dynamic levels.

Bow: What are dynamic levels?

String: Fancy words for loud and soft.

Bow: Tell me more.

String: If your player wants a big thick creamy tone, have her steer you across me slowly near the bridge. Ask her to sink some of her supported weight into you in such a way that I think you are heavy. Fat bow—fat tone.

Bow: That should be easy to remember. A fat dog is heavier and moves slower.

String: Right!

Bow: So you want me to move lighter and faster when my route is near the fingerboard?

String: Yes. Your player needs to understand she is dealing with three ingredients.

Bow: Three?

String: Yes. Speed, weight, and the distance from the bridge. Ask your player to experiment with you and to listen carefully.

Bow: Listen?

String: Yes. When she finds a beautiful tone, she should memorize the recipe—how much of each of the three ingredients she has used.

Bow: How?

String: By looking and feeling.

Bow: Then what?

String: When she changes the amount of one ingredient, she must change the amount of at least one other ingredient or possibly both.

Bow: Oh! Suppose the player has found a gorgeous tone in a bow track near the bridge?

String: If she wants or needs to move you faster, she should add more supported weight and/or move to a track farther from the bridge.

Bow: So everything is in proportion?

String: That is the secret! In general, slow heavy bows sound best near the bridge. Fast light ones near the fingerboard.

Bow: How many bow tracks are there?

String: Some players picture five or six. They are all invisible, of course.

Bow: I think I need to have a little chat with my navigator-pilot.

String: Good! She will learn to play well a lot sooner if she knows the principles I live by and respects them. She needs to steer you carefully and change weight and speed accordingly.

Bow: Everyone will be happy!

String: Right!

Bow: Wait! One more question! How in the world can my player think of all these things when she is making music? Haven't you heard of people playing from the heart? I would think all of her mind and heart should be focused toward molding the phrases and creating moods and colors.

String: Right! By concert time most of her attention will lie there. That is why all these things are worked out so carefully in practice, especially in the early stages of learning a piece. She will have a variety of tools at her command and be able to draw on any of them at will.

Bow: Terrific!

Three Look-Alikes
SCENE 140

TV Host: We have three look-alikes on our show today! Cameras, roll forward so our audience at home can see the printed music as I introduce our guests. Staccato! (*Applause*) Flying Spiccato! (*Applause*) Ricochet Bowing! (*Applause*) Studio audience, what do you say? Do they look alike?

Studio Audience: YES!

TV Host: Right! Each of our guests has dots above or below the heads of the notes, yet several notes are linked by a slur. This appears to be a great contradiction! Dots in this position indicate short notes. A slur binds notes together. Staccato, how can you slur and, at the same time, shorten the notes?

Staccato: A slur tells the string player that all of the notes within it are to be played in the same bow direction—either an up-bow or a down-bow. Usually the notes are played legato, but, when little dots or dashes are in the picture, the notes are to be separated. To a musician's well-trained eye they almost form a blazing neon sign which reads SEPARATE THE NOTES!

TV Host: How do you separate the notes?

Staccato: Ah! Now you are hitting on our differences! Each of us look-alikes has our own method.

TV Host: Staccato, what is your method?

Staccato: I'm the stop-and-go type. The player keeps the bow hair touching the string and his arm moves steadily along. He moves his hand and bow in a series of little short martelé strokes all traveling in the same direction.

TV Host: So the hair never leaves the string?

Staccato: Well, occasionally, a player will lighten the pressure so much that the bow leaves the string. Then, they call me Flying Staccato or Staccato Volante. But, if I fly, I travel at only a

very low altitude. Most people think of me as being very solidly on the string. In fact, I've been called "Solid Staccato."

TV Host: What about you, Flying Spiccato?

Flying Spiccato: I'm a real flier! My player makes a series of little spiccato strokes all going in the same direction. I prefer up-bows. He throws the bow on the string for each note so his hand and bow move in a row of little arcs, as though he is writing a string of u's backward. I can't go as fast as staccato. At times my player backtracks so the bow hits one spot of the hair over and over. Some people call me Jeté when we do that.

TV Host: Ricochet, I understand you bounce across the string. What makes you different than Flying Spiccato?

Ricochet: My player throws the bow on the string one time but, out of that one throw, he gets several notes! When the bow hits the string, he loosens his hold and lets the bow do all the work. It bounces across the string. I'm kinda a sputtery type. I do my best work if the hair is flat and the bow stick is not tilted. I prefer down-bows.

TV Host: If you all look alike on the printed page, who decides which of you will be chosen?

Staccato: Unless the composer has actually written in one of our names, the player decides. Of course, tradition plays a part. In an orchestra the conductor is the decision maker.

Ricochet: But I am usually the only one who shows up in orchestra music. My friends here specialize in virtuosic solo music.

TV Host: We thank the three of you for coming today. Let's take a commercial break. Please stay tuned. We will be right back with another exciting guest!

Diamond-Shaped Notes
SCENE 141

Sales Clerk: MUSICAL SUPPLY HOUSE—Mail Order Department. May I help you?

String Player: I'm telephoning to order some notes. I would like some of those that look like double stops but the top note is diamond-shaped.

Sales Clerk: Oh, those are artificial harmonics! They are listed on page 17 of our latest catalog.

String Player: Artificial? I wouldn't want anything artificial!

Sales Clerk: Artificial isn't really a good name for

them. Some people call them false harmonics. But, there isn't anything false about them either. They are real harmonics found in a harmonic series built on a pitch which is not an open string. I assume you have played natural harmonics.

String Player: Yes, at least four or five on each string.

Sales Clerk: Good! The open string served as the fundamental of the harmonic series. In artificial harmonics, the fundamental is a note stopped by a finger or thumb.

String Player: They sound genuine. I'll take a dozen. Do they come complete with instructions?

Sales Clerk: Yes, most of them do. In fact, the instructions are right on the staff! The bottom note, which looks like any normal note, indicates where you put your finger down solidly on the string. The upper note, which is diamond-shaped, tells you where to touch the same string lightly with another finger.

String Player: Just any finger?

Sales Clerk: It depends on the harmonic. Our most popular variety has the notes written a Perfect 4th apart. Violinists and violists use the first and fourth fingers. Cellists and bassists use the thumb and third finger.

String Player: What pitch does it sound?

Sales Clerk: Two octaves above the lower note. You see, the finger playing the lower note actually serves as a new nut. The finger touching the upper note causes the string to divide into four equal parts.

String Player: You say that some artificial harmonics do not come complete with instructions?

Sales Clerk: Yes. Some composers prefer to notate the desired pitch rather than give how-to instructions. They write a single note with a ° above it. It looks like a natural harmonic.

String Player: But how can I tell if it is a natural or an artificial harmonic?

Sales Clerk: If the pitch is not in the harmonic series of one of the open strings, it is artificial.

String Player: Do you stock other varieties?

Sales Clerk: Yes. One has the top note a Perfect 5th above the bottom note. It sounds an octave plus a fifth above the lower note. Another has the two notes a Major 3rd apart. It sounds two octaves plus a Major 3rd above the lower note.

String Player: I'll keep those in mind and call if the need arises.

Sales Clerk: Is there anything else I can help you with today?

String Player: Yes, I would like an eraser—one that erases the sound of an ugly note after it is played.

Sales Clerk: I'm sorry. To my knowledge no such eraser has been invented yet. Once a sound wave is created there is no way to erase it. That is why musicians practice so much. They practice carefully with much repetition so each note is perfect. If such an eraser is invented, you can be sure it will be featured on the cover of our catalog. Now, may I please have your name, address, and major credit card number?

Newsbreak
SCENE 142

Newscaster: WE INTERRUPT THIS PROGRAM TO BRING YOU THIS SPECIAL NEWS BULLETIN. Tension has been named the Number 1 Killer of potentially beautiful tones by the National Foundation for Tone Control. Statistics released today show that over 90 percent of those people who are unable to produce beautiful tones on stringed instruments first displayed tight thumbs. The nation's young musicians, their parents, and their teachers are cautioned to be on guard against this potentially hazardous symptom.

We now return you to the regularly scheduled program.

A Snake
SCENE 143

Violin: What's that snake doing inside of you?

Cello: Snake! Are you trying to scare me?

Violin: No! I saw your player drop a snake in one of your F holes.

Cello: Oh! That's my Dampit! It's a gadget my owner soaks in water before lowering into an F hole. It helps provide the humidity I need when the climate is too dry.

Violin: Do we need humidity?

Cello: Sure, our wood needs air and moisture like people! We breathe through our pores. If we live in a dry climate too long, we can get brittle and possibly crack. Besides, our tones are lovelier when we are not all dried out. You could have a Dampit, too. They make smaller sizes.

Violin: What did musicians do before someone invented the Dampit?

Cello: Some string players would put half of an apple or potato in their cases during dry spells.

Violin: Your player surely takes good care of you.

Cello: Oh, yes. I'm very lucky! She wipes me off with a soft cloth after every practice session. She is very careful that I don't get either too cold or too hot. She never leaves me in a car unless the temperature is very pleasant and she guards me from bumps. I've heard her say she wants to keep me nice for my next owners because I can outlive people.

Violin: I wish all players felt that way! We have long life expectancies if we are given a chance! Some old-timers two or three hundred years old are still being played. They are prized very highly and sound magnificent.

Cello: Good! Let's make a date to meet on A.D. October 20, 2286!

Press Conference
SCENE 144

Announcer: We are waiting here in the Press Room for Rapid Détaché to make his appearance. He has called this unexpected press conference this afternoon to make what he terms an important announcement. . . . Here he comes now! Accompanying him are Sautillé and Tremolo.

Rapid Détaché: Good afternoon, Ladies and Gentlemen. Thank you for coming. I wish to announce that Tremolo, Sautillé, and I have discovered that we are related. We are a family of bowings. We would like for this to be known publicly and for us to be treated accordingly.

Reporter A: How did you discover that you are a family?

Rapid Détaché: Recently we met at a rehearsal. The more we talked, the more we realized how many traits we have in common. So many, in fact, that we believe that we are related.

Reporter B: What are these traits?

Rapid Détaché: First, we are all short bow strokes. Second, we are all fast. There is not a pokey one in the group! Third, our motions and rhythm are repetitive. Each note is of equal time value. Fourth, the player gives her hand a little shake so that it moves in an eraser-type motion. The underside of her upper arm jiggles at a different angle. The elbow appears to float in one spot unless there is a string crossing. Fifth, one spurt of energy makes several notes.

Reporter C: Tell us more about that spurt of energy, Rapid Détaché.

Rapid Détaché: Oh, people do that lots of times in everyday life. Watch how you dust a table or polish the car. One action makes the next. The motion appears to be nonstop. If you were to work at every motion, moving to the left, then moving to the right, you would be exhausted after a very short time. Instead, people automatically balance their arms and give spurts of energy only when needed.

Reporter D: But you and Sautillé do not sound alike. Sautillé seems to have difficulty in staying on the string. May we hear how Sautillé feels about this?

Sautillé: Surely. It is true that I'm the jumpy member of the family. The player deliberately tilts her bow so that the frog end is a bit lower than when playing rapid détaché. That is, the lower half of the stick is dropped a bit closer to the neighboring string. The player wants the bow to have trouble staying on the string. It is an exciting effect.

Reporter A: Can we hear from Tremolo?

Tremolo: I have always known that my strokes were really baby détachés. I am proud to be an official member of the family.

Reporter B: What is the difference between you and Rapid Détaché?

Tremolo: I usually play many notes on one pitch and am extremely fast. Composers do not write out each one of my notes. They use a special symbol—three slashes across the stem of a note—to cue me in. Players tend to play my strokes nearer the tip of the bow. I give the music a special effect.

Rapid Détaché: If there are no more questions, we will go back to our music making. On behalf of the three of us, thank you for coming today.

An Insurance Policy

SCENE 145

Insurance Agent: What can I do for you?

String Player: I'm interested in buying some performance insurance.

Insurance Agent: What coverage particularly interests you?

String Player: Shifting insurance. I want to feel confident that I will play the top note in tune after a long ascending shift.

Insurance Agent: Good! I think our company has just what you need. I suggest that you read this policy carefully before buying it. Particularly note the conditions listed in small print. If you prefer, we can go over them together.

String Player: Yes, please read them to me.

Insurance Agent: This policy is effective only under the terms described below in regard to practice techniques:

- The insuree will know the letter names of the notes at the beginning and end of the shift and can give the name of the interval. (An exception will be made for the student who has not yet studied music theory.)

- He will sing both the bottom and top notes, first orally, later mentally.

- He will find a good balance on the finger playing the last note before the shift and, if there is enough time, he will vibrate beautifully on it.

- He will select a finger to travel on—the one playing the top note or the one playing the bottom note, depending on the nature of the phrase; if he decides to travel on the finger playing the top note, momentarily before starting the shift, he will tend to preshape his hand in the same shape required to play the top note. (Exceptions: Some shifts to notes high on the violin/viola fingerboard may require a shape change en route; also, some cellists/bassists may prefer to bring the thumb up while en route.)

- He will balance on the selected finger immediately before beginning the shift and remain balanced on it while traveling.

- He will lighten his hand and arm before beginning the shift and the weight will remain suspended throughout the travel; the selected finger and all those with a smaller number will dust the string lightly while moving.

- He will give a slight boost to his hand and arm to start them on their trip; the size of the boost depends on the length of the shift—the longer the shift, the greater the boost.

- He will shift at a speed appropriate to the tempo of the musical passage; in no case will there be jerks. The final determiner will be the player's singing voice; he will shift at the same speed he would sing the interval in the phrase in which it is located.

- He will allow the finger playing the top note to snap into the pitch on arrival; the live weight through the hand and arm will sink into the fingerboard as required for the size of the instrument. The larger the instrument, the more weight required.

- He will use a beautifully balanced vibrato on both the bottom and the top notes if time allows.

- He will isolate the interval and practice shifting from the bottom to the top note and back repeatedly in the manner prescribed in the clauses above. During the descending shift he will balance on the finger that played the top note.

- He will keep his ears alert to be sure that the sound is pleasing at all times.

- He will think optimistically throughout the practice period.

In actual performance the insuree is responsible only for playing the music expressively and maintaining a positive attitude. His practice habits will ensure the success of the shift.

String Player: Mercy! I had no idea shifting is so complicated!

Insurance Agent: Confidentially, it is not! How could so many people shift so well if it were that difficult to do? Remember insurance companies cover themselves for all conditions.

String Player: But, how can I think of all those things at once?

Insurance Agent: You can't! Just focus on one point at a time in your practice. Today specialize in balance, tomorrow the suspension of weight, and so on. Soon you will do these things automatically.

String Player: Oh! I don't believe I need shifting insurance after all. I will just practice carefully instead. I surely thank you for your time.

The Case of the Missing Bowing

SCENE 146

Private Eye: Hello! I wonder if you could help me. I am a private investigator. I'm working on the case of a missing bowing. Have you seen or heard of a bowing named sautillé recently?

First Person: What does it look like?

Private Eye: My client was unable to furnish a photo but she said that dots above or below the note heads signal that possibly sautillé bowing will be used.

First Person: Yes, I saw some of those in this neighborhood yesterday.

Private Eye: What was happening?

First Person: The bow was shooting right across the string in almost a straight line.

Private Eye (*somewhat disappointedly*): It stayed on the string?

First Person: Never left the string! It stopped dead between notes.

Private Eye: Did every note begin with an accent?

First Person: Right!

Private Eye: Did the notes follow each other at a rapid pace?

First Person: No, not too fast.

Private Eye: That sounds like a perfect description of martelé—another great bowing sometimes marked with a dot above or below the note.

First Person: Oh, yes. That was the name. I am sorry. I hope that someone else will be of more help.

*   *   *   *   *   *   *   *   *

Private Eye: Good afternoon. I'm a private eye. I'm searching for a missing bowing. Have you seen or heard of a short one recently? The name is sautillé.

Second Person: I don't know the name but I saw and heard a short, bouncy type this morning.

Private Eye: How did it move?

Second Person: It moved back and forth in a continuous motion. The bow didn't stop an instant. Always moving.

Private Eye (*enthusiastically*): Good clue! What part of the bow hair touched the string?

Second Person: Near the middle of the bow.

Private Eye: I believe we may be on the right track. Tell me, how were the bow strokes shaped?

Second Person: They were little arcs—like little smiles.

Private Eye (*disappointedly*): Oh. Sir, are you positive?

Second Person: I'm dead sure. I noticed that the bow hit the string right smack in the bottom of the arc—then the bow bounced off the string to complete the arc. The notes were lively but not terribly fast.

Private Eye: Too bad.

Second Person: Oh, it was nice! Happy-sounding little notes!

Private Eye: I'm sure. But your description tells me that you met up with spiccato bowing—not sautillé. Thank you very much for your time.

Second Person: I'm sorry to disappoint you. You might want to ask the guy who lives on the corner. He doesn't talk much but he usually knows everything that goes on in this neighborhood.

*   *   *   *   *   *   *   *   *

Private Eye: Good afternoon. I understand you have a sharp eye. I'm trying to track down a bowing called sautillé. Have you seen or heard it?

Third Person: Yip.

Private Eye (*speaking rapidly*): Here's a quick profile. Fast short strokes, nonstop—one motion seems to make the next. Played near the middle of the bow on the cello and double bass, above the middle on the violin and viola. Usually so fast that one impulse or one spurt of energy makes several notes. Jumpy type. The bow seems to want to leave the string. Often used when notes are repeated at the same pitch.

Third Person: Yip. That's it all right.

Private Eye: Where did you see or hear it?

Third Person: Next door.

Private Eye: When? Recently?

Third Person: Yip. Right now.

Private Eye: But what I hear is détaché.

Third Person: That's it. Sautillé in disguise.

Private Eye: Could you tell me more, please?

Third Person: Sautillé goes into disguise as détaché bowing when practiced slowly.

Private Eye: No kidding! When does it come out of disguise?

Third Person: When the player takes a faster tempo and slightly lowers the frog end of the bow so it's a little closer to the neighboring string. This makes the bow kinda jumpy feeling. The hair can no longer hug the string.

Private Eye: So that's it! Sautillé takes on a different personality in slow practice! One can always identify a spiccato or martelé stroke whether the tempo is slow or fast. But, of course, neither of those bowings can go nearly as fast as sautillé!

Third Person: Yip.

Private Eye: Thank you greatly, sir. I will report to my client that sautillé has been found. The case of the missing bowing is closed.

Coming Unglued
SCENE 147

Bass Bar: Oh, no! We have a buzz again! From where you are standing can you see light coming through the seams?

Sound Post: No, can't see anything from here. Remember last January how we saw a crack of light up around the upper bout on my side? It buzzed every time a G was played.

Bass Bar: Yeah. That's when we spent a night or so at the violin maker's shop getting the seams glued. Why don't they use better glue? This happens every year or so! If they can send a man to the moon, surely they could glue up our seams permanently!

Sound Post: Oh, didn't you hear why they use nonpermanent glue? They use that glue on purpose! With weather changes, wood expands and contracts. The instrument gets fatter or slimmer. Sometimes when it gets fatter some-thing has to give. If the glue holding the front and back to the ribs didn't let go, the front or back might crack.

Bass Bar: Oh! That is serious. Some cracks on the front or back require major surgery. Remember when the violin maker opened up our instrument in order to glue up a crack? He put a patch on the underside to help hold it together again.

Sound Post: Yes. That is another reason they use nonpermanent glue. When a violin maker needs to take our instrument apart, he is able to pry the seams open. Violin makers don't make incisions like people surgeons do.

Bass Bar: I also recall times we have had a buzz which was considered minor and required no surgery at all. Our player checked to see if a string had gone bad. One time the end of a string wrapped around a tuning peg in the pegbox was touching another string and buzzing. Also, several times the fine tuners down on the tailpiece got a little loose and started singing when certain pitches were played.

Sound Post: Do you remember when a seam was just a little bit loose and started buzzing? We couldn't see any light coming through at all but the violin maker discovered the problem when he gently knocked his knuckles around the edge of the top and back. One spot sounded a little different to him so he pushed in some glue, put on some clamps to hold the sides together tightly, and we were out of the shop in one day!

Bass Bar: I'm sure glad that our player doesn't get angry when there is a buzz. I've heard of that happening.

Sound Post: Yeah. Our guy is smart. He just realizes that this sort of thing happens and it is no one's fault.

A Miniseries Documentary
SCENE 148

MC: This evening we present Part Three of a four-part miniseries documentary called THE MAGIC OF THE BOW. Here in beautiful snow-covered Missoula, Montana, we will take a profile look at Détaché Lancé and some other members of the Détaché family through the eyes of our three guests—the Note, the Bow, and the String. Note, let's start with you. What is your viewpoint of Lancé?

Note: When I look up, I see two things hanging above my head—a dot and a line.

MC: Is this a signal for Détaché Lancé?

Note: Yes. But, if my stem goes up, the dot and line are suspended below my head. It means the same thing. The player can use this bowing even if there are no marks.

MC: That is good to know. Bow, how do you view Détaché Lancé?

Bow: I like it! It is fun getting off to a jackrabbit start!

MC: Is that typical of Détaché Lancé?

Bow: Yes. Lancé means darting. I move quickly at the beginning of a stroke, then slow down toward the end of it. Usually, I make a break between notes.

MC: Martelé also starts fast and has breaks between notes. Is this the same stroke?

Bow: Definitely not! Martelé begins with an accent and my stick gets pinched by the player's first finger and thumb. The sound comes on the release of the pinch.

MC: So that is the main difference. String, how do you react to Détaché Lancé?

String: Remember, I am so sensitive that I respond to how ever I am treated! The fast start with the bow gets me spinning enthusiastically. Then I calm down as the bow moves slower until it stops on me.

MC: What does the note sound like?

String: It is a short, unaccented note. Usually you find a group of these notes. Sometimes, they follow a group played Détaché Porté. This makes a nice change.

MC: What is the difference?

String: In Détaché Porté I start vibrating small, grow larger, then smaller again. The listener hears a swell on each note as the bow dips deeper into me and goes faster.

MC: Are the notes separated in Porté?

String: They give the impression of being separated because of the diminuendo at the end of each swell. Lancé's break is more definite.

MC: Note, do you have anything more to say about Détaché Lancé or any member of the Détaché family?

Note: I have a line above or below my head for Porté, an accent for Accented Détaché, but there is no special marking for Simple Détaché.

MC: We all know what accents are—but let's delve deeper into Simple Détaché. Bow, do you prefer to use a certain part of you for Simple Détaché strokes?

Bow: No. Simple Détaché can be played with any part and any length of me. The term simply means that a separate bow is used for each note. The strokes are smooth and there is no variation in pressure. Also, there are no breaks and the note has no special marking. It's simple!

MC: I've also heard people speak of Grand Détaché.

Bow: It resembles Simple, but in a Grand Détaché I use the full length of my hair!

MC: The Détachés are an interesting family of bowings. Thank you for being with us this evening. This concludes Part Three of our mini-series. Time now for a Public Service Announcement.

Sul Who?
SCENE 149

Tailpiece: What is making that weird sound? What's going on up there?

Bridge: Be calm! It's my favorite bowing—sul ponticello. My namesake!

Tailpiece: I thought your name was Bridge.

Bridge: Right! But in Italy all bridges are called "ponte," even the big ones that span the famous Tiber River of Rome.

Tailpiece: Is that bowing supposed to sound like this?

Bridge: Yes. When the composer wants a special effect created by bowing very close to the bridge with too much speed for the amount of pressure, she puts my name in the music! She writes "sul ponticello." Often it is a real mysterious sound, especially when it is combined with tremolo. Other times the tone is harsh and scratchy. But to me it is always gorgeous!

Tailpiece: So in violin music the composer writes "sul pontiviolin" and in double bass music "sul ponti-double bass?"

Bridge: Oh, no! It is always "ponticello." The English translation is "on the little bridge." Let's listen to that wonderful sound while we can because it will cease when the words "ordinaire" or "naturelle" appear on the printed music.

Court Case
SCENE 150

Quarter Note: Have you heard the news? We are going to court a week from Monday.

Half Note: No! What in the world have we done?

Quarter Note: We have been charged with fraudulent practice.

Half Note: On what grounds? We have just been sitting here putting in time.

Quarter Note: They say that we have deceptive packaging—that we look like a tremolo but are not tremolo. See those two little lines centered on your stem? I have two also. An inexperienced string player saw those little lines and started playing us as tremolo. He used very fast, short strokes and that got us into trouble! Of course, we both know that two lines indicate that our time values are to be filled up with repeated sixteenth notes. The musician is supposed to measure them carefully.

Half Note: Sure! If there were only one little short line slanted across our stems, I would represent four eighth notes and you two eighth notes. This is easy to remember because an eighth note has only one flag. Will a lawyer defend us?

Quarter Note: Yes. In Exhibit A she plans to show the judge what a page of music would look like if every one of our repeated notes were printed. She will make her plea on the grounds that barrels of ink and truckloads of paper have been saved by us. She will argue that a whole row of repeated notes on a page can make it much more difficult for the musician to read. On the other hand, we are neat, compact, and superefficient.

Half Note: But, what about the inexperienced string player who got confused and played us like a tremolo?

Quarter Note: Our attorney plans to explain that this would never have happened to an experienced musician. However, she will admit that there are many times that confusion exists when we have three little lines centered on our stems. In a slow passage even a veteran musician often cannot be sure whether the composer intended us to be played as a tremolo or as thirty-second notes. Traditionally he will ask himself or discuss with his colleagues, "Should this be an unmeasured or measured tremolo?" Some people prefer to say, "tremolo or non tremolo?" But, with three lines we usually are played as a real tremolo where the number of strokes crammed into our time values is anyone's guess!

Half Note: So you think we are in the clear?

Quarter Note: Absolutely! We are simply efficient paper and ink savers with no intention of deceiving anyone. They probably will end up giving us a gold medal for saving the nation's resources for future generations!

Opening a Savings Account
SCENE 151

Musician: I have come to open a savings account.

Banker: Good! We have several different kinds of accounts popular with musicians: Regular Savings, Endurance Savings, Fast Tempo Savings, and Slow Tempo Savings.

Musician: Please explain the last three. I know what a regular account is, of course.

Banker: The Endurance Savings works this way. If a musical passage tires you and you have difficulty getting through it, the goal is to build up endurance. In practice, don't stop at the end of a passage. Instead immediately repeat it without missing a beat. Gradually you will build up your endurance until you can play it through five or six times nonstop. Then, in a concert, you will have confidence that you will have plenty of endurance in reserve. In fact, you will probably spend only the interest and not dip into the principal.

Musician: Sounds good! Just the one I need! But, what about the others?

Banker: They work on the same concept. In a fast passage, rather than work it up just to the tempo you plan to use in a concert, go beyond it. You will never feel uneasy if the tempo is faster than intended because you will always have some technique in reserve.

Musician: And the Slow Tempo Savings Account?

Banker: The same principle! Have you ever been worried that you might run out of bow on a long note? This won't happen if you have at times practiced the phrase at a much slower tempo than you would choose. Remember: often a colleague—perhaps a conductor or a pianist—will set the tempo, not you! Knowing that you can play the music successfully at a tempo considerably slower will give you security. Of course, security is one of the strongest selling points of any kind of savings account.

Musician: I'll take all three!

Banker: Good! Please sign these little cards on the lines I have checked. I trust you realize that these are *investment* accounts. To keep them current you will need to invest time on a regular basis. The time is spent practicing.

In the Body Shop
SCENE 152

Viola: Mercy! You look in bad shape! What happened to you?

Cello: I have a broken neck! That is why I'm here in the violin maker's shop. A couple of days ago my fingerboard came unglued and fell off.

Viola: Oh, too bad! Your player didn't loosen the strings immediately?

Cello: No. She didn't know to do that and my neck snapped. The wood of our necks is not strong enough to hold up under that kind of tension without the support of the fingerboard. It is a shame because gluing on a fingerboard is only a minor operation. What are you here for?

Viola: A little crack developed on my front plate. The violin maker plans to squeeze in some glue and clamp me. I should be out tomorrow. I felt sorry for my player because she was afraid that maybe she had bumped me but the violin maker explained that weather conditions can also cause cracks. If he didn't squeeze in glue now, the crack might lengthen and I would be in for major surgery.

Violin: That's what I'm here for! They are going to take me apart at the seams and put a patch on the underside of my front plate. My crack is too long for the treatment you are having.

Cello: Did you see that double bass over there? It must have had a terrible accident! It looks like it should be in Intensive Care!

Violin: No big deal. The gut of its tailpiece broke so the bridge fell down and the strings are dangling. It looks like a disaster hit but that instrument should be in good shape soon. Probably the violin maker will need to reset the soundpost after he replaces the tailpiece gut, sets up the bridge, and tightens the strings.

Cello: How can he do that? The soundpost stands up inside the instrument!

Violin: He will stick a soundpost setter down through one of the F holes. There is not much room to work but somehow he always manages.

Cello: Why would he need to reset the soundpost anyway?

Violin: It usually falls down when all of the strings are loosened and the bridge is off. That is why people use a bridge jack when changing a bridge.

Viola: Like a car jack when a tire is changed?

Violin: Exactly the same principle! First, they slacken the strings just a little, then insert the bridge jack. When it is raised higher than the top of the bridge, the bridge is removed and another one slipped in under the strings. Then the jack is lowered and removed. Say, why are you here? You look perfect!

Second Cello: I'm here for a little cosmetic surgery. My fingerboard has a tiny bump that makes the A string sound twangy on certain notes when my player uses pizzicato. The violin maker will smooth it down. He said that lots of fingerboards have that sort of thing happen.

Bow: Aren't you going to ask about me? I had an emergency today.

Second Cello: What happened? You look fine. I assumed you were here to have a hair job. I think they call it rehairing.

Bow: No. Suddenly my player couldn't tighten my hair! She turned my screw but nothing would happen. I was helpless! I couldn't play at all!

Violin: Has your problem been diagnosed?

Bow: Yes. The threads of my eyelet were stripped.

Violin: Eyelet?

Bow: It is a little metal part with a hole threaded to match the screw. You can't see it unless the screw is taken out of the bow and the frog separated from the stick.

Second Cello: What caused the threads to strip?

Bow: Probably old age. Eyelets get worn down with use. However, the violin maker advised my player to hold the stick and frog firmly and quietly with the left hand while the right hand turns the screw to tighten my hair. He said it helps the screw and eyelet to last longer. I'm all fixed up now and am eager to get out of here!

Viola: Let's hope we all are out soon so we can get back to work! Our players need us!

Convention Program—Morning
SCENE 153
(Especially designed for cellists, but helpful to other string players)

Setting: A national convention of the American String Teachers Association

Moderator: The topic of our session today is Left Hand Extensions in Cello Playing. We have brought four of the world's greatest authorities who will contribute their ideas in a round table discussion. I am happy to present: 1st Finger (*applause*), 2nd Finger (*applause*), 3rd Finger (*applause*), and 4th Finger (*applause*). Each of

these experts, who have been involved in playing the cello for many years, will share with us information gleaned from on-the-spot experiences. Shall we begin with you, 4th Finger?

4th Finger (*hesitantly*): I am delighted to be here today and would be glad to share my knowledge with the dedicated teachers. However, after much deliberation I have decided that I must disqualify myself from this panel.

Moderator: Oh?

4th Finger: You see I almost never extend. The hand and arm just take me wherever I need to go. In fact, most of the time I determine their location because I insist on being comfortable. In other words, the side of the hand and I stay in line, I do not stretch out.

Moderator: I see. (*Pause*) Well, 3rd Finger, I think we are ready for you.

3rd Finger: I'm sorry. I'm in the same situation as 4th Finger. I almost never stretch. I accept whatever position is necessary to keep the fourth finger in line with the hand and arm. I just go with the rest of the gang. I, too, must disqualify myself.

Moderator: I'm sure you have plenty to contribute, 2nd Finger.

2nd Finger: I am sorry to disappoint you, Jerry, but I don't know what it feels like to stretch. I'm usually comfortably opposite the thumb or at least fairly near it. I really have no expertise in this area.

Moderator: Well, this leaves us in somewhat of a predicament. 1st Finger, do I dare ask you to contribute?

1st Finger: Indeed! I consider myself the only true authority on cello left hand extensions. I am the one who stretches back a whole step below the second finger so the cellist's hand can cover a distance of a Major 3rd from the first to the fourth finger on one string.

Moderator: You only stretch when the notes are on one string?

1st Finger: Oh, no! Extensions can be played on each string or a combination of different strings. I just cited the interval on one string as an example.

Moderator: How do you extend?

1st Finger: Feel me. I can make myself like rubber!

Moderator: Indeed! How do you do that? By relaxing?

1st Finger: That helps but it is not nearly enough! Look at my base knuckle. It is the one that joins me to the hand. Touch it. I'll show you what I do. (*Turning to the other fingers*) 2nd, 3rd, and 4th Fingers: Stay in your usual places on the fingerboard during my demonstration.

Moderator: Why, you are collapsing your base knuckle! It is moving closer to the cello neck while your tip rises slightly and makes a little arc back in the air. The tip is landing on the new note which is a whole step below the second finger. Now you are actually quite straight. Before your travels you were gently curved.

1st Finger: You are right! And you noticed I prefer air travel. I could have gone by surface but that tends to make me tense. Of course, I fly very low.

Moderator: I see that your wrist watch tilted a little when you did this low aerial maneuver. Now it appears to be turned somewhat toward the scroll.

1st Finger: Yes, the hand and wrist help me perform this feat by tilting ever so slightly. If they were in a square position, I could feel like an iron rod in this shape. Instead, I feel like stretched rubber.

Moderator: Now what happens?

1st Finger: If we are playing some fast notes, we fingers would just stay in this pattern as long as the music requires. But I can tell you it is quite a different story when the notes are longer!

Moderator: I'm sorry, our time is running out. Let's take this up at the afternoon session. Thank you. We will hope to see all of you immediately after lunch.

Convention Program—Afternoon

SCENE 154

(Especially designed for cellists, but helpful to other string players)

Setting: A national convention of the American String Teachers Association

Moderator: This afternoon's session is a continuation of the round table discussion begun this morning. It is entitled Left Hand Extensions in Cello Playing. We welcome back 1st Finger, 2nd Finger, 3rd Finger, and 4th Finger to discuss their experiences in playing the cello. This morning's session ended on a suspenseful note. 1st Finger had explained how to play fast notes in an extended position. His exact words were "But I can tell you it is quite a different story when the notes are longer!" 1st Finger, please continue.

1st Finger: On a stringed instrument players almost always use vibrato on the longer notes. In other words, if there is enough time to beautify a note with vibrato, they do!

Moderator: How does this affect you?

1st Finger: As individual fingers, we have a NO VIBRATO policy while in an extended position. An exception, of course, is a double stop. Now, look at the shape I'm in while extending. Note the relationship between my base knuckle and my pad. Do you think I could possibly vibrate in this position? No way! It would sound terrible!

Moderator: Perhaps if you tried harder and practiced three hours a day for ten more years.

1st Finger: Never! Look, it is miraculous enough that you people have been given the marvelous equipment called a hand. Don't ask us to do something we weren't designed to do! You don't ask a light switch to inflate a bicycle tire or a TV set to make ice cubes!

Moderator: A good point!

1st Finger: The human hand can do a lot of things but it must change its shape to perform different tasks. When you put a button through a buttonhole, your fingers look very different than when you shake hands!

Moderator: Yes.

1st Finger: I'll show you the shape I like to be when I vibrate but first take a good look at me in this extended position. Note my shape. See how the second, third, and fourth fingers are still in their usual places and the arm and hand still favor the fourth finger?

Moderator: Yes, and the thumb is still fairly opposite the second finger.

1st Finger: Good! Take a mental photo of this position. Now the other fingers will leave the fingerboard and I will play a note using a gorgeous vibrato!

Moderator: Beautiful! The vibrato is even and full. You look quite different now! Why, I do believe the whole hand and arm are balanced on your pad. Even the thumb, arm, hand, and the other fingers have moved back a little closer to you.

1st Finger: You are a good observer! Now describe my shape so the people who buy cassette tapes of the convention sessions will know what I look like.

Moderator: Your base knuckle is no longer collapsed. In fact, it is sticking out! A moment ago your base knuckle was lined up about halfway between your tip and the tip of the second finger. But now your base knuckle is closer to the cello scroll than your fingernail is. You really look and sound beautiful as you freely rock away! The other fingers are in the air near you and are also swinging. The vibrato is gorgeous!

1st Finger: Did you notice the elbow?

Moderator: Yes, the tip of the elbow didn't appear to move, but the forearm and wrist look quite different. They moved back to help you vibrate. Now they seem to favor you instead of the fourth finger.

1st Finger: Exactly! So, when the music has notes moving from the fourth finger side of the hand to the first finger side, the first finger tip always goes early to blaze the way. Then the forearm, wrist, hand, thumb, and other fingers join the first finger in its new place.

Moderator: And the reverse?

1st Finger: When moving from a first finger vibrato to the other fingers, the end of me stays on the note. But I collapse my base knuckle and move it down along with the forearm, wrist, thumb, and other fingers so they can reach their destination without stretching. Remember, I'm the only stretcher in the group! For an instant I am almost perfectly straight—

like I am pointing to our player's ear. The moment the new finger is in place, I let go and join the others. I snap into my new position, which is usually in the air riding along with the vibrato swing of the new note. Now my shape is curved.

Moderator: What would happen if you chose to remain on your note instead of joining the other fingers on the vibrato ride?

1st Finger: It would sound terrible! If my tip stayed anchored down some distance from the other fingers, the vibrato motion of the new finger would be restricted. We fingers have a slogan: GO FOR THE RIDE!

2nd Finger: That's our motto, OK!

3rd Finger: Yes. We cooperate with whatever finger plays the note. He gets himself in his favorite position to vibrate. We never fight him or hold him back. He needs freedom to balance and to move.

1st Finger: Right! And the whole hand vibrates between notes. That is, we move from one finger to another on a vibrato swing which is already headed in the direction we need to go. Our goal is to make the transfer from one finger to another with so much grace the listener has no idea that, as individual fingers, we refuse to vibrate on a stretched hand. She just hears some beautiful notes bound together to make a phrase.

4th Finger: Right! Of course, if we play double stops, that is a different matter.

Moderator: Playing double stops would make a great topic for our next convention! Thank you so much for an informative and interesting session.

INTERMISSION ENDS

7 Spotlight on Interpretation

Lo, the magic of interpretation! As though touched by a gilted wand, the lifeless black ink on the musical page becomes charged with life and reaches out to the hearts of people! Just as letters become syllables, syllables become words, words become sentences, and sentences become paragraphs, notes can be grouped, shaped, and colored by the performer to create a living language. Without this, music has no justification or meaning.

The following thirty-one Scenes are intended to be incorporated into the music the student is studying. They are suggestions as to ways the teacher can help the student gain an insight into making the music as expressive as possible. This, of course, is the ultimate goal.

SCENES FOR BETTER MUSIC MAKING

The Duke or the Clown
SCENE 155

Musical Setting: A melody

Teacher: "Suppose you are writing an opera or a musical. To which character would you assign this melody?

"Will the duke sing it? The clown? The young lover? The priest? The villain? The grieving nephew?"

After the student has selected the role, the teacher adds: "Picture that character complete with costumes and gestures as you play his song!"

Cue to Use

1. Anytime in the early study of a new composition.
2. Whenever the performance lacks style and personality.

Inner Drama

The most important element of any melody is the character. It determines the entire approach to the study of the music and should be identified early. The gestures used by the string player, especially in the bow arm, are chosen to match the mood of the music. It makes no sense to practice one set of gestures then change them later in the study. The clearer the final goal, the more direct is the route.

A Puzzle
SCENE 156

Before the lesson the teacher has written on a blackboard or paper the following letters:

elephantshavesixsetsofteethduringtheirlife timetheyneedsomanysetsbecausethefoodthey eatisverycoarse

"Can you make any sense out of this?"

After the word puzzle has been solved, the teacher explains: "Letters group together to form words. Words group together to form clauses and sentences. We do the same in music!

"How to group notes in music is not so clear cut. Sometimes one musician's grouping of notes will differ from another's. We call this 'interpretation.'

"However, one thing is for sure. We enjoy music the best when the notes fall into logical groups. No one wants to hear a series of single notes!"

Cue to Use

1. Anytime, except in the early training, the teacher wishes to emphasize the grouping of notes.
2. Whenever the student's performance sounds "notey."

Props

A blackboard or a paper prepared in advance.

Inner Drama

The grouping of notes is often what distinguishes the artist from a musician and the musician from a player. Some people have an uncanny ability to feel a logical grouping of notes which can reach the hearts of people. The teacher's primary goal in this scene is to trigger the student's thinking in this direction.

What? No Rehearsal!
SCENE 157

Musical Setting: A very rhythmic composition with a dance-like character

Teacher: "Bring out the rhythm of this piece so it is contagious!

"Watch how a stadium full of people can chant together! Without a single rehearsal strangers can stamp their feet in perfect ensemble!

"Good rhythm reaches everyone. Make your listeners feel it so much that they, too, want to move to the beat!"

Cue to Use

1. When the student's performance lacks rhythmic vitality.
2. Whenever an ensemble has difficulty in playing together.

Inner Drama

The capability of tens of thousands of football enthusiasts chanting and stamping together without lessons or rehearsals has proved to be a fascinating phenomenon to the teacher. If strangers with an infinite variety of social backgrounds, training, and occupations can feel the rhythm together so intensely, she asks why rhythm appears to be so difficult for some music students.

She believes that rhythm is in the core of all human beings. Through this scene she hopes to convince her students of its naturalness and its ability to unify a group of people. With the leadership of one person, total strangers in a concert hall can be brought together to form what appears to be a new living body with its own heartbeat. This body is called an audience.

A or B?
SCENE 158

Teacher: "Which do you like better? A or B?"

After the teacher sings or plays a phrase two ways and the student makes her choice, the teacher asks: "Why? What is the difference? . . . Now try playing it that way."

Cue to Use

Whenever the teacher does not like the student's phrasing.

Inner Drama

Often a student will play a musical phrase with an interpretation that does not seem desirable to the teacher. Perhaps the flow of the musical line is broken or stress is given to certain notes which the teacher considers relatively unimportant. Or, possibly, the student overlooked vibrating on an important note.

In this scene either A or B will be an imitation of the student's phrasing although it will not be labeled as such. The other performance will be closer to the teacher's ideal. Usually, when the student is able to listen objectively to someone else sing or play the music, her choice is quick and decisive. Thus, the teacher is able to convert the student to his phrasing by drawing on the student's own musical instincts.

A Big Fat O
SCENE 159

Teacher: "Picture the letter O—a big fat one! Let's say it—O. Notice how our lips form a circle. The air from our lungs seems to flow through a nice round tube. Shall we sing an O?

"Now, with our instruments let's search for that beautiful, round sound. I can almost feel an air column flowing from my back through a big round flexible hose to my hand and on to the bow. Even my vibrato feels freer. Listen for a round, full tone! Every part of the wood in your instrument will shiver!"

Cue to Use

Anytime to improve the student's tone, especially if it tends to have a thin, nasal, or strident quality.

Inner Drama

The teacher realizes that few goals in life are achieved accidentally. She believes that the very act of stating or affirming a goal is the first step toward achieving it. She feels that the main reason some string players have such extraordinarily beautiful tones is that their desire for them is strong.

The teacher's plan is to identify a worthy goal and to make positive suggestions toward attaining it. Who wants to listen to music performed on a stringed instrument if the sound is not beautiful?

The Magic of the Upbeat
SCENE 160

Musical Setting: A phrase beginning with an upbeat

Teacher: "The upbeat is like a giant hook! It reaches out and pulls us into the phrase. There is a magic to the upbeat!"

Cue to Use

Anytime to help give movement to a phrase beginning with an upbeat.

Inner Drama

The feeling of movement is one of the prime characteristics of a phrase played by an artist. One person can play a phrase that seems to move like a living thing. Another will play the same phrase at the same tempo but the feeling of motion is missing.

The teacher believes that the secret of the artist partially lies with the upbeat—not only the upbeat that is often found at the beginning of a phrase but also a note or group of notes within a phrase that simulates the energy of an upbeat and directs the movement forward to the following first beat. The suggestion of a hook in motion, especially when reinforced by the teacher's gesture, emphasizes the active quality of the anacrusis. It can be realized in string playing by a slight increase of the intensity in the vibrato and in the speed and pressure of the bow during the

note or group of notes identified as the upbeat. This signals to the listener that the phrase is moving on and seems to point to the direction. A successful upbeat in no way gives the impression that it could be the last note of the phrase. It is a real generator of motion in much serious music.

A Kaleidoscope of Colors
SCENE 161

Musical Setting: A note of long rhythmic duration

Teacher: "Let's make one long note a kaleidoscope of colors! Change the bow direction when you please. I will play an accompaniment with changing harmonies. Listen carefully to my part and keep varying your vibrato and bowing so one color melts into the next!

"Our colors may become lighter or darker, the tone louder or softer but one thing for sure, nothing will stay the same!

"Now let's play this long note in your piece. Give it life!"

Cue to Use

Anytime, after the student has a pleasing vibrato, that the music calls for one long sustained note.

Inner Drama

A characteristic of all life is that nothing stays the same for long. Some kind of action is continually going on. Air is exhaled and inhaled, the heart beats, the sap flows, the leaves rustle, the stream rushes on.

The teacher hopes to make the student aware that changing colors during a long sustained note is desirable. This keeps the music alive and, after all, giving life to the music is the ultimate goal.

Left hand and arm variables in making color changes include the portion of the finger tip or pad that contacts the string, the hand elevation, and the size and speed of the vibrato. Right hand and arm variables include the distance from the bridge that the bow hair contacts the string, the amount of bow hair used, the speed of the bow, the amount of pressure released through the bow to the string, and the character of the player's gestures.

The Beginning and the End
SCENE 162

Teacher: "Suppose I handed you a paper filled with words but there was not a single capital letter or punctuation mark on the page! Just one word after another! What would you do first?

"Right! Mark the beginning and the end of each sentence so the message would make sense! Every word belongs to a group. The question is to decide *which* group.

"We treat music the same way. First, we determine where a phrase begins and where it ends. Notes, like words, fit into groups. Let's do that now with our music."

Cue to Use

When the teacher feels it is appropriate to discuss phrasing.

Inner Drama

Without question the first step in shaping a beautiful phrase is to identify where it begins and where it ends. This is more difficult than it sounds when one looks only at a violin, viola, cello, or double bass solo part.

Unlike some other instrumental music in which the phrases are often clearly indicated, the string player's part is covered with bowing marks. The slurs in string music have usually been inserted by an editor along with his other bowing and fingering marks. They are his suggestions as to which notes are to be played in one direction of the bow.

It is not intended that the slur be interpreted as an audible grouping of notes. The fact is that, in order to mold a convincing phrase, the transition from the last note of a group of slurred notes to the first note of the next bow may need to be as smooth as the transition from one note to another within the slur. Disguising the bow changes audibly is often the goal in practicing. Thus, unless a musical phrase is preceded and followed by a rest, the printed page offers limited visual clues as to the beginning and the end of phrases.

The art of determining the grouping of notes has traditionally been passed on from teacher to student in a live teaching situation. Students who have the opportunity to hear concerts and recordings absorb the traditions and get the "feel" of phrasing faster than those without listening experiences. Hearing the piano part, if there is one, along with the string part is an absolute necessity since the harmonies, and most especially the cadences at the end of phrases, are the best cues of all. Fortunate, indeed, is the string student who has a parent or teacher who can play the piano with him in the early study of a new piece. The final decision about phrasing of any part in an ensemble should be postponed until the whole music is heard and studied unless one has a good model to imitate.

Pass the Peanut Butter
SCENE 163

Musical Setting: Two successive phrases, or fragments of a phrase, which are identical

Teacher: "Suppose at the supper table tonight you say, 'Please pass the peanut butter.' If you have reason to say it a second time, how would you say it?"

Time is given for the student to respond.

"Yes, there are many ways you could say it, ranging from a plea to a demand. But, one thing you can count on—the second time will be different from the first!"

Cue to Use

Whenever a student plays two identical phrases, or groups of notes, the same way.

Inner Drama

The teacher's goal is to stress a basic principle adhered to by all artists: a repeated phrase or motive is not played the same way the second time. Perhaps there is no better example of natural expressiveness than in the human speech under the most ordinary circumstances.

The possibilities of varying the nuances and intensity are virtually unlimited to the string player. Even a new bending of the phrase or molding of a note can communicate, as does the raising of a corner of a speaker's eyebrow. Not to be overlooked is the possible linking of two notes by a portamento, sometimes called a slide, although it is not marked in the music. This form of a glissando, if tastefully done and sparingly used, can add warmth and expression to a repeated phrase.

Special Words—Special Notes
SCENE 164

Musical Setting: A phrase in which certain notes to be brought out have already been identified

Teacher: "We can bring out notes by playing them louder. But there are also other ways—just as in speech there are different ways we bring out words.

"We can take a little more time on a note. For example: 'Waiting in line took *so-o-o* long.'

"A note can become important by making it softer than the surrounding notes. 'It was a *tender* moment.'

"A slight hesitation before playing a note can make it seem special. 'The sunset was absolutely (*pause*) beautiful.'

"Change is the important thing! Change something—the speed or width of the vibrato, the bow speed, the bow pressure, the amount of articulation, the timing—something! Make special words and special notes different than those which surround them!"

Cue to Use

Anytime, except in the very early training, to make the music more expressive.

Inner Drama

Language is the most universal form of human communication. In every language the communicator stresses certain words or syllables to make the communication tie between people stronger. Since stressing a word or musical note through increased volume is the most obvious method of highlighting special words or notes, the teacher's goal is to provide more tools for expression.

In his effort to help the student make the most of special notes, the teacher particularly is on the lookout for an anticipation. He believes that it offers the possibility for an unusually expressive moment and that, in many instances, it should sound more beautiful, more loved, and no softer than the longer note it anticipates.

The Prima Donna
SCENE 165

Musical Setting: A melody that requires a singing, expressive quality but is indicated p

Teacher: "Picture the prima donna of a Verdi opera when you practice this melody! In her long velvet dress she walks to center stage. As she opens her mouth, rich golden tones flow out to the top balcony.

"Don't worry about the *p* marking now. Play the melody big and expressively. You can easily cut it down to a solo *p* later."

Cue to Use

1. In the initial approach to almost any melodic phrase requiring a singing quality.
2. Anytime the student's playing sounds inhibited or lacks a carrying quality.

Inner Drama

The teacher's observation is that most string students are quick to obey the *p* markings because their orchestra directors have emphasized this. Obeying the dynamic indications is of paramount importance in all ensemble playing because of the need to balance the parts. However, from experience the teacher has found that it is far more effective in the initial study of a melody to change the overall dynamic markings of *mp*, *p*, or *pp* temporarily to *f* or *mf*.

When no restrictions are imposed, the musician is better able to discover the natural grouping of notes, a feeling for the shape of the phrase, and a love for the music. After the string player identifies with the melody and it has become meaningful to him, reducing it to a smaller scale is comparatively easy.

An added benefit is that the workability of the position and approach is checked. The act of playing forte on a stringed instrument without producing a strident, harsh sound is usually proof that the technical approach is correct. On the other hand, it is possible to produce soft, pleasing sounds when the power flow is blocked. Thus, a harmful habit could be established and the potential expressive power limited. The teacher's goal consistently is to make sure that there is no blockage so the student is able to play loud or soft as he desires and the music indicates, not because of technical limitations.

On occasion the teacher may wish to change the prima donna to a dramatic tenor.

The Needle of the Meter
SCENE 166

An imaginary fan-shaped meter is permanently installed on a wall of the studio or classroom. As she talks, the teacher points to the extreme sides of it and to the current location of the needle.

"Let's take a look at our meter! Today the far left side is labeled _____. The far right side has the word _____. (*The reader will find suggested labels at the end of this Scene.*) When you played that phrase, the needle was about in the center. Play it again and move the needle over farther to the left!"

As the teacher suggests that the needle be moved, she gestures with her own straight hand to imitate a quivering needle inching over toward the left.

Cue to Use

Whenever the teacher is tempted to use a negative word in describing a student's playing but desires to avoid it.

Inner Drama

The studio meter has two magical characteristics. First, the labels can be changed to meet any situation. Second, the teacher can use a negative word in order to make the message very clear, yet she has not insulted the student's playing. Thus, there is no reason for the student to identify his own playing with the unpleasant word.

The observing parent or teacher soon learns that people tend to live up to the image associated with them. The child who has been labeled "neat" seldom has to be told to hang up his clothes. The "punctual" person is almost never late. The "average" person remains average. Since most musicians and music students have a very personal identification with their playing, the attachment of negative labels during a music lesson is definitely something to avoid.

The possibilities for labels of the extreme sides of the meter are virtually unlimited. Though many times the descriptive pair of words will have a positive/negative connotation, this is not always the case. Some suggested labels are ele-

gant/coarse, serious/carefree, frisky/sleepy, easy/labored, mellow/harsh, graceful/clumsy, bold/cautious, silky/rough, dancing/sluggish, pompous/humble, velvet/sandpaper, elegant/rugged.

Energizing Music
SCENE 167

Musical Setting: A phrase that needs to sound more energetic

Teacher: "Listen! I will say the same sentence two times at the same loudness and at the same speed."

The teacher recites a sentence such as "The University of Texas at Austin is an exciting and dynamic place!" The first time he says it clearly but with no accents. The second time he gives accents and spurts of energy at the beginning of some of the words.

"What is the difference?"

The students will soon discover that the accents and spurts of energy dramatically changed the sentence so it became charged with energy.

"The same is true with music! Sometimes we string players cannot play as loudly as we would like. Our instruments can never sound as loud as a brass instrument, piano, or pipe organ. But we can always energize the music through extra spurts of energy and bow speed at the beginning of some notes. This gives the impression that we are playing louder when we have already been playing as loudly as we can!"

Cue to Use

Anytime, except in the very early training, the teacher wishes to help energize the student's performances and to add contrast.

Inner Drama

The teacher has the impression that in each decade more new concert halls are made larger and that there are more concert grand pianos in use. Yet, the string player is equipped with a beautiful, sensitive instrument which has changed very little over the past few hundred years.

Though the volume of the string tone can increase as the string student progresses, limitations are always present. With the method of energizing described in this scene, the impression of greater power can be conveyed to the audience.

Painting a Picture with Sound
SCENE 168

Musical Setting: A long diminuendo on one bow stroke

Teacher: "Picture standing in the middle of a long straight road and looking off at a distance. Its outside boundaries grow closer and closer together until they finally come together. It is like the symbol used for a diminuendo.

"Now let's paint the picture with sound. Begin loud enough that you will have somewhere to go! Gradually suspend your arm weight and slow down the bow. At the same time tilt the stick away from the bridge so fewer hairs touch the string.

"Your vibrato will become smaller and quieter so it matches the vibrations of the string. The road fades to nothing at all."

Cue to Use

Anytime after the vibrato is well established and the teacher thinks that the student is ready to play a beautiful diminuendo. It can be modified for a crescendo.

Inner Drama

The teacher believes that producing a carefully graduated diminuendo is a learnable skill as are

most other skills in making music. She does not stress this early in the training, however, because she prefers to avoid the required suspension of live weight until the tone is well developed and the technique secure.

At some point the teacher will explain to the student that not all diminuendos marked in the music should go to nothing. Many times the composer uses this symbol to indicate an inflection or a slackening off of volume. Dropping to nothing in the middle of a phrase would spoil the contour and make no sense out of the musical line.

The opposite expressive device, known as a crescendo, is made by adding energy through increasing both the speed and pressure of the bow to get the string to vibrate wider. The bigger the spin, the bigger the volume. As the width of the string vibration increases, the vibrato, too, should become wider so the tone will not become strident. Learning to make a big crescendo with a down-bow takes more concentration than an up-bow crescendo, but it pays high dividends in expressive music making.

The Invisible Orchestra
SCENE 169

Teacher: "Suppose you have your own ninety-piece orchestra! Conduct this phrase so the musicians will play it exactly the way you feel it!"

As the student conducts, he and the teacher sing.

"Good! Now use the same convincing gestures when you bow."

Cue to Use

1. When the student's playing lacks expression due to inexpressive gestures.
2. When the student's gestures do not match the mood of the music.

Inner Drama

The gestures used by an expressive conductor and an expressive string player are surprisingly similar. Through trying to communicate to his invisible orchestra, the student is able to disassociate himself from any existing problems or distractions. Observations about the conducting motions can be made. With their transferral to bowing, often a more expressive style is immediately apparent. Who would dare to conduct a ninety-piece orchestra in a boring manner?

Specialist in What?
SCENE 170

Musical Setting: A rest of long duration

Teacher: "Remember, a rest on a page of music is not an accident! The composer put it there for a reason!

"Imagine a long rest being interviewed. When asked about his occupation, his answer would be, 'I'm a specialist in dramatic silences.'

"Hold your audience during long rests! Move your body as little as possible. Silence and stillness go hand in hand."

Cue to Use

Anytime the student appears busy or restless during a long rest.

Inner Drama

The teacher has observed the manner in which artists can hold their audiences spellbound during a rest. He believes that moments of silence are an integral part of music and can add repose, suspense, and drama to a performance. The teacher's goal is to help the student learn to respect the potential expressive power of what appears to be nothing at all!

The Little Man in the Back Row
SCENE 171

Musical Setting: Two successive notes of the same pitch

Teacher: "Think of the little man in the back row of the audience! Be sure he hears that there are two distinctly separate notes. Stop the sound of the first note a bit early or make a diminuendo. Bring in the second one with a fresh start!

"If the composer had wanted one long note, you can be sure he wouldn't have bothered to write two!"

Cue to Use

Anytime, except in the very early training, notes are repeated at the same pitch.

Inner Drama

The sustained tone is one of the most attractive features of a bowed instrument. Unlike a piano or harp, an instrument which uses a bow can make the end of a note as loud or louder than its beginning. Thus, it is possible to play amazingly legato. However, this should not be the goal in the execution of repeated notes—a situation which demands articulation.

If the second note is to be played with the correct rhythm, setting the stage for its entry must come during the time value of the first note. A number of possible methods of finishing the first note include: diminish the volume by lightening the bow pressure, guide the bow off the string

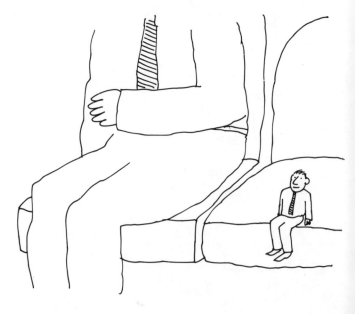

like an airplane on a runway, bounce or lift it off the string, or stop it on the string. Also, changes in the size and speed of vibrato or in the bow speed can help make a difference between the end of the first note and the beginning of the second. Separation by silence or contrast is the secret of sending two notes, not one, to the listener in the back row.

A Baffling Situation
SCENE 172
(Especially effective for groups)

Musical Setting: A simple piece of a march-like character in which articulation is a must, preferably one unfamiliar to the students

Teacher: "Let's read this piece, making it as smooth as possible."

After the performance, the teacher remarks: "Something just doesn't seem right! . . . Let's try humming it. They say it is good for instrumentalists to sing."

But, after the humming, the teacher again appears puzzled and dissatisfied. "Let's try humming it loud and fast! Maybe that will give it more life. . . ."

Again disappointment is expressed. "Something seems missing. . . . Let's try singing on 'oh.' That should make it sound better."

But again the teacher is disappointed. He continues by leading the singing of the piece on "ah," then on "e-e."

"What possibly could be wrong? Nothing seems to sound right!"

Undoubtedly, one of the students will suggest that the notes need articulation although that term may not actually be used.

"Good idea! Let's sing this piece using the word 'dough.' . . . Wow! It sounds great! Now, let's try the word 'toe.' . . . That adds even more energy! . . . Try 'ko.'"

Immediately following each singing performance the students will play the opening phrases on their instruments, searching out just the right amount of bow articulation to match the articulation of the words. Preferences will be expressed.

"What have we learned from this? . . . Many musical phrases sound beautiful when they are played smoothly but others need more articulation. Articulation adds energy!

"Our language consists of both vowels and consonants. The consonants provide the articulation as well as make many more words possible. Our expressive powers would be limited, indeed, if we spoke only in vowels!

"This piece demands a generous dose of consonants. Let's examine another piece and decide how it should be articulated."

Cue to Use

Anytime the teacher wishes to stress the need for articulation and has time in the lesson or class for such an approach. It was not designed for the very young student.

Inner Drama

The approach described in this scene can be stimulating to a class of students, particularly of junior and senior high age. Many students are attracted to puzzle solving and take pride in finding solutions. It can offer a welcomed change to the established routine. One can expect that such an episode is not forgotten quickly and may possibly influence a student for many years.

Surprise!
SCENE 173

Musical Setting: A phrase repeated several times in a composition; however, one time some notes are changed

Teacher: "This phrase starts like the others but it changes! What is the difference?"

After the differences are pointed out, the teacher adds: "Suppose we said, 'The tree is green . . . the tree is green . . . the tree is a *wonderful living thing.*'

"Bring out the new notes as we did the new words. Don't let them slip past unnoticed. Perhaps use a little faster bow or more intensity in the vibrato? Just when the listener thinks she knows what you are going to say, surprise her!"

Cue to Use

Anytime there is a change in a phrase which has been repeated several times in a composition.

Inner Drama

Most music has repetitive phrases although they are not necessarily consecutive. The wise interpreter performs the music in a manner that makes the organization of notes and phrases as clear as possible to the listener. This organization is called the *form* of music.

The reader may wish to refer to *Special Words—Special Notes*, Scene 164, and *A Kalei-*

doscope of Colors, Scene 161, at this time for suggestions as to various means of bringing out certain notes.

Jody
SCENE 174

Musical Setting: A succession of two-note slurs in which the second note of each group is the same pitch as the first note of the following group

The teacher sings the passage using a two-syllable name for each two-note slur. For example, "Jo-dy, Jo-dy, Jo-dy."

"Bring out the first note louder than the second! During the second note, make a quick diminuendo. Release some of the first finger pressure on the bow stick and slow down the motion. This will help each group to stand out like a name!"

Cue to Use

Anytime to make musical sense out of a sequence of two-note slurs found in the Musical Setting described above. It can also be used for an appoggiatura or a suspension.

Inner Drama

Most two-syllable words which have the stress on the first syllable will work in this scene. Some words invite a more beautiful resonance than others; however, a student's name, such as Karen, Sarah, Kristin, Carol, Laura, Debbie, or Julie, will serve the purpose and can add a personal touch to the lesson.

The initial practice of détaché porté bow strokes of the same durational value as required by the two-note slurs helps. After the student gains a feel for the pulsing-type action, the second note can be added by the left hand. It is possible to give the feeling of separation between the groups without actually stopping the bow. Although the bow changes may look smooth and the motion continuous, the groups will sound separated because of the diminuendo on each second note.

Using one vibrato impulse on the first note, allowing it to carry through to the second note, adds further expression. Thus, the vibrato is recharged at the beginning of each group and the left hand will feel slurred. Devising a fingering in which the shifts are made between the groups also helps.

After the student learns to play the series of two-note units effectively, the teacher will encourage her to mold the entire phrase into a good contour. The reader is advised to refer to *Lost Slur*, Scene 134, and *A Dynamic Landscape*, Scene 175, at this time.

Appoggiaturas and suspensions can be power packed with expression when the player leans on the nonharmonic tone. *Jody* can help with the inflections in these, too.

A Dynamic Landscape
SCENE 175

Musical Setting: A melodic phrase

Teacher: "Suppose you are an artist and you have been asked to give your interpretation of the dynamics of this phrase in the form of a landscape. How would you draw the horizon? As a mountain sloping up one side and down the other? A series of small hills, each one a bit higher? A steady incline going right to the end? A decline. . . ?

"Just don't draw the horizon of a Kansas wheatfield! It, of course, has its own golden beauty but does not make a good phrase. Give each musical phrase an interesting dynamic contour!"

Cue to Use

Anytime the teacher feels that the student is mature enough to understand the concept of molding a phrase without using a model. The very young, of course, learn best by imitation.

Props

The teacher may wish to have a pad and pencil in hand when talking about the shape of a phrase. It can be helpful to sing while drawing. As the line unfolds, the phrase takes on a special meaning.

Inner Drama

Concert artists do not always agree on the dynamic contour of a phrase and, in fact, tend to seek out individuality. However, it appears that almost all agree that a phrase should be shaped dynamically and that the contour does not always follow the pitch line. They also agree that a phrase should have a definite arrival point toward which the music flows, then moves away, much like inhalation and exhalation. This variety of interpretation keeps music alive. No performance is an exact replica of another and none should be boring.

En-cy-clo-pe-di-a
SCENE 176

Musical Setting: Several consecutive notes of equal durational value, for example, four or more quarter notes, eighth notes, or sixteenth notes

The teacher starts telling a story in which he uses a number of large words well known to the students. With each multisyllabic word he gives equal stress to every syllable, as though the word were spoken by a robot. Despite the jerky, machine-like quality, he tries not to slow down on the selected words and takes special care to make the remainder of each sentence flow. An example follows:

"When I was a student at the *un-i-ver-si-ty*, I consulted the *en-cy-clo-pe-di-a* often. It has a wealth of information about almost everything, varying from the *rhi-noc-er-os*, to *Na-po-le-on Bo-na-parte*, to *re-fri-ger-a-tors*.

"Why are you laughing? Is this *ri-di-cu-lous*?"

With the teacher's guidance the students will discover that one reason long words sound so fluent in normal speech is that one impulse—one spurt of energy—makes several syllables. Even when the principal accent is in the middle or near the end of a word, the speaker feels that the word rolls off his tongue and that he does not have to recharge each syllable.

"Note the difference! Let's pronounce each word both ways but try to keep the same tempo. *Un-i-ver-si-ty*: university. *En-cy-clo-pe-di-a*: encyclopedia. . . .

"And notice how we bring out one or two syllables much more than the others! Now play this group of notes so it sounds like one long word, not four or five individual syllables. . . . Good! Talk through your instrument!"

Cue to Use

Anytime a group of notes, such as those described in the Musical Setting, sound more like notes than music and lack a feeling of movement.

Inner Drama

The teacher has witnessed dramatic improvement in a student's performance after an explanation such as the one depicted in this scene. He believes that most people are innately musical but that some need a little more guidance than others in transforming notes into music. Reducing the number of impulses and adding life-giving inflections can do wonders.

Apparently no infallible all-purpose rule exists to help either a student or a professional in determining which notes to bring out. Some musicians find it helpful to sing the music with as much feeling as possible, then analyze which notes were instinctively stressed. Others move or dance to the music to determine its natural music flow. Some "try, try again," first placing the emphasis on one note, then another. They cull those that do not sound right until the possibilities of choice are narrowed, then eventually make a decision. Often it takes weeks or months of "living" with the music and, even then, the decision can change with a flash of insight. The musician may feel a phrase differently today than yesterday. And who knows what tomorrow will bring?

This lack of standardized interpretation is what makes a musical performance a creative art. Any convincing interpretation comes from within the player and can be dictated by the heart at the moment.

At the Composer's Desk
SCENE 177

Musical Setting: A trill

Teacher: "Suppose you are a composer and this is your composition. You are sitting at a desk working on your manuscript.

"Why did you write 'tr' above that note? Were you trying to make it more exciting with a trill? Suspenseful? Or did you simply want to dress up the note with something very beautiful?"

After the student has made her decision the teacher continues: "Good! Give it that character! A trill played dutifully and mechanically is disappointing to both you and the listener. Give it a reason to be there!"

Cue to Use

Anytime a student plays a trill in a lifeless, mechanical manner. With modifications it can also be used with other ornaments, such as a grace note, a turn, or a mordent.

Inner Drama

The teacher believes that there is no better way to gain an understanding than to put oneself into the role of another individual. He is mindful of the Indian prayer: "Grant that I may not criticize my neighbor until I have walked a mile in his moccasins."

Though the subject of criticism is not the one at hand, the student's visualization of herself as the composer should give her insight helpful in working toward an effective interpretation.

The Thumb and the Tongue
SCENE 178

Musical Setting: Music which has on the string bowing that needs articulation

Teacher: "I think this music needs more articulation. How do you say 'T'?"

The students soon discover that the tongue presses against the alveolar ridge just back of the upper teeth. When it releases suddenly, there is a tiny explosion of sound resulting in a "T."

"To make a T-sound with the bow, push the thumb up against the bow stick toward the first finger as if you were pinching it. The T-sound comes on the sudden release of counter-pressure. The *thumb* is to bowing what the *tongue* is to speech!"

Cue to Use

Whenever the teacher wants the student to become more aware of articulation.

Inner Drama

The use of a plosive consonant in this scene is an example of the teacher's fascination with the relationship between music and speech and the application of everyday life principles to the playing of a stringed instrument. He believes that string teachers have barely begun to explore these areas and that many new discoveries will be made by future generations. Ideally, not only will the standards of string playing be raised to new heights but also the time spent in learning to play these beautiful instruments will be shortened.

Although the teacher recognizes that repetition is necessary in acquiring any manual skill, he believes that often more hours than are necessary have been used because of a lack of knowledge and advancement in string pedagogy. Time, after all, is the most precious of all commodities.

J. R. Is—
SCENE 179

Musical Setting: Two consecutive phrases which are almost identical, but the second has more notes

Teacher: "This is an add-a-note phrase! We have lots of add-a-word sentences! 'It is nice. It is *very* nice.' 'The chili is hot. The chili is *piping* hot!'"

As she continues, the teacher signals for the students to complete each second sentence.

"The pumpkin pie is delicious. The pumpkin pie . . . The puppy is hungry. The puppy . . . J. R. is mean. J. R. is . . .

"We always bring out the added word! The same is true in music. The new notes add interest to the phrase!"

Cue to Use

Anytime to make the Musical Setting described above more expressive.

Inner Drama

Through this scene the teacher helps the student to become aware of the form and structure of music and its relationship to another communication device called speech. Whether notes are added or simply changed, the differences are usually stressed.

For ideas about methods of bringing out notes the reader may wish to refer to *Special Words—Special Notes*, Scene 164, at this time.

Wake Up a Sleeping String
SCENE 180

Musical Setting: A note beginning a phrase marked p *or* pp

Teacher: "Move the bow a little faster at the beginning of the stroke when starting this soft note, then slow it down.

"Think of it this way. The string is just lying there asleep. To make a beautiful sound it must vibrate freely. Something has to convince it to start spinning. Move the bow lightly but fast enough that the string knows exactly what it is supposed to do!"

Cue to Use

Whenever a soft note does not speak or has a poor tone quality, possibly due to lack of free vibrations.

Inner Drama

Since piano or pianissimo notes are played with light bow strokes in a lane near the fingerboard, sometimes not enough energy is transmitted to the string to activate it. The teacher has observed that a bow stroke that does not sound good at the beginning seldom improves as it continues. The initial triggering of the vibrating string is by far the most important part of the bow stroke. It is impossible to color the tone and make it expressive if the string hasn't started to vibrate. There is simply nothing there with which to work.

Naturally the student may overreact to the advice in this scene and start the bow too fast. This could result in either too loud a volume or a surface-like sound. If so, adjustments can be made. Exaggeration of the teacher's advice is all part of learning. There is no need to be embarrassed because one responds too well to instructions!

The Purple Cow
SCENE 181

Musical Setting: A phrase or group of notes repeated consecutive times, either at the same pitch or sequentially at different pitches; in its third appearance the phrase is extended

Teacher: "Suppose I say, 'The purple cow is over there. The purple cow is over there. The purple cow is over there in the pasture.'"

As the teacher talks, she gestures.

"Did you notice how I made the words flow onward in the third statement? The word *there* became the link to the words *in the pasture*. You knew that I was not going to stop and start all over again.

"Let's hear you play these three phrases again. Bind the last long phrase together. Which note will serve as the link? Sustain that tone with your bow, perhaps even make a crescendo, and keep your vibrato alive. Signal to the listener that you have more to say!"

Cue to Use

Anytime to make the phrases or group of notes described in the Musical Setting clearer and more meaningful.

Inner Drama

The teacher recognizes that consciously or unconsciously the listener tries to organize sounds to make sense. Once a pattern is established, such as pausing two times after the word *there* in the above example, one expects a pause the third time. Thus, most speakers would make an effort to show that the phrase is not finished. In music the pausing or lessening of volume the third time would make four phrases instead of three and the music would likely sound choppy.

The possibilities of helping the music student in interpretation by relating the spoken language to music appear to be virtually unlimited.

The Ghost Upbeat
SCENE 182

Musical Setting: A phrase that begins on the first beat of a measure

Teacher: "Every phrase has a ghost upbeat whether it appears to be there or not! Picture a conductor lifting his baton during an upbeat. Your music will become more expressive!"

Cue to Use

Anytime a student's playing sounds blocky.

Inner Drama

The teacher is a great believer in the magic of the upbeat. He is convinced that the conductor's baton rising before the downbeat does far more than serve as a preparatory motion to get the ensemble to commence together. He feels that it creates a feeling of movement so vital in a music performance.

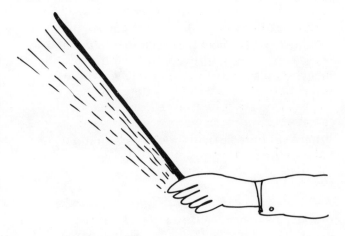

For some years the teacher has observed that string students often sound more musical when playing in an excellent orchestra than in a solo performance. He believes that some of this is not solely due to the superior interpretative ability of the conductor or the fact that a group of stringed instruments tend to sound richer than one. It is his impression that the movement of the conductor's arm and baton is mirrored in the string player's right arm and bow motions. Picturing the ghost upbeat helps the player to know how to play the first note. It also tends to free her motions.

Peter Piper Picked
SCENE 183

Musical Setting: A fast passage or, most especially, a fast run

Teacher: "True or false? . . . *When we speak faster, it becomes more important to make every syllable clear and distinct.* . . . If you are not sure of your answer, let's do some research!"

The teacher suggests that a student go to the far end of the room and make a statement, preferably something with many consonants, such as "Peter Piper picked a peck of pickled peppers."

"Good! Now say it twice as fast!"

The student will soon discover that good enunciation and articulation are essential to make fast-spoken messages understandable. If the student is not able to say it quickly and clearly, the teacher can advise:

"Practice saying it slowly, emphasizing the beginning of every syllable. Spit out the consonants! Soon you will be able to make it clear and distinct.

"The same is true in music! When we play fast, we must be very sure that each individual note stands out. Let's return now to your music and practice making the beginning of every note super clear!"

Cue to Use

Whenever more articulation is needed in fast passages.

Inner Drama

Any musician can testify that many hours of practice have been devoted to making fast notes distinct and clear to the back row listener. The player who makes every note stand out is usually commended for her technique. However, when

this characteristic is missing, the technique is generally regarded as lacking in development.

If one considers that every note has a beginning, a middle, and an end, only the beginning of a note of very short duration is heard unless it is followed by a rest. By the time the string responds, the next note is being played. Thus, if the beginning is not audible, there is no note. When the responsibility lies with the left hand, a tapping action of the fingers can help with articulation.

As in most other things, exceptions in articulation can be made. The interpreter may choose to have some blurring of notes in order to create a special mood or effect. Typical examples can be found in impressionistic music. In most music, however, clarity is looked on as an admirable trait.

Mouse House
SCENE 184

Teacher: "Some words start with a little explosion of energy, then they are on their own! WOW! . . . HEY! . . . HI! . . . Now you say them. . . . Notice how the air shoots out of your mouth. Your work is over!

"Other words are created by an ongoing process. Say MOUSE HOUSE. . . . Notice how the air seems to move around in your mouth.

"If our music is to sound as though it has lyrics, we need various kinds of words. We already have Rodgers—now we need Hammerstein! Let's experiment with these sounds on our instruments."

Cue to Use

Whenever the teacher feels the student is sophisticated enough musically to be interested in experimenting with the various nuances in sound.

Inner Drama

With the mouse house–type notes the player will continue to refuel the bow stroke by pulling and creating more resistance as it journeys across the string. In the WOW!-type notes the player releases the energy and the bow travels across the string on its own momentum with little reinforcement from the player. It coasts, yet the motion is not necessarily ballistic and fast moving as in martelé bowing, nor does it always begin with a noticeable accent. Often the WOW!-type note is a single-note introduction to a composition.

Naturally there are many words and notes which do not fit into either of these two categories, but looking for places in the music to use them can be fun. Besides, they certainly aid in humanizing the music!

The Reluctant Farewell

SCENE 185

Musical Setting: A diminuendo on the last note of a movement or composition

Teacher: "The artist adds a final touch of drama to his closing diminuendo. He leaves the tip of the bow on the string for a moment after all motion ceases. Everything is still. Then, leading with the wrist, he slowly lifts the frog end of the bow. The tip is the last to move as though it is reluctant to leave the string it loves so much."

Cue to Use

Anytime, except very early in the training, that the teacher feels that an emphasis on a closing diminuendo is appropriate.

Inner Drama

The teacher believes that the performer is obligated, within limits, to provide a visual aspect of a performance which matches the mood of the music. A hasty lifting of the bow after a long diminuendo can spoil a magic moment for the person whose eyes are focused on the musician. In fact, any quick gesture at such a moment can have a jarring effect. At the appropriate time, silence and stillness are sacred partners.

THE CURTAIN DROPS

8 Closing Notes

The houselights go on as the curtain drops. *The String Play* is over but tomorrow it all begins again.

What makes this drama a never-ending production? Other plays eventually close even after a record-making number of performances. Why does this one go on and on?

- THE STRING PLAY is built on time-honored values.

- Its plot centers on people helping other people through music.

- Its theme is the realization of the enormous potential of the human mind and body, neither of which was designed by humans.

- Each act is one of re-creation; yet every generation has the potential to far surpass the preceding one.

- Each scene is grounded on the faith and conviction of the worth of the overall goal.

- Its spotlight focuses on the beauty in the hearts and minds of both the performers and the listeners.

- Its platform is built on the strength of the ageless columns called learning, giving, and sharing.

- This is the drama of love.

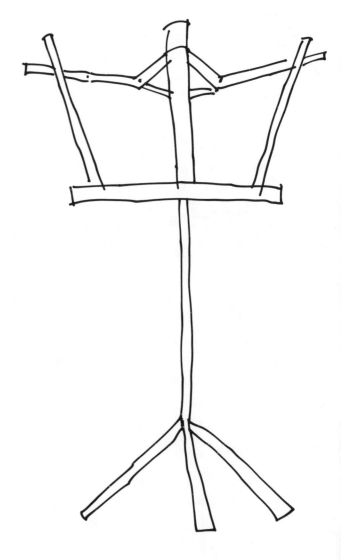

Cue Sheets

The suggested scenes listed after each cue are generally in the order of their relevancy. In some instances the exact words of the cue will not be found in the scene.

1. WORD CUES RELATED TO BOWING

Accented détaché
   18. Boom-m-m
      Also see 136, 21, and 148.

Accents
      See Cue Sheet 6: *Accents.*

Alignment of the hand and arm
   14. Salting a Sweet Potato
    6. Kangaroos and Roadrunners
      Also see 19, 52, 40, 31, and 9.

Angle of the bow
   16. Focus Here!
   22. Colorful Skyways
      Also see 9, 133, 31, 6, 55, and 144.

Arm level
      See this Cue Sheet: *String Crossings; Elbow.*

Articulated notes within one bow direction
   36. Poking Balloons
  140. Three Look-Alikes
   39. Dear Gabby

Articulation
      See Cue Sheet 6: *Articulation.*

Balanced action
    3. Scrubbies
   47. Take a Holiday!
      Also see 14 and 144.

Ballistic action
   11. Shooting Arrows
    6. Kangaroos and Roadrunners
      Also see this Cue Sheet: *Martelé.*

Beginning of the bow stroke
   12. Five Dollars for the First Inch
  180. Wake Up a Sleeping String
  183. Peter Piper Picked
      Also see 16, 29, 31, 42, and 178.

Bow as an extension of the arm
   43. Leaving Fingerprints on the String
    1. Coconut Cream Pie

Bow changes
      See this Cue Sheet: *Legato bowing.*

Bow distribution
    8. Spotlight on Bowing
    4. A Pattern
   20. Glow in the Dark
      Also see 27 and 151.

Bow hold
  111. Campaign Promises
      Also see 52, 24, 32, and 132.
      Also see this Cue Sheet: *Touch.*

Flexibility in the hand and fingers
108. A Prisoner of One Tight Joint
  7. Spreading Mayonnaise
 82. Putty Hands
 24. Go Ahead—We'll Catch Up!
 35. Suntan Oil and Contact Paper
 41. Garden Gloves
     Also see 9 and 85.

Fluidity of motion
 99. Rusty Knees, Rusty Elbows
 85. Straight Lines from Arcs?
     Also see this Cue Sheet: *Flexibility in the hand and fingers.*

Flying spiccato
140. Three Look-Alikes

Flying staccato
140. Three Look-Alikes
     Also see 132.

Focus
 16. Focus Here!
 30. A Hunk of Cheese
 31. Mary Poppins Landings
 33. Pouring Maple Syrup
     Also see this Cue Sheet: *Sounding point.*

Fouetté
136. Mail Order Accents
     Also see 137.

Grand détaché
148. A Miniseries Documentary

Harmonics
138. Cloned
     Also see Cue Sheet 3: *Harmonics.*

"Hooked" bowing
 25. Two for the Price of One!

Jerky motions
 21. The Archer Takes Time

Jeté
140. Three Look-Alikes

Legato bowing
 17. Pea Soup
  7. Spreading Mayonnaise
 37. Ships at Sea
 24. Go Ahead—We'll Catch Up!
 41. Garden Gloves
     Also see 162 and 137.

Louré
130. Kneading Bread Dough

 40. Give It a Heartbeat!
     Also see 135, 134, and 137.

Martelé
 11. Shooting Arrows
 29. The Race Horse
 34. Hurry Up and Wait!
 42. Pea Pod
 21. The Archer Takes Time
146. The Case of the Missing Bowing
     Also see 148, 135, 136, 18, 39, 119, and 137.

Monotony in bowing
 37. Ships at Sea
 20. Glow in the Dark

Off the string bowings
114. The String and I

On the string bowings
114. The String and I

Paintbrush type stroke
 24. Go Ahead—We'll Catch Up!
 41. Garden Gloves

Passive hand
 35. Suntan Oil and Contact Paper

Patterning
  4. A Pattern

Persistent bowing flaw
 97. Self-Correcting Ears

Personality in the bow stroke
 28. The Thud and the Bounce
     Also see this Cue Sheet: *Expressive gestures.*

Piqué
 25. Two for the Price of One!

Placing and lifting the bow
 31. Mary Poppins Landings
 16. Focus Here!

Ponticello
149. Sul Who?
     Also see 135 and 137.

Portato
     See this Cue Sheet: *Louré.*

Power flow
 14. Salting a Sweet Potato
 19. A Good Bridge
 35. Suntan Oil and Contact Paper
 40. Give It a Heartbeat!
     Also see 9, 33, 165, and 130.

Also see this Cue Sheet: *Ratio of the speed, weight, and distance from the bridge.*

Whipped stroke
See this Cue Sheet: *Fouetté.*

Wrist
19. A Good Bridge

2. VIDEO AND AUDIO CUES SIGNALING SPECIAL NEED IN BOWING

Does the tone sound hard? Do the fingers appear rigid or inflexible?
35. Suntan Oil and Contact Paper
Also see Cue Sheet 1: *Flexibility in the hand and fingers;* Cue Sheet 3: *Tone; Vibrato.*

Is the thumb not opposite the second finger? Or does it appear tight? Or caved in?
See Cue Sheet 1: *Thumb; Bow hold.*

Does the hand grip the bow tightly? Does the tone lack sensitivity?
See Cue Sheet 1: *Touch.*

Do the finger joints collapse?
See Cue Sheet 3: *Strengthening the hands.*

Does the wrist appear rigid or collapsed?
19. A Good Bridge

When playing fast separate bows, do the elbow and upper arm move in the same direction as the hand and bow? Does the music sound labored?
23. The Ladybug Ride
47. Take a Holiday!
Also see Cue Sheet 1: *Balanced action.*

Does the arm get tired from playing?
See Cue Sheet 1: *Tired arm.*

Does the bowing motion, in general, lack fluidity?
See Cue Sheet 1: *Fluidity of motion; Flexibility in the hand and fingers.*

Does the arm appear to move in an unnatural manner?
4. A Pattern

Does it appear that the tip is not in the student's control?
See Cue Sheet 1: *Control of the tip.*

Is the sound surfacey? Does the bow slide around on the string so the distance between the bridge and the contact point varies for no apparent musical reason?
See Cue Sheet 1: *Contact with the string; Distance from the bridge; Sounding point; Focus.*

Does the student play in one part of the bow most of the time? Does the bowing appear sluggish?
See Cue Sheet 1: *Speed of the bow; Bow distribution; Equal volume in all parts of the bow.*

Does it appear that possibly the hand and arm are not properly aligned? Does the power line from the player's back appear to be broken? Is the tone not large and full?
See Cue Sheet 1: *Alignment of the hand and arm; Tone building; Power flow; Weight.*

Does the tone sound weak in certain parts of the bow? Particularly at the tip?
See Cue Sheet 1: *Equal volume in all parts of the bow; Pronation; Focus.*

Does the student lack awareness of the ratio between pressure and speed and their relationship to the sounding point? Does the tone lack quality?
See Cue Sheet 1: *Ratio of the speed, weight, and distance from the bridge.*

Do the notes not sound clear?
See Cue Sheet 6: *Articulation; Consonants.*

Does the student need help in finding the proper angle of the bow and position of the arm on a particular string? Does the tone lack a ringing quality on this string?
See Cue Sheet 1: *Angle of the bow; Placing and lifting the bow; Routes of the bow.*

Does the student need help with string crossings?
See Cue Sheet 1: *String crossings.*

Does the student treat the thickest string the same as a thinner string?
117. Go on a Diet

Does he have a problem with a rhythmic pattern, bow distribution, or the shape of a bow stroke?
8. Spotlight on Bowing
4. A Pattern

Does he need help in articulating two or more notes in one bow direction?
See Cue Sheet 1: *Articulated notes within one bow direction.*

Does he appear to be using excessive or restrictive motion?
See Cue Sheet 1: *Size of the motion.*

Does a dotted rhythmic figure lack vitality?
25. Two for the Price of One!

Do the student's eyes focus on the bow hold most of the time?
See Cue Sheet 1: *Watching the bow.*
Also see 16, 9, and 1.

Does the string fail to respond at the beginning of a bow stroke?
See Cue Sheet 1: *Beginning of the bow stroke.*

Are the changes in bow direction rough? Or is the melodic line broken because there is a lack of sustaining quality?
See Cue Sheet 1: *Legato bowing; Pulling action; Control of the tip.*

Does the bowing lack personality? Is there not enough variety?
See Cue Sheet 1: *Personality in the bow stroke; Expressive gestures.*

Does the style of the preparatory motion fail to forecast the mood of the music?
See Cue Sheet 1: *Preparation.*

When the bow stroke is partially on the string and partially off, does the motion fail to keep the same character throughout? Does the tone fail to ring?
119. A True Marcel Marceau

Does the student tend to run out of bow on long slow strokes?
See Cue Sheet 1: *Slow bow strokes.*

Is there a need to emphasize better ensemble playing?
See Cue Sheet 6: *Ensemble precision.*

Does it take several notes for the student to get into a passage which requires a different style of bowing than the previous passage?
28. The Thud and the Bounce
91. The Dark Window

Does the tone lack a variety in colors?
See Cue Sheet 6: *Variety of tone colors.*
Also see Cue Sheet 1: *Monotony in bowing; Speed of the bow.*

Do the harmonics fail to speak clearly?
138. Cloned

Is there a persistent flaw in the sound that the student obviously is not hearing?
97. Self-Correcting Ears

Does the student need help with specific kinds of bowing?
See Cue Sheet 1: *Accented détaché; Collé; Col legno; Combined staccato; Détaché; Détaché lancé; Détaché porté; Expressive détaché; Flautando or flautato; Flying spiccato; Flying staccato; Fouetté; Grand détaché; "Hooked" bowing; Jeté; Legato bowing; Louré; Martelé; Piqué; Ponticello; Portato; Rapid détaché; Ricochet; Sautillé; Simple détaché; Slurred staccato; Spiccato; Staccato; Staccato volante; Sulla tastiera; Sul tasto; Sur la touche; Tremolo; and Whipped stroke.*

3. WORD CUES RELATED TO THE LEFT HAND

Accents
136. Mail Order Accents
66. The Man on the Flying Trapeze

Alignment of hand, wrist, and arm
See this Cue Sheet: *Shape of the hand, wrist, and arm.*

Angle of the hand
68. Shock Absorbers

Arch of the hand
See this Cue Sheet: *Base knuckles.*

Articulation
183. Peter Piper Picked

Artificial harmonics
141. Diamond-Shaped Notes

Balance
74. Walking Forward
75. Walking Backward
76. Stepping over a Mud Puddle
77. Stepping Back over a Mud Puddle
78. The Good Camper
154. Convention Program—Afternoon
109. Learning to Race
Also see 145 and 51.

Balanced action
53. Rattling the Matchbox

Base knuckles
51. Strange Little Animal

Restricted motion
106. No Owner's Manual
 98. Marble Statues

Ringing tone
119. A True Marcel Marceau

Rolling the hand
 57. The Roman Arch
 53. Rattling the Matchbox
 62. The Light Show
 74. Walking Forward
    Also see 78 and 89.

Runs
 59. The Traveling Sequin
    Also see 101.

Shape of the hand, wrist, and arm
 51. Strange Little Animal
 57. The Roman Arch
 52. The Magic Staircase
 71. A Homing Pigeon
 53. Rattling the Matchbox
 60. Doorbells and Doorknobs
    Also see 86, 55, 70, 74, 75, 76, 77, 78, 82,
    and 118.

Shifting
145. An Insurance Policy
 56. The Optimist
 58. The Springboard
 61. Take a Lesson from a Dog
 63. Leaving for an Appointment
 64. A Speck of Lint
 67. Guiltless
 85. Straight Lines from Arcs?
    Also see 59, 62, and 85.

Slide
163. Pass the Peanut Butter

Strengthening the hands
 96. The Plastic Gobbler
 69. Pitching the Tent

Stretching
 65. Another Lesson from a Dog
    Also see 76, 77, 78, 153, and 154.

String Crossings
 55. Hidden Double Stops
 75. Walking Backward
    Also see 76, 77, and 86.

Supporting muscles
 70. Rattling the Bones

Sur une corde
117. Go on a Diet

Tension in the hand
 48. A Fuzzy "Pom-pom"
 65. Another Lesson from a Dog
 73. The Dance of the Double Stops
 56. The Optimist
    Also see this Cue Sheet: *Flexible hand and
    fingers; Thumb.*

Thumb
 50. Adam's Apple
142. Newsbreak
108. A Prisoner of One Tight Joint
115. Three Cheers for Leftie!
    Also see 118, 128, and 48.

Thumb position
 69. Pitching the Tent
    Also see 81.

Tone
 49. Rubber Cushions
 68. Shock Absorbers
 86. The First Note of the Piece
159. A Big Fat O
    Also see this Cue Sheet: *Vibrato.*

Touch
 49. Rubber Cushions

Trills
118. The Good Trillers
177. At the Composer's Desk
 89. 7:05 A.M.

Vibrato
 53. Rattling the Matchbox
 62. The Light Show
 72. Match Mates
128. Call the Authority
 70. Rattling the Bones
 68. Shock Absorbers
154. Convention Program—Afternoon
 49. Rubber Cushions
 57. The Roman Arch
 78. The Good Camper
 74. Walking Forward
 75. Walking Backward
 76. Stepping over a Mud Puddle
    Also see 136, 109, 77, 64, 55, 66, 130, 23,
    4, 27, 168, 35, 174, 160, 161, 164, 171, 173,
    and 181.

Weight
    See this Cue Sheet: *Balance.*

Weight suspension
51. Strange Little Animal
64. A Speck of Lint
109. Learning to Race
    Also see 58, 145, and 168.

4. VIDEO AND AUDIO CUES SIGNALING SPECIAL NEED IN THE LEFT HAND

Does there appear to be tension in the hand? Is the thumb tight? Does the tone sound hard?
    See Cue Sheet 3: *Tension in the hand; Flexible hand and fingers; Thumb; Touch; Tone.*

Does the student complain that her fourth finger is too short? Does the line between the elbow and the fingers appear broken? Do the fingers point up when not in use?
    See Cue Sheet 3: *Shape of the hand, wrist, and arm; Fourth finger.*

Does the student roll her hand?
    See Cue Sheet 3: *Rolling the hand.*

Are her motions jerky, particularly in runs and shifts?
66. The Man on the Flying Trapeze
59. The Traveling Sequin
63. Leaving for an Appointment

Does the elbow appear stiff?
99. Rusty Knees, Rusty Elbows

Does the student wait until she touches the fingerboard to shape the hand?
60. Doorbells and Doorknobs

Is it difficult for the student to move her fingers quickly? Are the fingers straight or base knuckles sunk in?
    See Cue Sheet 3: *Fast fingers; Fast and slow technique differences; Strengthening the hands; Curved fingers.*

Does the student get off to a slow start in a fast passage?
101. Ready—Set—HOLD!

Does the vibrato look and sound tight? Does it stop between notes?
53. Rattling the Matchbox
70. Rattling the Bones
68. Shock Absorbers
128. Call the Authority

Also see Cue Sheet 3: *Vibrato; Flexible fingers; Thumb.*

Does the student appear to keep the same hand balance when playing notes that require vibrato as for those that go past too quickly for an effective vibrato?
    See Cue Sheet 3: *Balance; Fast and slow technique differences.*

Does the vibrato appear to be the correct motion, balanced, and rhythmically even but still not beautiful?
72. Match Mates
68. Shock Absorbers
128. Call the Authority

Does the student's vibrato lack variety?
84. A Green Rainbow
72. Match Mates
168. Painting a Picture with Sound

Does the student need help in binding the notes together in string crossings? Are there noises between notes?
55. Hidden Double Stops
75. Walking Backward

Does a cello student who can vibrate well on isolated notes need help in making the vibrato beautiful when playing notes requiring extensions?
78. The Good Camper
153. Convention Program—Morning
154. Convention Program—Afternoon

Does the student's shifting seem heavy or awkward? Is the intonation inaccurate?
58. The Springboard
61. Take a Lesson from a Dog
145. An Insurance Policy
64. A Speck of Lint

Are there intonation problems in techniques other than shifting?
    See Cue Sheet 3: *Intonation; Rolling the hand.*

Is it difficult for the student to play successive double stops and chords in tune? Is tension present?
73. The Dance of the Double Stops

Does the student appear to be using excessive or restrictive motion?
89. 7:05 A.M.
106. No Owner's Manual
98. Marble Statues

Do trills sound labored or mechanical?
118. The Good Trillers
177. At the Composer's Desk
 89. 7:05 A.M.

Are the harmonics not clear?
See Cue Sheet 3: *Harmonics*.

Is there a persistent problem which the student obviously does not hear?
 97. Self-Correcting Ears

5. WORD CUES RELATED TO THE INSTRUMENT

Amplitude of the string vibrations
 35. Suntan Oil and Contact Paper
 72. Match Mates
117. Go on a Diet
       Also see 168.

Bass bar
147. Coming Unglued
120. The Life of a Soundpost

Bow
125. League of Bow Hairs
152. In the Body Shop
112. Traffic Violation
114. The String and I

Bridge
133. Long Distance
131. Bondage
152. In the Body Shop
107. A Letter to the Editor
149. Sul Who?
120. The Life of a Soundpost

Bridge jack
152. In the Body Shop
131. Bondage

Buzz
147. Coming Unglued

Cracks
152. In the Body Shop
147. Coming Unglued

Dämpfer
131. Bondage

Dampit
143. A Snake

Endpin
129. Born at the Blacksmith's

F holes
127. My Security Guard
152. In the Body Shop
131. Bondage

Fine tuners
124. From the Heart of a Tree
147. Coming Unglued

Fingerboard
152. In the Body Shop

Fingerboard nut
133. Long Distance

Glue
147. Coming Unglued
120. The Life of a Soundpost

Hair
125. League of Bow Hairs

Humidity
143. A Snake

Label
107. A Letter to the Editor

Mute
131. Bondage

Neck
152. In the Body Shop

Peg compound
124. From the Heart of a Tree

Purfling
127. My Security Guard

Resonance
113. Eight Coats

Screw and eyelet
152. In the Body Shop

Scroll
127. My Security Guard
124. From the Heart of a Tree

Seams
147. Coming Unglued
152. In the Body Shop

Sordino
131. Bondage

Soundpost
120. The Life of a Soundpost
147. Coming Unglued
152. In the Body Shop

Sourdine
131. Bondage

"Strads"
107. A Letter to the Editor

Strings
114. The String and I
117. Go on a Diet
121. Going to Pieces?
124. From the Heart of a Tree
119. A True Marcel Marceau
138. Cloned
133. Long Distance
      Also see 120.

Sympathetic vibrations
119. A True Marcel Marceau

Tailpiece
152. In the Body Shop
124. From the Heart of a Tree

Temperature
107. A Letter to the Editor
152. In the Body Shop

Tuning Pegs
124. From the Heart of a Tree
147. Coming Unglued

Varnish
113. Eight Coats

Weather conditions
143. A Snake
152. In the Body Shop
113. Eight Coats
107. A Letter to the Editor
147. Coming Unglued

Wood
113. Eight Coats
143. A Snake
124. From the Heart of a Tree
      Also see 147.

6. WORD CUES RELATED TO MUSICAL INTERPRETATION

Accents
136. Mail Order Accents
167. Energizing Music
      Also see 18, 21, 135, and 148.

Anticipations
164. Special Words—Special Notes

Appoggiaturas
174. Jody

Articulation
172. A Baffling Situation
178. The Thumb and the Tongue
183. Peter Piper Picked
171. The Little Man in the Back Row
      Also see 18, 36, and 135.

Bringing out certain notes
164. Special Words—Special Notes
134. Lost Slur
176. En-cy-clo-pe-di-a
173. Surprise!

Character
155. The Duke or the Clown
105. The TV Store
 80. TV Game Show
 90. Imagination, Inc.

Color
      See this Cue Sheet: *Variety of tone colors.*

Consonants
 18. Boom-m-m
172. A Baffling Situation
178. The Thumb and the Tongue
183. Peter Piper Picked

Contour of the phrase
175. A Dynamic Landscape

Crescendo
168. Painting a Picture with Sound

Diminuendo
185. The Reluctant Farewell
168. Painting a Picture with Sound
      Also see 119, 136, and 174.

Dotted rhythm
 25. Two for the Price of One!

Dynamics
175. A Dynamic Landscape
      Also see 136, 139, 112, 114, and 165.
      Also see this Cue Sheet: specific terms for dynamics.

Energy
167. Energizing Music
180. Wake Up a Sleeping String
      Also see 168, 172, and 184.

Ensemble precision
157. What? No Rehearsal!
 45. What, No Hair?
102. Catching the Beat

Expressive gestures
See Cue Sheet 1: *Expressive gestures.*

Extended phrases
181. The Purple Cow

Fast playing
183. Peter Piper Picked

Form
173. Surprise!
179. J. R. Is—

Forte or fortissimo
See Cue Sheet 1: *Tone building.*
Also see 72 and 167.

Forte-piano
136. Mail Order Accents

Glissando
163. Pass the Peanut Butter

Grace notes
177. At the Composer's Desk

Grouping of notes
156. A Puzzle
162. The Beginning and the End
176. En-cy-clo-pe-di-a
Also see this Cue Sheet: *Phrasing; Relating to language and speech.*

Humanizing music
184. Mouse House
176. En-cy-clo-pe-di-a

Identical, successive phrases
163. Pass the Peanut Butter

Imitation
95. The Xerox Machine

Impressionistic music
183. Peter Piper Picked

Impulses
176. En-cy-clo-pe-di-a
Also see 174.

Modified repeated phrases
173. Surprise!
179. J. R. Is—
181. The Purple Cow

Monotonous music
See Cue Sheet 1: *Monotony in bowing.*

Mood of the music
155. The Duke or the Clown
166. The Needle of the Meter

66. The Man on the Flying Trapeze
Also see Cue Sheet 1: *Expressive gestures.*

Mordent
177. At the Composer's Desk

Movement
160. The Magic of the Upbeat
176. En-cy-clo-pe-di-a
182. The Ghost Upbeat
181. The Purple Cow

Personality
155. The Duke or the Clown

Phrasing
162. The Beginning and the End
175. A Dynamic Landscape
158. A or B?
165. The Prima Donna
176. En-cy-clo-pe-di-a
Also see this Cue Sheet: *Relating to language and speech; Grouping of notes; Upbeats.*

Piano or pianissimo
180. Wake Up a Sleeping String
165. The Prima Donna

Portamento
163. Pass the Peanut Butter

Relating to conducting
169. The Invisible Orchestra

Relating to language and speech
164. Special Words—Special Notes
156. A Puzzle
162. The Beginning and the End
163. Pass the Peanut Butter
173. Surprise!
174. Jody
179. J. R. Is—
184. Mouse House
181. The Purple Cow
18. Boom-m-m
176. En-cy-clo-pe-di-a
178. The Thumb and the Tongue
42. Pea Pod
Also see this Cue Sheet: *Consonants; Vowels.*

Repeated notes and phrases
171. The Little Man in the Back Row
163. Pass the Peanut Butter
Also see this Cue Sheet: *Modified repeated phrases; Extended phrases.*

Scene Index by Name

Scene Index by Number